GARLAND STUDIES IN

AMERICAN POPULAR HISTORY AND CULTURE

edited by

JEROME NADELHAFT
UNIVERSITY OF MAINE

A GARLAND SERIES

Garland Studies in American Popular History and Culture
Jerome Nadelhaft, series editor

EARLY AMERICAN WOMEN DRAMATISTS 1775–1860

ZOE DETSI-DIAMANTI

GARLAND PUBLISHING, Inc.
A MEMBER OF THE TAYLOR & FRANCIS GROUP
NEW YORK & LONDON / 1998

Library of Congress Cataloging-in-Publication Data

Detsi-Diamanti, Zoe, 1966–
    Early American women dramatists, 1775–1860 / Zoe Detsi-
Diamanti.
        p.   cm. — (Garland studies in American popular history
and culture)
        Includes bibliographical references and index.
        ISBN 0-8153-3304-8 (alk. paper)
        1. American drama—Women authors—History and criticism.
2. Women and literature—United States—History—19th century.
3. Women and literature—United States—History—18th century.
4. American drama—19th century—History and criticism.
I. Title. II. Series.
PS 338.W6 D48 1998
812'.2099287—dc21
                                                                98-45560

To Yanni

Contents

Acknowledgments

I would like to express my heartfelt appreciation to my professors at Aristotle University, E. Georgoudaki, S. Patsalidis, and E. Sakellaridou, whose moral support and direction, their sense of humanity and humor, their understanding and suggestions have been most meaningful and invaluable.

For research assistance and funding, I owe special debts to the Fulbright Program of Greece and the Program of Hellenic Studies at Princeton University.

I am also grateful to the Princeton Department of Rare Books and Special Collections, the New York Public Library, the Billy Rose Collection at Lincoln Center, and the Columbia University Library.

Finally, I would like to express my gratitude and my love for my husband and parents, who played a huge role in my ability to write this book.

Early American
Women Dramatists
1775–1860

CHAPTER 1

Introduction

Although contemporary feminist criticism has mainly focused upon American women playwrights of the twentieth century—women like Rachel Crothers, Susan Glaspell, Lillian Hellman, and Sophie Treadwell,—there is evidence that a feminist tradition rooted deep in the nationalistic and democratic impulses of the American nation existed more than a hundred years before these women started writing. It may come as a surprise to some readers that a significant but overlooked number of women playwrights vitally contributed to the development of early American drama.

Scholars are increasingly calling attention to writings by early American women dramatists and a number of recent studies have focused on Mercy Otis Warren, the writer of the American Revolution, best known for her propaganda plays, and actress-playwright, Anna Cora Mowatt, whose brilliant comedy of manners, *Fashion* (1845), has become part of the American canon. In addition, Amelia Howe Kritzer's collection has gathered in one volume eight plays by early American female dramatists, while Kathleen Nichols' earlier study briefly discusses the dramatic work of a number of American women playwrights who actively participated in the dramatic activity of late-eighteenth and nineteenth-century America.[1] Finally, in her 1995 *American Women Writers and the Work of History, 1790-1860*, Nina Baym points to women's extensive writing about history between the founding of the American nation and the onset of the civil war. Chapter 9 of this study looks briefly at a substantial number of historical plays published by American women before 1860.

The task of resurrecting lost American women playwrights, of locating any significant number of extant texts written by women for

the stage proved to be particularly arduous. Most of the plays had fallen
into obscurity and were accessible only on microprint and in rare book
collections. Therefore, when I came across the plays of Mercy O.
Warren, Judith S. Murray, Susanna H. Rowson, Margaretta V.
Faugeres, Caroline Lee W. Hentz, Anna C. Mowatt, Sidney F.
Bateman, Frances Wright, Julia Ward Howe, and others, I hoped to
bring to focus the dramatic writing of a few of the invisible but
pioneering women in American theater. The plays in this book have
been drawn from the obscure corners of early American theater history,
where they have lain for many years, they vary considerably in
dramatic form—some of them are exceptionally stageworthy,—and
actually highlight the experiences, ideas, hopes, and aspirations of some
of the most educated and socially active women of the American
nation.

In restricting myself to female playwrights in early American
society, I seek to stress, on the one hand, the cultural and historical
specificity of their writing, and, on the other, the interrelation between
these women's dramatic attempts and the formation of an American
national and literary identity. Acknowledging, however, that the
variations among individual women can be as great as those between

Like their male contemporaries, early American women
playwrights wrote on a variety of topics and employed a variety of
dramatic methods and techniques-ranging from propaganda plays to
social comedies, melodramas and romantic tragedies. In their majority,
women dramatists of the late-eighteenth and early-nineteenth centuries
reveal an extraordinary critical awareness of the various social,
economic, and political transformations that were taking place in
America at the time their plays were written. Affected by major social
events, like the War of Independence, the industrial revolution,
abolitionism and the first women's movements, they center their work
around urgent social issues and changing ideological and cultural
values. In some cases, their plays deal with the various social, political,
and economic problems of women at that time—their inferior status,
the restrictions of options as to education and the professions, and
certainly the restrictions imposed upon their sexuality. Although many
American women tried to write for the theater, only a handful of them
managed to bring psychological insights of their own gender into their
plays and explore new areas of women's lives, alternative social roles
and definitions.

In restricting myself to female playwrights in early American
society, I seek to stress, on the one hand, the cultural and historical
specificity of their writing, and, on the other, the interrelation between
these women's dramatic attempts and the formation of an American
national and literary identity. Acknowledging, however, that the
variations among individual women can be as great as those between

men and women, I avoid making any arbitrary generalizations and focus primarily upon the works of white, urban, middle-class women. My study covers the period between 1775 and 1860, a time when American men and women struggled to define themselves and their place in response to the radical economic and institutional transformations which characterized that period. Based on the assumption that women's experience of the world differs from men's, I try to show that the plays of my study are sites of gender inscriptions as well as collective evidence that late-eighteenth and nineteenth-century men and women were affected differently by the economic, political, and social changes that were taking place in America at that time. Neither after the American Revolution nor in the Age of Jackson did women share the historical experience of men. On the contrary, they experienced status loss, sexual repression, and limited role choices.

Taking into consideration the social dimensions, cultural ideals, and literary determinants that shaped these women's writing, I have examined the texts in relation to the cultural environment of early American women, to historical change, as well as to the shaping force of economic and political factors. Thus, the first important theories of the New Women's History, such as the works of Linda Gordon, Gerda Lerner, and Carroll Smith-Rosenberg, provided me with a theoretical basis for the study of women's experiences and role options in relation to the social and political structures as well as to the private world of feelings and personal relations. [2] Increasingly, then, I turned my attention to a number of comprehensive studies which examined American women's relation to the late-eighteenth- and nineteenth-century social arrangements and institutions, the prescriptive norms and socialization processes, as well as their own personal experiences and psychological development. Of particular use and interest to me were Barbara Welter's pioneer analysis of American women's social roles in the nineteenth century, Nancy F. Cott's study of "woman's sphere" in New England, and her invaluable collection of primary documents, which offer full expression to women's voices and experiences throughout three centuries of American women's social history. [3]

Furthermore, I used a number of significant studies on women's history, like Mary Beth Norton's systematic account of women's lives in the late eighteenth century, as well as the comprehensive works by Catherine Clinton, Ellen Carol Dubois, Eleanor Flexner, Linda K. Kerber, Aileen S. Kraditor, Carroll Smith-Rosenberg, and Page Smith. [4]

My study of the American middle-class woman has also centered upon specific information concerning women's life cycle, the experiences of adolescence, marriage, childbirth, child-rearing duties and housekeeping responsibilities, celibacy, old age and death. An analysis of female sexuality offered me the opportunity to explore the prevalent sexual norms and cultural values, the social attitudes towards puberty, menstruation, pregnancy, menopause, the various medical tracts, as well as women's own attitudes towards their sexuality.[5]

Thus, studying women's cultural and historical experiences in the late-eighteenth and nineteenth-century American society, their status as family members and as workers, their educational options and their struggles for autonomy and emancipation, has been the first step towards an understanding of the interrelation between a female complex social reality and women's writing. For the analysis and interpretation of the themes and structures of early American women's dramatic literature, I used the theoretical models proposed by current American feminist critics, such as Elaine Showalter, Josephine Donovan, Annette Kolodny, and Lillan S. Robinson.[6] The theoretical problems that preoccupied my mind while I was working on this project,focused on the question of women's relation to the dominant male literary and dramatic canon, women's access to the symbolic systems of language, their thematic concerns and aesthetic devices.[7]

While choosing to write about a group of neglected American women playwrights, I have also been preoccupied with theoretical questions that are relevant to women's access to the public theatrical art and to the coded representation of feminine consciousness, female experience and reality. Do these women conform to or challenge the dominant male ideology in their plays? Do they interpret themes of social interest in a different way? Do their plays fit into the dominant canon? What playwriting techniques do they use?[8] Because I work in the theater, rather than in literary criticism, I have also focused upon the uniqueness of theater as representational art and collaborative work. The importance of theater as medium of culture led me to an exploration of the ways theater produces and communicates meaning as well as reflect the ideological workings of the dominant culture.[9] Drama, as a form, is essentially more public and social than all the other literary arts and actually offers the female playwright "greater potential for effecting social change" (Hart 2). One of the most remarkable aspects of these plays by early American women is the pioneering spirit in which they foreground female characters and the frequency with which they challenge male cultural, social, political, and intellectual discourse.

It is not at all accidental that these women chose to present their opinions and ideas in dramatic form addressing a community of spectators, in defiance of the warning generally given to women to avoid drawing attention to themselves. It reflects their awareness of the highly politicized nature of theater as well as the acknowledgment that the stage offered them direct, though compromised, access to public life and activity. They powerfully reached out to a community of spectators succeeding in integrating women's voice in the wider ideological frameworks of republicanism, democracy and individualism. Early American women playwrights may not be radical feminists, but in most cases, their plays reflect the status of American women within the larger social processes and ideological changes that were taking place in American society in the late-eighteenth and early-nineteenth centuries.

AMATEUR EFFORTS: MORAL DIALOGUES AND DRAMATIC SKETCHES.

American women playwrights published in every field of letters: they wrote histories, essays for periodicals, political pamphlets, juvenile literature, translations and adaptations of classic plays and popular novels and, of course, original plays. However, in order to present as full a picture as possible of women's early dramatic writing, it is important to add that American women proved really adept at moral dialogues, pastorals, and dramatic sketches. In most cases, these dramatic pieces were published anonymously, they were essentially religious and moral in theme, and were usually intended for the instruction of young ladies. It can be argued that these dramatic attempts greatly resembled the conduct books, or advice manuals for women that were published in profusion in America at that time, as they tended to emphasize the proper behavior of young ladies, the observance of etiquette, religious values and domestic principles. For example, *May Day; or, The Celebration of the Return of Spring* (1819) is a play written for the *Amusement of Young Girls on the First Day of May.* Interspersed with songs and ritual dances, this dramatic piece celebrates "the return of spring: that season which clothes the fields with green, and causes all nature to smile at the return of the great fountain of light." The moral and religious message becomes clear as the Queen of May compares the cycle of the seasons to the cycle of human life and invites the girls to join her, "with hearts overflowing with love and gratitude to the ruler of the universe," in the celebration of the return of Spring.

The great majority of these dramatic sketches were mainly amateur efforts, not intended as commercial plays, but rather to be performed in private theatricals, or by students in the Female Academies, or, as in the case of *Catherine Brown; or, The Converted Cherokee* (1819), by church missionary groups. Being mostly instructive and intensely moral, these plays usually employ an all-female cast of characters aiming primarily at instilling solid principles in young girls. For example, *The Search After Happiness* (1794), a pastoral drama by a Lady in Connecticut, clearly aims at giving advice and moral guidance to young ladies. All the characters are women, who, for their own personal reasons, have left their homes and past lives in their search after happiness. In the play, the world of "courts and cities" with "its folly, pomp and deceit" is sharply contrasted to the beauty and innocence of nature. The play touches upon the detrimental impact of wealth, fashionable amusement, and flattery on the character of young ladies, while, at the same time, it stresses virtue, good judgment and domestic accomplishments.

There is no action in these dramatic pieces, just long and sometimes wearisome discussions, and very little concern about structure, plot and character development. The unidentified author of *The Misfortunes of Anger* (1798), for example, appears to be conscious of the weaknesses of her own dramatic creation as she herself explains in the preface to her play that she did not "intend her dramatic dialogues to be performed; well aware that the length of the scenes in some places, and the simplicity of plot in all, would render them flat and heavy in representation." It is true that the contemporary reader may regard these plays as just naïve efforts towards dramatic creation, lacking polish and fine characterization, with obvious deficiencies and weaknesses. However, before we hastily dismiss these amateur efforts as worthless and unimportant, let's consider that these dramatic dialogues indicate something of the breadth of our definition of dramatic writing by women. What's more, in a few cases, this type of drama does reveal some of the writers' interests, perspectives, their ideas regarding the didactic power of drama itself, as well as their own definitions of American womanhood. Regardless of ideological intentions, these plays show intellectual depth and represent a woman's milieu meaningfully.[10]

WOMEN AND EARLY AMERICAN THEATER.

It can be argued that women significantly contributed to the creation of a distinctively American drama and were in fact really active and successful in developing early American theater. For example, Mercy Otis Warren, one of the earliest American female playwrights, was the first one, even among male dramatists, to turn to propaganda plays in an attempt to provide an outlet for her deepest patriotic feelings as well as exhort the people of her country to adhere to republican principles. Like Warren, Susanna H. Rowson, a well-known actress in the late eighteenth century, also worked within the domain of republican ideology and employed its rhetoric in her work while she sought to establish a relationship between the ideological framework of democracy and egalitarianism and women's experiences and reality.

Probably the first professional female playwright in America, Louisa Medina enjoyed an astounding career by adapting contemporary fiction for the stage. Medina wrote a significant number of plays over a five-year period which held the American stage for almost a generation after her death. Without question, she created some of the most popular and spectacular melodramas of the 1830s. Furthermore, Charlotte Barnes' success as a woman dramatist and as an actress was second only to that of Anna Cora Mowatt whose *Fashion* is the most frequently anthologized play by an American woman. A closer look at the plays written by early American female playwrights reveals that, in some cases, their work ranks among the best that America can offer for the late eighteenth and early nineteenth centuries. For example, Arthur Hobson Quinn observes about Julia Ward Howe that "with any real encouragement she could have contributed plays to our stage that would have enriched our literature as well as our theater" (367).

However, the public nature of the theater and its complicated and male-dominated network of operation, along with its association with immorality, discouraged many talented women from venturing into the field, forcing them to choose less 'public' and more 'respectable' modes of writing, like poetry and fiction. The relegation of women dramatists to the claustrophobic domestic sphere of private activity together with their own awareness of the conventional notion that literary women relinquished the much-cherished feminine virtues which made up the ideal of 'True Womanhood,' were the main factors why some of them chose to hide behind anonymity. Although it appears that the use of a male pseudonym was not common, identifying oneself as a playwright involved great risks. Mercy Otis Warren published her propaganda plays anonymously, Sarah Pogson Smith always wrote under 'A Lady,' whereas Judith Sargent Murray initially had her two plays produced as the work of 'An American Lady,' although she later published them in *The Gleaner* under her feminine pseudonym, Constantia. But the problem still remained and the women who publicly associated themselves with the theater jeopardized their and their families' reputations and often had to defend themselves against social and religious biases. Anna Cora Mowatt, among other women playwrights, expressed support for the theater and its people and commented on the force of the prevalent anti-theatrical attitudes. In her best-selling *Autobiography of an Actress* (1854), she felt compelled to prove how unfounded the prejudices of the people and the church were against the acting profession and the theater in general.

For some of the women who chose to associate themselves with the theater either as actresses or playwrights, or both, the decision was often spurred by financial need. Despite its obvious drawbacks, the theater was one profitable area of enterprise open to women. The vocational possibilities of the stage profession afforded women the opportunity to receive a comparatively good salary, to compete with men on an equal basis of talent and public appeal, and even reach positions of management in the theater.[11] On the other hand, however, by engaging in a profession that was so loudly and frequently condemned, female performers had to relinquish the most important attributes of 'True Womanhood' by which a woman was judged and appraised in society. Their virtue was constantly at stake since their "co-sexual work place meant that they enjoyed freedoms unknown to women of other socially sanctioned occupations"(Davis 69). The woman who dared to aspire to the unconventional role of actress and/or playwright certainly deviated from the ideal image of womanly purity, modesty, and religiousness. Even the female public orators who addressed mixed audiences in their work for abolition and temperance were harshly criticized. Anna Cora Mowatt was attacked by the press in

1842 for appearing publicly before men and women. Eric Barnes, her biographer, points out that "it was bad enough that Mrs. Mowatt should read poetry in public, but that she should do so before mixed audiences seemed nothing less than depravity" (84). Frances Wright was so severely criticized for appearing in public that she often needed a bodyguard to protect her against hostile members of the audience.

What is really amazing, however, is the fact that, despite the odds, the majority of early American female playwrights somehow 'exposed' themselves to the public world in various ways. Some of them were actresses, like Rowson, Bateman, Barnes, Medina, Kemble, and Mowatt, while others, like Warren, Wright, Howe, Murray, and Ellet, were already committed to public causes and were active social reformers and radical freethinkers. There is also a number of them, like Hentz and Faugeres, who published in other genres—poetry and fiction—and occasionally tried their hand at drama. These women's access to the politicized public world, effected through playwriting, acting and lecturing, is really crucial. The fact that these women decided to take some action during periods of political, economic, and social upheaval is extremely significant. Their audacity to enter the public world of discourse challenged, in a sense, the social construction of 'reality' that kept women to the recesses, that kept women silent.

A starting point for the interpretation of these women's work has been an extensive reading of a large number of late-eighteenth—and nineteenth-century plays by American male dramatists and a thorough examination of the male dramatic codes of the period.[12] My purpose has been twofold: first, I wanted to place these women within the general social, political, and theatrical framework of their time, and second, to define those facets of their work that threaten male authority and offer a female-gendered perspective on a number of social and political issues. In her brilliant critical study of women's writing, Joanna Russ provides the term "The Double Standard of Content" as she argues that the socially-constructed differences between men and women are reflected in their art (40). Recognizing that women's positioning within existing social, familial, and ideological structures differs fundamentally from that of men, I have sought to read the texts as a "double-voiced discourse, containing a 'dominant' and a 'muted' story" (Showalter 1986: 266). The shape my argument takes is informed by the question: how do these women manage to give an explicitly feminine voice to their dramatic creations and actually project their experiences and feelings onto the all-male screen of ideological framework and social institutions in early American society? Realizing that the social and ideological conditions of textual production play an important role in determining the limitations and aspirations of an individual text, I endeavor to link the analysis of the plays to broader questions of social, political and cultural change, as well as embark on an exploration of the aesthetic and ideological significance of these plays within the broader dramatic framework of styles and conventions. Finally, and bearing in mind Josette Feral's observation that women writers "are still confined to the masculine mode unless they shatter traditional discourse," I avoid making any arbitrary speculations regarding the existence of a uniquely or specifically feminine discourse in the plays (549). Rather, I look into the ideological and structural dimensions of my texts without reducing them to the single authenticating source of authorial consciousness or arguing for a necessary relation between 'women's writing' and linguistic experimentation and marginality.

Hopefully, this work will prove of value in many ways. First, it will offer a comprehensive view of early American women's involvement in the theatrical activity of the time and their active participation in the creation of a distinctively American drama. Second, it will make available the dramatic writing of women such as Susanna Rowson and Frances Wright whose novels and essays, respectively, have been extensively studied. Third, it will present, through the plays, the brief biographies of the writers and the historical background of textual production, aspects of early American women's lives, experiences and aspirations. Finally, it will fill in some of the still sparsely occupied space in feminist theater criticism and will bring to feminist critics' as well as to historians' attention the work of some of the relatively unknown, but pioneering, women in American theater.

SUMMARY OF CHAPTERS

In the chapters that follow, I have grouped the authors according to their major concerns, with consideration for subject matter and genre. Every chapter includes units that provide information about the social, political, and theatrical context of the time and addresses specifically the changing nature of women's status during the various stages of

American cultural development. I have also attempted to briefly discuss a number of plays by early American women dramatists in order to shed some light on the social, political, and ideological interests they articulate, while the core of my study centers around a close examination of the plays by Warren, Rowson, Mowatt, Bateman, Howe and Wright, as representative examples of the dramatic techniques and thematic concerns employed by women playwrights in the period between 1775 and 1860.

My first chapter, "The Metaphors of Freedom: Republican Ideology and Women's Rights in the Plays by Mercy O. Warren and Susanna H. Rowson," is structured around an examination of the social and political context of the American Revolution as well as an investigation of drama as a primary means of political expression and protest. For one thing, the War of Independence kindled the development of an explicitly nationalistic dramatic tradition in America. Moreover, the propaganda plays written during the decade of social and political upheaval echoed the republican rhetoric of the time and vigorously reflected the national identity of an emerging nation. Finally, the democratic sentiments of the American Revolution provided the first important link between women's writing and the demand for women's rights.

Mary V. V.'s Tory satire, *A Dialogue Between a Southern Delegate and His Spouse on his Return from the Grand Continental Congress* (1774), as well as the plays by Judith S. Murray and Margaretta V. Faugeres, which were written during the revolutionary and post-revolutionary war period, attempt to raise some questions about women's rights and social status in early American society. However, it is in Warren's propaganda plays and her romantic tragedies as well as in Rowson's comedy that gender constitutes an integral part of the plays' subject matter. As a matter of fact, Warren's and later Rowson's writing consciously manipulated the traditionally masculine forms of political satire, romantic tragedy, and farce in an attempt to respond to the broader questions of social, political, and ideological transformations. Evidently inspired by the American Revolution and its ensuing egalitarian rhetoric, their plays can be read as sites where Warren and Rowson connect national to sexual politics and actually enter the debate for equal rights. Without rejecting the dominant republican discourse and the prevailing theatrical rhetoric of the time, both playwrights raise questions about the place of women in American society and actually inculcate a strong sense of the female self and consciousness in their works.

This need to integrate women's voice into the male-centered social and political systems, to construct an alternative image of femininity, actually constitutes the main axis of my second chapter: "Industrial Capitalism and the Status of Middle-class Women in Mid-Nineteenth-Century American Family: Anna C. Mowatt's *Fashion* and Sidney F. Bateman's *Self.*" It should be noted that for a number of playwrights in the first half of the nineteenth century, the developing American social landscape provided incomparable opportunity for social commentary. Various aspects of American social life, American manners and mores as well as the American business world and fashionable life were caricatured in a number of plays, especially farce-comedies. However, in Mowatt's and Bateman's plays, a most powerful social criticism of the nineteenth-century industrial ethos of material success and individual progress meets with the dramatists' acute frustration at the blatant exclusion of women from the generally accepted belief in the equal chance of social and economic advancement for all people. Combining aspects of farce and melodrama, the plays elaborate on the social values and contemporary social problems of the American society. Written within the context of the increasingly commercialized economy in Jacksonian democracy, the plays take the new industrial ethic to its full consequence by exposing the pervasiveness of the threatening image of dissolution in social, human and gender relations.

Compared to the works of contemporary male American dramatists, Mowatt's *Fashion* is the best structured social comedy written in America in the nineteenth century. Although the impulse to satirize the ambitious parvenu and fashionable life seems to have been present since Royall Tyler's *The Contrast* (1787), *Fashion* and *Self* are the only plays which focus upon the ideological vulnerability of American society and actually court with a new system of democratic values which would successfully embrace American women as well.

Finally, in my third chapter, "Gender Perspective and Ideology in Frances Wright's *Altorf* (1819)and Julia Ward Howe's *Leonora* (1857)," I look closely at the significance and popularity of the romantic tragedies written in America in the early part of the nineteenth century with particular emphasis on the poetic dramas by American women—more specifically, the work of Charlotte Barnes, Elizabeth Ellet, Caroline Hentz, Frances Kemble and others. Focusing upon distant places in older times, the majority of the verse dramas written by American playwrights elaborated on a political theme of noble rebellion against tyranny, reflected the democratic spirit of the Americans, and actually dealt with the universal struggle of love with duty and honor. Following the romantic trend of the time, while, at the same time, augmenting the female tradition initiated by Warren and her heroic tragedies, American women dramatists wrote plays that emphasized the power of the common man, the concept of universal freedom, and the heroic qualities that all Americans admired.

Examining Wright's *Altorf* and Howe's *Leonora* against the backdrop of poetic tragedies written at the time, it became apparent that both plays represented more than a romantic view of historical events in faraway places and times, or of the universal issues of freedom and patriotism. Written within the context of the first organized social and political protests by middle-class women in the first half of the nineteenth century, the plays are built upon a successful blending of the conventional pattern of poetic drama with the issue of women's contradictory relation to early American society.

NOTES

1. Baym, 1995: 187-213; Kritzer, 1995; Nichols, 1991; Scullion, 1996.
2. Gordon, 1986: 20-30; Lerner, 1975: 5-14, 1986; Smith-Rosenberg, 1975: 185-98.
3. Welter, 1976; Cott, 1977, 1986.
4. Clinton, 1984; Dubois, 1978; Flexner, 1975; Kerber, 1980; Kraditor, 1968; Smith-Rosenberg, 1985; Smith, 1970.
5. For a sustained analysis of sexual behavior in the United States, see D'Emilio, 1989; Hartman, 1974. See also Degler, 1974: 1467-90; Rosenberg, 1973: 131-53; Smith-Rosenberg, 1973: 332-56.
6. Donovan, 1989, 1987: 98-109; Kolodny,1986: 499-51, 1986: 46-62; Robinson, 1986: 572-82; Showalter, 1978, 1986: 125-43, 1982: 9-35, 1991.
7. Moers, 1977; Spacks, 1976.
8. Armstrong, 1992; Greene, 1985; Jacobus, 1979; Jones, 1981: 247-63; K. Miller, 1981: 36-48; Reinelt, 1992.
9. The representation of women on stage, the construction of women as objects of desire—as objects of the 'male gaze'—their absence as subjects of dramatic works, led feminist dramatic critics to derive some of their insights from the fundamental notions of Lacan's rereading of Freudian psychoanalysis.

See, for example, the works of Austin, 1990; Case, 1988, 1990; Davis, 1989: 59-81; De Lauretis, 1984; Diamond, 1989: 58-72; Dolan, 1988, 1993; Hart, 1989; Kaplan, 1981, Wandor, 1986. I also found the French feminist critics' writings really stimulating. Their focus on the acts of reading and writing as subversive, political, introduced me to a more rigorous theoretical stance. See, for example, Cixous, 1981: 245-67; Irigaray, 1985, 1985; Kofman, 1985; Kristeva, 1986: 471-84.

10. Of course, there were a few women who continued to write moral dramatic sketches well into the nineteenth century and had them published under their own name. For example, Caroline H. Gilman wrote *Isadore*, a dramatic dialogue in two scenes, which was published in her *Tales and Ballads* (Boston: W. Crosby, 1839). Isabella Oliver Sharp includes two instructive dramatic dialogues, *Philander and Lucinda*, and *Frances and Mila*, in her collection of *Poems, On Various Subjects* (Carslile: A. Loudon, 1805). Finally, plays based on Bible history were highly didactic dramatic pieces built around a religious theme and conveying a message of morality and Christianity. See, for example Louisa J. Hall's *Miriam* (Boston: Crosby and Nichols, 1850) and *Hannah, the Mother of Samuel, the Prophet and Judge of Israel* (Boston: J. Munroe, 1839), as well as Eliza L. F. Cushing's *Esther: A Sacred Drama* (Boston: J. Dowe, 1840).

11. For more information regarding the acting profession in America in the late-eighteenth and nineteenth centuries, see Chinoy, 1987; Dudden, 1994; Johnson, 1984; G. Wilson, 1966.

12. For a comprehensive compilation of the plays written and produced in America in the late-eighteenth and nineteenth centuries, see Berquist, 1963; Brown, 1903; Chorba, 1951; Clark, 1940-49; Dunlap, 1963; Hill, 1934; Hixon, 1977; Hoole, 1946; Ireland, 1860-7; Meserve, 1965, 1980; Tompkins, 1908; Roden, 1900; Wegelin, 1905; A. Wilson, 1935.

CHAPTER 2

The Metaphors of Freedom
Republican Ideology and Women's Rights in the
Plays by Mercy Otis Warren and Susanna Haswell
Rowson

> Theater is one of the rhetorical figures imported from England and
> used by colonists, and later by American-born writers, to express
> their version of life in the New World (Richards 1991: xi).

I: DRAMA AND POLITICS: PROPAGANDA PLAYS IN REVOLUTIONARY AMERICA

In the study of early American drama, one cannot help noticing that for
many years America remained an English colony both intellectually
and culturally.[1] The early period of American drama has been viewed
by critics and historians with suspicion, often doubting its value and
labeling it as the "stepchild of the British art form, a second-rate copy"
(Spritz 3). It is true, however, that American theater took a long time to
establish an identity of its own, to attain full maturity, and finally to
occupy a position in the world drama equal in merit and prominence to
that of the European. The evolutionary process of an American theater
in the wilderness of the new continent was extremely slow and painful.
Quite a few years elapsed before America could actually boast of
popular native playwrights and great American hits. Although the first
settlers brought with them a rich dramatic heritage, "the incredible
hardships of the early years of settlement left no time or desire for
dramatic entertainment" (Wright 176). The pioneering spirit of the
early colonists, the urge to explore and tame the vast virgin land, all
contributed to regarding any distraction from the tasks of survival in a
hostile environment as mere wasteful luxury.

However, apart from the new nation's literary dependence upon England and the living conditions of the colonists, the most important reason conducive to the early neglect of drama was the religious nature of the Puritan New England colonies. Religious opposition against theatrical activity manifested itself in legislature that prohibited any form of playacting and even in overt hostility against the stage and the people related to it. The prevailing scorn of the theater derived mainly from the Puritan fear that "the presence of a playhouse and players would undermine the sentiments which the pulpit was trying to instill into the hearts of the colonists" (Moses 25). The Puritans repudiated the theater for showing profane, licentious stories detrimental to personal morality and spirituality, and succeeded in perpetuating an image of the theater that bore the stigma of indecency and iniquity.

The Puritan attack on the 'evils' of the stage stemmed primarily from their general dissatisfaction with the church of England. The theater for the Puritans was reminiscent of the religious rituals of Anglo-Catholicism. Richard Moody explains that "in the act of driving symbolism out of the Anglican church—for symbolism smacked of 'Popery'—they discovered that symbolism was at the base of theatrical entertainment" (25). So, they despised drama for what it was: a symbol, a concrete representation of life. The Puritans attacked the stage because it aped reality, it portrayed an illusion. Besides, they clearly recognized the etymological relationship between the hypocrite and the actor.[2]

Nevertheless, despite the principal factors that impeded the growth of theater and drama in America, we do find evidence of faint instances of theatrical activity. Unfortunately, before 1750, the record of dramatic performances is extremely insufficient.[3] By the time of the Revolution, however, an atmosphere conducive to drama and the arts in general had appeared. As the colonies developed into social and commercial centers, an intellectual elite slowly began to emerge from the upper classes. In 1766, the Southwark Theater in Philadelphia, the first permanent playhouse in North America, was erected. Existing evidence proves that by the 1770s there was a number of plays written by American authors as well as a newly-formed audience for legitimate theater in the colonies.[4]

During the Revolutionary War, a considerable change occurred in theater activity and the writing of plays in America. In October 1774, the Continental Congress suspended all public entertainment.[5]

Although there is no record of professional theater during the Revolution, playgiving did not entirely disappear. Plays were presented not by professional companies, but by the soldiers themselves. In fact, the British troops were especially active as they presented profitable shows presumably for the benefit of war victims and soldiers' widows. Despite the fact that these military players were basically amateurs, they played a vital part in the history of American theater by continuing theatrical activity in the colonies and by presenting plays never before seen in America, such as *The Rivals* and *The School for Scandal*.

Although the limitations imposed by the Revolutionary War tended to generally stultify cultural, intellectual, and artistic advances, drama in America underwent a recognizable change while it entered a new phase in its development. As the American War of Independence drew nearer, "the foundation had been prepared for an elevated treatment of American struggles and sacrifices" (Richardson 26). The colonists began to express their ideas vigorously in newspapers, in privately printed material, in sermons, political orations, and pamphlet plays. On the one hand, the ardent Patriots sought to incite citizens to rise up against British rule, while on the other, the Loyalists tried to warn Americans of the horrors of rebellion and the prospective loss of a well-established social and political order. During the decade of the explosive political events, Patriotic and Loyalist sentiments found expression in the satire, vilification, and caricature of the propaganda/pamphlet plays written at the time.[6] These plays, which proved particularly effective as literary weapons of attack, offer invaluable information to the historian of the American Revolution since they depict the social and political upheaval of the late-eighteenth century in a strikingly unvarnished, direct, and straightforward way. Taken as an aspect of social and political history, these propaganda plays reveal with historical authenticity and emotional vividness colonial reactions to actual events and fully dramatize a period of turmoil and anguish.

Although the plays do not follow the traditional patterns of plot and characterization—the events of the Revolution are just being reported and the characters, prominent figures of the time, are just being caricatured—they are unique as a particular genre of persuasion that effectively served its purpose: to encourage the combatants, to expose and ridicule. Norman Philbrick attempts to defend these propaganda plays against the accusation that they cannot be categorized as literary and artistic works by arguing that the uneven writing and the lack of polish of the pamphlet plays preclude an evaluation of them as works of literature, but these very qualities, of rough-hewn style and personal commitment, raise them above the criticism that might dismiss them as eccentricities of dramatic literature (3). The heightened emotionalism and partisan fervor of the plays stimulated by the writers' personal involvement and growing commitment to the political cause made up for their lack in artistic merit. The genre to which these propaganda plays are most closely allied is the English political drama of the last quarter of the seventeenth century and the first quarter of the eighteenth. Although the English political plays were better dramas, in the sense that they followed a strict and recognizable dramatic pattern, an analysis of the structure of the pamphlets of protest drama printed during the Revolutionary period reveals that they were primarily intended for reading, not for performance, aiming at securing adherents to their particular viewpoint.

It is safe to infer that within the world of stirring political and social events drama held a unique position. The late-eighteenth-century theatrical discourse effectively echoed the dominant rhetoric of the American Revolutionary period. One of the reasons why the majority of writers chose the pamphlet play as their primary means of expression and protest is located in the very nature of drama itself. The writing of propaganda plays was closely related to the immediacy and impact of dramatic dialogue on the listener or reader. As maintained by Walter J. Meserve, "conversation was a valued part of daily life; a long speech did not provide the same appeal"(1977: 65). The dramatic representation of a historical event, imbued with a certain political or philosophical persuasion, strengthened the power of the rhetorical confrontations of the characters, while the explosion of conflicts and emotions could easily be accommodated in the polemical nature of the subject matter.

The satirical farce proved to be the most effective dramatic mode for protest. Responsive to a particular event, the dramatists of the Revolution created emotionally biased satires which projected their own anger and indignation, while, at the same time, assaulted political adversaries in bitter terms. Among the most prominent dramatists of the period who championed the cause of the Patriots were Mercy Otis Warren, Hugh Henry Brackenridge, and John Leacock.[7] Although their plays show weak dramatic structure, little concern for plot and characterization, they are excellent examples of the patriotic writing done in the period of the American Revolution.[8]

By rejecting the aesthetic imperative for the sake of propaganda purposes, late-eighteenth-century Americans turned towards a theater grounded in a fusion of political/historical events and a new ideological discourse in an attempt to inspire a national consciousness among Americans. The potential, and later the reality, of the American War of Independence forced both Tory and patriot playwrights to use their literary talent in order to define themselves and their cause, to look into the nature of events and issues in a powerful way, and to develop their arguments in an easily accessible form of entertainment. Although the American theater in the nineteenth century was an undisputed form of mass entertainment, the American plays written during the Revolutionary period show a conception of the theater as a place where political matters could be contained.[9]

II: POST-REVOLUTIONARY PERIOD: SOCIO-POLITICAL/ IDEOLOGICAL CHANGES AND WOMEN'S STATUS

Military victory over England was soon followed by the emergence of a distinctly American social landscape. The revolutionary war brought about certain changes in the social customs and political institutions of the newly-born nation. America's secession from the Empire kindled feelings of social democracy and republican fervor. The dynamic growth of Americans into self-knowledge actually meant two things: first, they had to recognize themselves as a republic, purged of the frivolity and corruption of the English class-bound monarchy, and, second, they had to establish liberty, democracy, virtue and reason as the widely-accepted cultural and social myths of the new republic.

The egalitarian principles of the Declaration of Independence stimulated new ideas about society and government and assured equal rights to all citizens. Social democracy was enhanced by the new nation's continuous attempts to eliminate the remaining shackles of medieval inheritance laws, the pervasive influence of an established church, the guild systems of employment, and other measures and laws that discriminated against the masses. The egalitarian sentiments unleashed by the war reflected, in many respects, the work of seventeenth- and eighteenth-century political philosophers, particularly of John Locke and Thomas Paine. In this dawning democratic age, the first attempts towards the abolition of the institution of slavery resulted in notable gains. Although the extension of the doctrine of equality to blacks remained incomplete—in fact, it was sacrificed to political expediency in an attempt to maintain national unity—quite a few northern states either abolished slavery outright or provided for the gradual emancipation of blacks.

However, the great questions of political liberty and civil freedom, of the relationship between democratic theory and social order, were questions that painfully ignored gender. As Linda K. Kerber argues, "a careful reading of the main texts of the Enlightenment in France, England, and the colonies reveals that the nature of the relationship between women and the state remained largely unexamined" (1980: 15).[9] Although late-eighteenth-century Americans were familiar with Enlightenment thought, the new social order they envisioned was more directly influenced by the literature of the Commonwealth and Radical Whig Opposition. The major ideological concerns of their political theory were rooted in assumptions that gave explicit attention to commercial growth and financial stability as well as to the need to limit the powers of the crown. American Whigs failed to integrate the concept of the proper relationship between women and the body politic into the egalitarian rhetoric following the Revolutionary War. As a result, American women found themselves in a position peripheral to the world of politics and decision making, excluded from the new republican ideology that proclaimed unbounded freedom of the individual, educational and economic opportunities for all groups of society. Although American men were unlikely to raise questions about women's political and social roles, the War of Independence as well as the developing ideology of republicanism altered women's own self-perceptions and encouraged their sense of involvement in the public realm. According to Gerda Lerner, "it was inevitable that, sooner or later, women would ask: If all men are created equal, why not women?"(31).

During the Revolution, however, women played a role of considerable significance. On the one hand, the war heightened the political consciousness of American women, while, on the other, it disrupted the conventional eighteenth-century 'feminine' functions. Women joined patriotic organizations, such as the "Daughters of Liberty," they made clothing for the soldiers, they worked in hospitals and provided care for the wounded, and at times they even took up guns. Furthermore, revolutionary circumstances had another especially striking effect upon women. Although most women's prewar experiences had been solely domestic, now, there was the time when women were forced to engage in unknown areas of endeavor. While their menfolk were away serving the army, they alone had to manage family property, they had to earn money in order to provide for their families, and generally undertake tasks and handle business affairs that fell outside their prescribed feminine sphere. Elizabeth Ellet, in her volume *The Women of the American Revolution* (1848), highlights the significance of the role that women were called upon to play in a period of political tensions and social changes:

> patriotic mothers nursed the infancy of freedom. Their counsels and their prayers mingled with the deliberations that resulted in a nation's assertion of its independence,. . they willingly shared inevitable dangers and privations, relinquished without regret prospects of advantage to themselves, and parted with those they loved better than life, not knowing when they were to meet again. It is almost impossible now to appreciate the vast influence of woman's patriotism upon the destinies of the infant republic (78).

For the first time, women were not frowned upon for venturing into the predominantly male sphere of politics. On the contrary, "the talk of rights and freedom set at least a few ladies to reflections on the rights of their own sex" (Smith 66). The pervasiveness of egalitarian sentiments, which, eventually, became codified in the Declaration of Independence, as well as the recognition of the significance of the political and social contributions made by women, gave impetus to the expression, in private correspondence, on the one hand, and in print, on the other, of a number of demands for women's rights. As the historian Linda K. Kerber points out, "if American women were to count themselves as the daughters of Liberty, they would have to invent their own ideology" (1980: 32). The concept of egalitarianism provided women with a solid theoretical basis for their arguments for political, social, and educational opportunities. According to Mary Beth Norton, "white women, who in the mid-1760s offered profuse apologies whenever they dared to discuss politics, were by the 1780s reading widely in political literature, publishing their own sentiments, engaging in heated debates

over public policy"(156). In 1776, Abigail Adams, in a letter to her
husband, issued the warning that:

> if perticular care and attention is not paid to the Laidies, we are
> determined to foment a Rebelion, and will not hold ourselves bound
> by any Laws in which we have no voice, or Representation (Norton
> 226).

The most important publication, however, came from the other side of
the Atlantic, but was widely read in America. It was *A Vindication of
the Rights of Woman* (1792), which was written by Mary
Wollstonecraft, an English lady who first saw the logical connection
between the American democratic values and women's rights. In her
major feminist treatise, Mary Wollstonecraft was particularly
outspoken about women's inferior legal status:

> I really think that women ought to have representatives, instead of
> being arbitrarily governed without having any direct share allowed
> them in the deliberations of government (145).

Similar arguments were voiced by native-born American women, like
Judith Sargent Murray, editor of *The Gleaner* (1790s), who "instead of
resting her case for investing girls with self-confidence on their need to
make an intelligent choice of a marital partner, she stressed rather the
preparation for their own independent future" (Norton 254). Murray is
also known for her feminist treatise "On the Equality of the Sexes,"
which was published in the *Massachusetts Magazine* in 1790. By
focusing on examples of highly-esteemed women whose actions
bespeak their merit, Murray elaborates on the idea that women are
equal to men, they are equally ingenious, "unsurpassed in bravery and
patriotism, possessed of eloquence, energy, loyalty, and heroism, and
entirely capable of supporting the toils of government" (Field 68). Also,
in later essays in *The Gleaner*, Murray continued defending women's
intellectual potential, stressing, at the same time, the importance of
education and economic independence for women. Finally, one of the
very few American men who, quite early, felt the need to address the
issue of women's equal rights was James Otis, the brother of Mercy
Otis Warren. In his pamphlet, *The Rights of the British Colonies
Asserted and Proved* (1764), James Otis asks: "are not women born as

free as men? Would it be infamous to assert that the ladies are all slaves by nature?" (Kerber 1980: 30-1).

With respect to its impact on women, the republican context of the Revolution positively redefined the American woman's role as mother and wife only. Stemming from the belief that the fate of the new republic depended largely upon the existence of virtuous citizens, it then followed that women could play a major role in instilling moral and patriotic sentiments into their children. The American Revolution "gave rise to the 'Republican mother' whose patriotic duty it was to nurture and guard the morality of the sons and daughters of the new Republic" (Nicolay 2). According to the new ideal of 'Republican Motherhood', American women were increasingly considered custodians of values and active promoters of public morality. The republican emphasis on motherhood had considerable implications for the status of women in the newly-born nation. In her very interesting article, Ruth H. Block observes that:

> what did change as a specific consequence of the American Revolutionary experience was that the feminine notion of virtue took on a political significance it had previously lacked. Americans never altogether abandoned the idea that the populace of the republic should be virtuous. Instead, they relegated the production and maintenance of public virtue to a new realm, one presided over largely by women (56).

Americans' ideal of the republican woman definitely required better formal instruction in order to enable her to bring up her children in an atmosphere of patriotism and virtue. The years immediately after the American revolution witnessed major improvements in female education.[10] A number of female academies opened, especially in the North, that prepared young ladies not for the traditional male professions—medicine, law—but to become better wives and mothers. One of the earliest American educational reformers, Benjamin Rush, argued that the education of American women should bear no resemblance to that of British women since it served specific social and patriotic purposes. According to Rush, "female education should be accommodated to the state of society, manners, and government of the country in which it is conducted" (181). Although Rush proposed a far more academic curriculum than the one offered by dame and adventure schools, which mainly stressed ornamental accomplishments, he, nevertheless, made it pretty clear that the ultimate purpose for women's scientific studies was better management of households.

Reformers seeking to improve female education in America in the 1780s and 1790s had to confront the old anti-intellectualism, the conventional objections to advance education for women. Deep-rooted in the Americans' consciousness was the assumption that, on the one hand, female intellect was far weaker than men's, and, on the other, academic study could turn woman into an unenviable anomaly, an "unsexed" creature. Progressive educational reformers, however, like Susanna Rowson, attempted to circumvent the pervasive opposition to women's academic education by insisting that improvement in education would make women better wives and mothers as well as more self-reliant, self-disciplined and rational citizens. Rowson's contribution to education for women was invaluable. She wrote a series of textbooks on geography, history, mathematics, literature, spelling and science, "at first only for the use of her own students, but they were so excellent and there was such a dearth of similar material, that they were soon published and used all over the Northeast for 50 years or more" (Turner 17). Rowson was one of the first teachers of young women to offer formal instruction in elocution and dramatics. Mary M. Turner explains that "her young ladies were well-educated, polished, grateful and charming, ready to enter society with conversation and accomplishments, rather than simpers and silences" (17).

On the whole, the most significant social change in the early republic that greatly affected women was the expansion of educational opportunities. However, the development of the feminine ideal of the republican woman, invested with patriotic significance, proved to be tremendously illusory since "a woman's competence was not assumed to extent to the making of political decisions. Her political task was accomplished within the confines of her family. The model republican woman was a mother" (Kerber 1980:228). Political action and decision-making continued to be inherently masculine. The egalitarian spirit of the Revolution, the developing public ideology of individual responsibility and morality as well as the need to secure and perpetuate civic virtue, all contributed to an enlargement of women's *domestic* role. By being literate, self-reliant (within limits, of course), untainted by the frivolities of fashionable behavior and superficial activities, the model republican woman placed her learning at her family's service and had the ultimate responsibility for the moral development of the male citizens of the Republic.

Consequently, in terms of women's legal and political rights, the birth of the Republic brought little or no changes at all![11] The anti-republican implications of the legal limitations placed upon women within marriage survived long into the new nation's maturity and actually reinforced women's political weakness and status of social dependency. However, in the atmosphere of republican ideology, American women started to question some of the hitherto unchallenged fundamental assumptions that governed their existence. Although the traditional legal system that colonial women inherited from England remained firmly entrenched in America, an increasing number of women demanded more egalitarian marital relationships, reciprocal affection and esteem in matrimony. The wider availability of divorce, the deliberate postponement of matrimony indicated that women were no longer willing to accept unquestioningly the traditional patriarchal attitudes towards marriage. In essence, the revolutionary era in America marked a number of tremendous social and political changes that awakened eighteenth-century women to an awareness of their subordinate status and constrictive sphere of action, and, in a way, "provided the women's rights movement with its earliest vocabulary" (Norton 299). While the promise of the Revolution proved to be essentially male-centered, the democratic sentiments of the Declaration of Independence were revised and appropriated in women's texts resulting in the drawing up of the first women's rights manifesto: The Declaration of Sentiments' (1848).

III: PLAYS BY WOMEN IN REVOLUTIONARY AND POST-REVOLUTIONARY AMERICA

In her brilliant book, *A Room of One's Own*, Virginia Woolf locates the major difficulty that women writers have faced throughout history in the fact that "they had no tradition behind them"(76). For the late-eighteenth century women playwrights, there was little in the way of a homegrown, distinctively American, dramatic tradition to draw on, let alone a female dramatic precedent upon which to built. However, the new code of values growing out of the American revolutionary experience gave a number of women writers the opportunity to use their own writing as an extension of the American republican spirit in an attempt to integrate women's voice into the newly-established democratic institutions. Aware of the broader questions of social and cultural change as well as of the great potential of drama in shaping democratic and nationalistic sentiments, women playwrights used the public forum of drama as a means to define their position in the social and political systems of the American nation. In some cases, their plays move beyond the simple commentary on national/political issues and the celebration of the American ideals of freedom and democracy, and actually constitute a conscious effort to establish a relationship between the late-eighteenth-century social and political climate and women's experience and reality.

We get the first glimpses of women's critical awareness of the fact that their own positioning within the existing social, cultural and ideological structures differs fundamentally from that of men in the plays written during the Revolutionary War period. Mary V. V.'s Tory satire, *A Dialogue Between a Southern Delegate and His Spouse on his Return from the Grand Continental Congress: A Fragment Inscribed to the Married Ladies of America by their Most Sincere and Affectionate Friend and Servant* (1774), constitutes one of the first explicit attempts towards the exploration of gender-specific concerns regarding the problem of women's social status and political experience. The writer openly questions the relationship between national and sexual politics offering a lively political-domestic argument with proto-feminist connotations. As the title itself describes, the play is a brief dialogue between a husband and his wife—there is no plot and no traditional pattern of writing is followed. The theme of the play is based upon the decision of the Whigs to send provincial delegates to an assembly in Philadelphia in order to discuss the punitive measures England had taken against Massachusetts as well as the various wrongs perpetrated by the mother-country. There seems to have been a tendency among the most conservative of the delegates to strengthen the relationship between England and America in order to avoid reaching a breaking point. But, this attitude towards conciliation between the two countries was thwarted by the more radical American Patriots, people like Sam and John Adams. The satire of the piece is an amusing one, based upon the popular farcical piece of domestic squabble, and the emotional tone of the play mainly rises from the deeply-felt indignation of the wife against the First Continental Congress of which her husband is a member. What is under attack in the play is the resolution of the

Continental Congress which defies Britain and which actually threatens to drag Americans into a major conflict with the mother-country. While reading the play, it is interesting to observe the wife's comments regarding the possibility of women making political decisions since they are less inclined than men to take actions that threaten the safety of the family. When the angry husband orders his protesting wife to "Mind thy household affairs, teach thy children to read, and never, Dear, with politics trouble thy head," she sarcastically replies: "Because Men are Males, are they all Politicians?"

As will be shown later in this chapter, Mercy Otis Warren, one of the earliest and most prolific American female writers, was the first one to establish a relationship between the ideological framework of democracy and egalitarianism and women's experiences and reality in her propaganda plays, and later in her romantic tragedies. While employing the republican rhetoric of the time, she successfully incorporated nationalistic comments and patriotic sentiments in her work in an attempt to raise questions about women's social status and their political rights in early American society.

When the political upheaval of the Revolutionary War was over, the people of the new nation started to repeal their anti-theater laws, a number of resourceful managers opened new theaters, and, before the turn of the century, a distinctly American drama made its appearance. The tendency of American dramatists in post-revolutionary era was to insert nationalistic sentiments in their themes and help people identify with the new democratic values. Although the partisan satires of the Revolution had disappeared, American drama continued its role, on the one hand, as a social and political commentator and, on the other, as a means of entertainment and moral instruction. As would be expected, the kinds of plays written at the time reflected an increasing interest in historical events as well as a strong patriotic feeling for the new country. Numerous plays from poetic tragedy to farce-comedy gained some popularity through their democratic spirit and patriotic sentiment. Taking into consideration all the dramatic works that were produced in America at that time, it appears that the early American playwrights' sense of nationalism found expression in the devices and techniques of seventeenth- and eighteenth-century English heroic tragedy and comedy.[12] From Thomas Godfrey's *The Prince of Parthia* (1765) to William Dunlap's *Andre* (1798), and to John Daly Burk's *Female Patriotism; or, The Death of Joan D' Arc* (1798), the writing of poetic drama continued well into the nineteenth century and actually became the mark of the serious dramatist. It seems that, in the wake of the Revolution, early American playwrights employed accepted romantic material for two reasons. First, by transcending time and space in their plays, they managed to treat effectively the universal themes of tyranny/oppression versus the ideals of liberty, freedom, and the dignity of common man. Second, the romantic spirit of the Revolution, the ever-growing faith in the power of the people to shape their destiny, in human rights and democracy, was successfully incorporated in the romantic tragedies' poetic speeches, heroic personages, noble sentiments and fights for freedom.

The successful American Revolution and its ensuing egalitarian rhetoric inspired a number of women playwrights to dramatize national issues and historical events and elaborate on themes of noble rebellion against tyranny. For example, in her farce-comedy, *Slaves in Algiers; or, A Struggle for Freedom* (1794), Susanna H. Rowson focuses on an urgent national affair: the American war with the Barbary Coast pirates, and actually centers her work around a most pressing political issue: the enslavement of American citizens by the pirates of North African States.

Augmenting the female tradition initiated by Warren and her heroic tragedies, *The Sack of Rome* and *The Ladies of Castile* (1790), American women dramatists began to write plays that emphasized the power of the common man, the concept of universal freedom, and the heroic qualities that all Americans admired. Margaretta V. Bleecker Faugeres exhibits her political idealism as well as her belief in human freedom and uncompromising human values in her five-act romantic tragedy *Belisarius* (1795). Written in the wake of the American Revolution, Faugeres offered *Belisarius* to the John Street Theater to be performed but it was eventually refused. The play emphasizes politics, patriotism and the ideals of liberty, dignity, and integrity, while employing the devices and techniques of 17th and 18th-century English heroic tragedy. Although *Belisarius* is overweight with long rhetorical speeches and exaggerated poetic diction, the playwright manages to convey the characters' passions and suffering, their emotional turmoil as well as their intense conflicts. The play is set in Rome and the hero, Belisarius, once a brave and victorious general, has been imprisoned and blinded by the emperor, Justinian, and his wife Theodora who, together with their vain and pompous courtiers, represent the corrupt side of political power. On the other hand, the citizens of the Empire unite with the soldiers in an attempt to free Belisarius and rebel against Justinian. The scene in which Belisarius talks to the riotous crowd and prevents a revolution attests to Faugeres' explicit attempt to convey a message of pacifism. This is particularly enhanced in the third act of the play where the Prince of Bulgaria offers Belisarius the opportunity to avenge his injustice by leading the Bulgarian troops against Justinian promising him at the same time immense wealth and power. However, in a truly Christian manner, Belisarius refuses saying that he no longer hates Justinian and that it is only "peace I love" (III, i). *Belisarius* also transmits a message of anti-materialism as it exposes the vanity of pomp and fame and maintains the sacredness of the simple, ordinary human life. Towards the end of the play, the emperor repents of his actions and, through the agency of his nephew Tiberias, apologizes to Belisarius and so the two men are reconciled.

It is interesting to note that Faugeres' female characters are caught in a world of male politics, of power, competition, and hostility, and act accordingly. The play presents two powerful women,—the Empress Theodora, and Julia, the woman who loves Belisarius,—whose high social status inevitably entails public power. Theodora is responsible for Belisarius' imprisonment while Julia consciously manipulates the Prince of Bulgaria and uses her influence to make him appoint Belisarius commander of his troops. The play ends with most of the female characters dead or having gone mad, while it becomes apparent that the women find themselves implicated in male power structures that in most cases victimize and depersonalize them.

Judith Sargent Murray also tried to explore the impact of the liberal democratic promise of independence and equality on the social and political status of American women in her play *Virtue Triumphant* (1798). As has already been mentioned, in terms of women's legal and political rights, the egalitarian principles of republicanism brought little or no changes at all. Women's political weakness and social dependency, especially within marriage, survived long into the new nation's maturity. Under the common law the colonists had inherited from England, married women had an unambiguously subordinate role and were legally and financially dependent on their husbands. However, in the atmosphere of republican ideology, American women gained some control over the selection of a husband, and actually started to demand more egalitarian marital relationships, mutual affection and respect in matrimony. Murray's *Virtue Triumphant* stresses egalitarian marriage principles and equality between the sexes. The play was performed at the Federal Street Theater in Boston, March 2, 1795, under the title of *The Medium; or, The Happy Tea Party*. It is included in the third volume of *The Gleaner*, and is introduced as the work of the obviously imaginary correspondent 'Philo Americanus.' The authorship of the piece was attributed to Murray's husband, John Murray, but publicly denied by him in *The Centinel*, March 4, 1795. *Virtue Triumphant* was not favorably received by the American audiences of the time. Perhaps that was due to the fact that the play reveals little dramatic skill on the part of the playwright; Murray's writing style is somewhat stilted and dull as she tends to insert many scenes that have nothing to do with the development of the story.

The play is about Ralph Maitland and his idea that everyone should adapt to a 'medium' of conduct and never, on any occasion, move to extremes. Maitland is really upset with his son, Charles, who has gone beyond that medium by being extremely attentive to Eliza Clairville. Charles has publicly declared his intention to marry Eliza and his devotion to her actually governs his every thought and action, thus making him a most unrealistic, colorless character in the play. Eliza Clairville also embodies some of the typical qualities of the late-eighteenth-century stage-heroine: she is the virtuous maid of unknown parentage who eventually succeeds in proving herself the social equal of Charles and his family. However, Maitland's objections quickly vanish when he meets her and is duly impressed by her, as well as when he finds out that the wealthy Colonel Melfort is her uncle. Following the trend introduced by Tyler's *The Contrast* (1787), Murray attempts to satirize the current fashions and manners through her secondary characters, people like Captain Flashet, an empty-headed boastful fellow, and Miss Dorinda Scornwell, a vain young lady of fashion, who looks down on anyone from a lower social class and "prefers cards to conversation, a ride to a book, and the ball-room to the play house" (II, iv). However, the significance of the play lies in Murray's portrayal of Eliza, her heroine. Despite her shortcomings as a stock character, it appears that Murray intended her as the stereotype of the self-assertive, independent woman who adamantly declares that: "Eliza Clairville will never unite herself to a man, whose family detests her" (II, i). Although Eliza, in a highly conventional way, gains her social and financial status through a male relative, her wish to be treated with respect and be viewed as equal to her future husband lies in her already internalized egalitarian principles as well as in her rising expectations about marriage.

Equally interesting, however, are the farce-comedies or social comedies that were written in America in the late eighteenth century. The trend toward farce-comedy, which actually began with Royall Tyler's *The Contrast* (1787) and continued with William Dunlap's *The Father; or, American Shandyism* (1788), Susanna H. Rowson's *Slaves in Algiers* (1794) and John Murdock's *The Triumphs of Love; or, Happy Reconciliation* (1795), generally focused upon social, political, and historical events in an attempt to improve American manners and morals and castigate social foibles and vices. John G. Hartman, in his very interesting work about the development of American social comedy, explains that social comedy frequently "seeks to satirize some particular social craze of the moment, or to reveal for our amusement the embarrassment individuals suffer because of the very conventions and institutions which they themselves have built up and supported" (1). In her preface to *Slaves in Algiers; or, A Struggle for Freedom*, Rowson makes a point by stating that "it has been my endeavor, to place the social virtues in the fairest point of view, and hold up, to merited contempt and ridicule, their opposite vices" (ii).

A little social comedy written in 1785, two years before Tyler's *The Contrast*, satirizes those wealthy or social-climbing republicans who, in true British fashion, became members of the Tea Assembly, a club where men and women could socialize playing cards and dancing. The play, *Sans Souci, Alias Free and Easy; or, An Evening's Peep into a Polite Circle,* is a farce in three acts, and has been attributed to Mercy Otis Warren, but there is no hard evidence of her authorship. *Sans Souci* reiterates a most appealing late eighteenth-century theme: the contrast between the affectation of British manners and fashions and American republican virtues and morals. Bearing a liberal amount of nationalism and moralizing, the play is extremely didactic in that it seeks to warn Americans of the pervasive influence of foreign vices, such as card-playing for money in public. Like most satires written in America at that time, *Sans Souci* substantially lacks in theatrical skills; the plot is extremely weak—just a combination of a few of scenes with satiric comments—and there is total absence of character development. However, it could be argued that its merit lies in the faithful depiction of the social biases of the day. The play is set in the "Metropolis of

Massachusetts," and the characters, who are simply social caricatures (Mr. and Mrs. Importance, Madame Brilliant, Jeremy Satirist, Dr. Gallant, Young Forward, Little Pert, Republican Heroine, et al.) are used as instruments for the playwright's satire. In the opening scene, both Young Forward and Little Pert agree that "fashion and etiquette are more agreeable to [their] ideas of life—this is the independence [they] aim at—the free and easy air which so distinguishes a man of fashion" (I,i). As would be expected, the rest of the play deals with the moral threat that the new entertainment, called Sans Souci, poses for Bostonian society. The Republican Heroine, the voice of morality and righteousness in the play, exclaims: "I could scarcely believe it possible, that this country, particularly this town, whose name stands foremost in the annals of America, should so early plunge into the utmost excesses of dissipation . . . I could hardly refrain from tears when I entered the Hall, to see the respectable inhabitants of this metropolis, so wantonly introducing a custom of public card playing, even at so early a period after the war" (II,i).

Another farce written at the time is Mrs. Marriott's *The Chimera; or, Effusions of Fancy* (1795). The play was performed in Philadelphia at Southwark Theater on November 17, 1794, with Marrriott acting the heroine, Matilda. The playwright was a member of the old American company who had arrived in the States from Edinburgh, and had joined the company two months prior to the opening night of her play. *The Chimera* was not favorably received by either the public or the critics, and the *New York Magazine* called it "a farce certainly unequaled by anything except its own prologue." This can easily be explained because Marriott, faithful to the spirit of the times, touches upon the familiar and much-celebrated ideals of liberty, democracy and patriotism in her prologue. However, the vehemence of the prologue does not really make up for the play's tremendous inadequacies: weakness of plot and dialogue, lack of character motivation and credibility of theme. The story, which takes place in contemporary England, is about Matilda, a young girl, who pretends to have lost her senses because her father, Sir Lambert Martin, has promised her hand to the "old and lame" Lord Aberford. In her fits of madness, Matilda is fond of invoking names of minor classical deities in an attempt to scare Lord Aberford off. In a really ludicrous scene, Matilda pretends to stab Lord Aberfod with a fan who, convinced that he has been mortally wounded signs his property over to Captain Rupert, his nephew and

Matilda's true love. Before the play ends, it is made quite clear that Matilda's purpose has been to gain one kind of chimera, an ideal marriage with Captain Rupert. It should be noted that Marriott satirically tackles the problem of female education as she stresses the impact of "these foolish books" on the frail mind of young women. [13]

IV: MERCY OTIS WARREN'S PROPAGANDA PLAYS, *THE ADULATEUR* (1773) AND *THE GROUP* (1775): AN EMERGING FEMINIST CONSCIOUSNESS

Probably the first woman playwright in America and a pioneer among early American writers, Mercy O. Warren successfully tackled political issues in her plays and revealed her unswerving devotion to republicanism. An eminent literary figure during the Revolution, she cleverly used her pen to satirize people and events as well as influence the political thought and consciousness of the Americans. [14] Lester H. Cohen rightfully regards her as "the most formidable female intellectual in eighteenth-century America"(xvi). She was one of the first American dramatists who managed to visualize an independent country with virtuous and freedom-loving citizens, and succeeded in setting up her ideal into dramatic form. A witty satirist, she manipulated the theatrical rhetoric of the time to voice her loyalty to the American cause, to comment on political events, and to express the British-American conflict.

For a woman of the eighteenth century, Warren's uncommon preoccupation with political and intellectual matters can certainly be attributed to the fact that she was the daughter of Colonel Otis, the sister of the distinguished patriot leader, James Otis, and the wife of General James Warren. Born the third child of the prosperous Otis family, she had the opportunity to study under her uncle, the Reverend Jonathan Russell, when he prepared her brothers for college. She was allowed to use her uncle's library, thus becoming familiar with the Greek and Latin classics, the works of Pope, Dryden and Milton, and the plays of Shakespeare and Moliere. In 1754, at the age of twenty-six, she married James Warren, a Harvard graduate and a Massachusetts political leader. As the conflict between the American colonies and the royal home government intensified, Warren's house in Plymouth, Massachusetts, became the meeting place of some of the most ardent supporters of the revolution and democracy. Thus, living at the center of revolutionary activity in New England, Warren was unavoidably drawn closer to public affairs since she was present at all the political discussions that took place in her home and had the opportunity to meet important public figures such as Samuel Adams and John Adams, who later became the second President of the United States (1797-1801).

Constantly encouraged to write by her husband and her close friends, who considered her an intellectual prodigy, Warren finally entered the War of Belles Lettres. As Walter J. Meserve points out, Warren "rallied to the Patriot cause with a fury that distinguishes her writing during the revolution. She was no middle-of-the-roader; what she thought she spoke or wrote. Her effect as a gadfly during the early years of the Revolution cannot be underestimated" (1977: 67). A close observer of the strenuous political activity during the Revolution, Warren decided to turn to propaganda plays in an attempt to provide an outlet for her deepest patriotic feelings as well as exhort the people of her country to adhere to republican principles. Theater-historian George O. Seilhamer observes that Mercy Warren was, among American writers, "the first to adopt the dramatic form as a vehicle for political satire"(3). Her work was recognized by her contemporaries and her plays, published in pamphlet form, swiftly circulated among the reading public.[15]

Warren's satires were primarily intended as weapons against political and personal oppression for all people.[16] Her writing projected the democratic values and principles of republicanism while, at the same time, aimed at stirring up "hatred for the Tories of Massachusetts and admiration for the American Revolutionaries" (Robinson 131). When Warren made her debut as a satirist, she appeared to be acutely aware of the social and political context in which she wrote. She also displayed an unparalleled talent and genius in that she elaborated on two interrelated concepts: human history and human nature. However, in her attempt to expose the Tories' folly and corrupted nature, Warren used satire so flagrantly that she, herself, felt really uneasy and uncomfortable with her work. In a letter intended to reassure her feelings of apprehension about the picture she had drawn of the Tory politicians in *The Group*, John Adams clearly urges her to continue her most valuable work:

> My most friendly regards to a certain Lady, tell her the God Almighty
> has entrusted her with Powers for the good of the World, which in the

Cause of his Providence, he bestows on few of the human race. That instead of being a fault to use them, it would be criminal to neglect them (Robinson 136).

In an era dominated by democratic principles, Warren's understanding of the power of the emerging language of republicanism was intimately associated with her own feminist consciousness in a developing social and political context. Warren's use of the republican idiom, which was mainly spoken by the prominent white, male, educated political figures of the late-eighteenth-century, encourages another view of republican rhetoric as the site where an articulate female intellectual challenges the immutability of women's role and status in early American society. Warren, as a member of the culture who might least expect to benefit from republican principles and institutions, uses the potential of the republican paradigm as a means to express her own complex identity as woman, writer, and committed republican.

Her plays indisputably reveal Warren's fusion of patriotic sentiments, her ethical and cultural background, as well as her own awareness of her gender position in the American society of the time. According to Lester H. Cohen, Warren performed "a kind of literary republicanism, one filled with poetic conceits and the coy blushings of the woman who speaks of politics daringly, only at the risk of sacrificing (or pretending to sacrifice) her conventional feminine pose" (1983: 488). Warren was definitely aware of the fact that, by writing political farces, not only did she step out of her prescribed feminine sphere, but she also presumed to occupy a subject position reserved for men only. Born into a society where women were trained in obedience, chastity, maternal love, and repression of personal desires and ambitions, it is easy to imagine Warren's feelings of guilt and apprehension as far as her literary creation was concerned. This must have been the main reason why she never openly desired to have her work published. It was her intimate friend, John Adams, who brought her work forward to the public, anonymously of course.[17]

In 1772, excerpts from Warren's first propaganda play, *The Adulateur*, were printed in the radical paper *The Massachusetts Spy* on March 26 and April 23, and, later, in 1773, a revised five-act version of the same play was published anonymously in pamphlet form. *The Defeat* appeared in the *Boston Gazette* in two installments (May 24 and July 19, 1773), while her most successful satire, *The Group*, appeared both serially in the *Boston Gazette* and the *Massachusetts Spy* in 1775 and in full editions in Philadelphia, Boston, and New York. Like her male contemporaries, Warren emphasized public and private virtue as the genius of republican ideology while she presented the historical events as a powerful struggle between two opposing political and moral principles: between liberty and arbitrary power, and virtue and corruption. In a letter to Abigail Adams in 1774, Warren revealed that dramatic expression was particularly suited to her needs for political and moral instruction:

> I think that the Follies and Absurdities of Human Nature Exposed to Ridicule in the Masterly Manner it is done by Moliere may often have a greater tendency to reform mankind than some graver lessons of morality (Richards 225).

Far from being apolitical, Warren followed the historical events of the American Revolution closely and organized her plays around a most insightful political analysis. Her plays are filled with the powerful language of public virtue mixed with Warren's apparent didacticism. Reading her propaganda dramas, it cannot be denied that Warren saw and understood well the complex implications of the political and social issues involved in the quest for democracy. It is not surprising that in all her dramatic creations she opted for the limitless interplay of moral and ideological contradictions.[18] Although the central trajectory of her plays is largely determined by the dominant thematic polarization between right and wrong, it appears that Warren uses a particular historical event as a point of departure for the discussion of more generalized, diachronic issues. To the modern reader these satires in dialogue, then called propaganda dramas, may appear particularly wearisome with their constant references to classical myth, world history and political figures. However, the wealth of these references show evidence of Warren's intellect and education and actually increase the weight of her political arguments.

What distinguishes her plays from the rest of the propaganda dramas of the time is the fact that Warren's republican language is not only used to explain history and politics, to comment and ridicule, but also serves as the space where the republican ethics of virtue meet the traditional role of women as the "moral pillars of society."[19] In a letter to her son Winslow, Warren argues that as a woman, mother, and writer, she functions as the bearer of republican values, the transmitter of patriotic sentiments:

> My duty and my inclination leads my whole attention to one great point—to form the minds, to fix the principles, to correct the errors, and to beckon by the soft allurements of love, as well as the stronger voice of reason, the young members of society (peculiarly my charge) to tread the path of true glory instead of the hackneyed vulgar walks crowded by swarms of useless votaries, who worship at the pedestal of pleasure or bow before the shrine of wealth (Cohen 1983: 495).

This is precisely her point of departure—the celebration of democratic values and ideals—which, in fact, clears a new space for the merging of the newly-established social reality and women's status. It appears that Warren treats the political events of the time from a mainly ethical standpoint. The tension between right and wrong, the juxtapositions of virtue and corruption, of tyranny and freedom, of wealth/power and the dignity of common man are prevalent in her plays. Alice Brown argues that for Mercy Warren "there was never a middle course. Life, and even political life, was right or wrong. There were moral blacks and whites; there were no grays"(153). In *The Adulateur*, for example, dramatic intensity is achieved through the depiction of the major moral conflict between Rapatio's tyrannical government and the group of Patriots led by Brutus. Set in Upper Servia (Boston), *The Adulateur,* a five-act tragedy in blank verse, was written after the "promiscuous death and slaughter" (II,i) of Americans, what is known as the Boston Massacre (1770).[20] The chief satire of the play is directed against Rapatio—as the name itself suggests, he is the rapacious one,—who is in fact Thomas Hutchinson, the last Tory Governor of the State. Jeffrey H. Richards remarks about Warren's portrayal of Hutchinson that "she was ruthless in exposing [him] as a Machiavel (1995: 85).

The characters in the play are drawn in strong contrast—the unscrupulous Tories and the virtuous, heroic Patriots. The political divergence of the opposing factions is subordinated to their moral antithesis, which is given particular emphasis in the play. Although Warren's black/ white dialectic appears to be rather simplistic and limiting, she, nevertheless, manages to highlight the importance of the moral aspect of human nature. So blunt and straightforward is Warren's

satire that when we are first introduced to Rapatio and his allies we
become instantly aware of their villainy and repulsive nature:

Rapatio

Hail happy day! In which I find my wishes,
My gayest wishes crown'd. Brundo retir'd,
The stage is clear. Whatever gilded prospects
E'er swam before me—Honor, places, pensions—
All at command—Oh! my full heart! 'twill burst!
Now Patriots think, think on the past and tremble
I'll make the scoundrels know who sways the sceptre
Before I'll suffer this, I'll throw the state
In dire confusion, nay I'll hurl it down,
And bury all things in one common ruin.
O'er fields of death, with hasting step I'll speed
And smile at length to see my country bleed (I, ii).

Rapatio meets opposition in the figure of honest Brutus, the leader of
the Patriots, who becomes the voice of morality and righteousness in
the play:

I sprang from men, who fought, who bled for freedom
From men, who in the conflict laugh'd at danger;
Struggl'd like patriots, and through seas of blood,
Waded to conquest.—I'll not disgrace them.
I'll show a spirit worthy of my sire.
Tho' malice dart her stings;—tho' poverty
Stares full upon me;—tho' power with all her thunder
Rolls o'er my head,—thy cause my bleeding country
I'll never leave—I'll struggle hard for thee,
And if I perish, perish like a freeman (I, i).

Despite the obvious deficiencies of *The Adulateur* and *The Group*
-weak plot, inadequate structure, absence of character development-
Warren's propaganda plays do not merely reflect her personal beliefs
and political convictions, but also, through the characters' important
monologues, generate an optimistic vision of an American republican
future as long as the American citizens adhere to the principles of

virtue, reason, and self-discipline. For example, in *The Adulateur*, Warren prophesies victory and a free country with virtuous citizens:

Brutus

... While thou my country, shall agin revive,
Shake off misfortune, and thro' ages live,
See thro' the waste a ray of virtue gleame,
Dispell the shades and brighten all the scene,
Wak'd into life, the blooming forest glows,
And all the desart blossoms as the rose.
From distant lands see virtuous millions fly
To happier climates, and a milder sky.
While on the mind successive pleasures pour,
Till time expires, and ages are no more (V,iii).

More than any of her contemporary protest writers, Warren identified republicanism with its ethical tenets. The republic of which she dreamed was one in which public and private virtues flourished. As Brutus proudly declares in *The Adulateur*, "We've done as patriots ought—like men who scorn the name of faction—men who nobly act from sense of honor"(II,i). Although the authority and legitimacy of the republican rhetoric are taken for granted in all the patriotic pamphlets written in the 1770s, Warren's writing points increasingly to the combination of individual vices with the larger political and moral processes. What emerges from the careful reading of Brackenridge's *The Battle of Bunker's Hill*, and *The Death of General Montgomery*, and Leacock's *The Fall of British Tyranny* is the need, on the one hand, to record in theatrical form the events leading up to the Revolutionary War in an attempt to attract allegiance to the American idea of liberty, and, on the other, to show the rightful anger and indignation of an embryonic nation against the enemies of democracy and freedom. However, Warren's plays reveal a greater awareness of republicanism as a complex system of politics and ethics which could only be sustained by public virtue and morality as well as commitment to democratic values and the ideal of liberty:

Brutus

... While from our fate shall future ages know,

Virtue and freedom are thy care below (*The Adulateur* I,i) .

Warren's preoccupation with right and wrong, virtue and vice, takes a most incisive form in both her protest plays. She employs nature imagery in an attempt to reinforce her arguments and philosophical concerns and to artistically implicate the natural order into her ideological schema:

Brutus

Oh! patriots rouse. The distant branches lop'd
The root now groans—let not the thought of power,
Ungenerous thought! freeze up the genial current (I, i).

In *The Adulateur* as well as in *The Group*, Warren develops strategies to establish various levels of inner conflict and actually move beyond political turmoil and military action in order to present us with powerful insights into human nature, into the characters moral codes, their consciences, their decisions and choices. In *The Adulateur*, apart from the stark contrast between the virtuous Patriots and the evil Tories, bombastic language is employed to describe some of the Tories' inner tensions as they waver between glory/wealth and loyalty to their country. Even ruthless Rapatio is smitten by his conscience:

Destroy their boasted rights, and mark them slaves
To ride triumphant o'er my native land,
And revel on its spoils—But hark! it groans!
The heaving struggles of expiring freedom!—
Her dying pangs—and I the guilty cause:—
I shudder at the thought—why this confusion?
The phantom conscience, whom I've bid alien—
Can she return? O let me, let me fly!
I dare not meet my naked heart alone (IV,ii).

In *The Group*, a polemical farce in two acts, Tory politicians become the target of the sharp shafts of Warren's wit and poignant observations. Warren presents thinly disguised portraits of such Tories as Peter Oliver and Daniel Leonard, and focuses upon a specific historical event, the appointment of a Counsil by the King rather than through election by the Assembly, thus resulting in the abrogation of the charter of Massachusetts. The play attacks those councilors who, after the abrogation of the colonial charter, accepted royal appointments to the Massachusetts Council, thereby depriving locals of the right to vote. It is particularly interesting to note that the characters in the play are all members of the Council while the Patriots are physically absent. The reason for such an artistic decision is, as B. Franklin explains, "that the government's men need no foil. They are so venal and spineless that introducing their adversaries would blur the play's focus and would divert the reader from the group's villainy" (xiv). Warren's play focuses upon each of the mandamus councilors and successfully projects their corrupted nature and moral laxity through an in-depth study of their personal confessions:

Hateall

Compassion ne'er shall seize my steadfast breast
Though blood and carnage spread thro' all the land;
Till streaming purple tinge the verdant turf,
Till ev'ry street shall float with human gore,
I Nero-like, the capital in flames,
Could laugh to see her glotted sons expire,
Tho' much too rough my soul to touch the lyre (I, i).

Although there is very little physical action in *The Group*, dramatic effectiveness arises from Warren's device to penetrate the consciences of the Loyalists and expose their villainy:

Monsieur

So great the itch I feel for titl'd place,
Some honorary post, some small distinction,
To save my name from dark oblivion's jaws,
I'll hazard all, but ne'er give up my place,
For that I'll see Rome's ancient rites restor'd
And flame and faggot blaze in ev'ry street (II, i)

Like Monsieur, all of them at some point in the play decide to betray the American cause for personal gain. Hazlerod declares that for fame and wealth he could "give [his] tears and conscience to the winds" (I,i).

So absolutely selfish and base the Loyalists are presented to be that they are unable to recognize a higher cause and purpose in life other than power and glory. Beau Trumps, shamelessly states that "there's nought on earth that has such tempting charms as rank, show, pomp, and glitt'ring dress" (II,i). Warren appears to be primarily concerned with avarice, wealth, corruption, and self-aggrandizement. She fears that her idealized republic will eventually disappear in the midst of political compromise, personal ambition and false values. By focusing upon the priority of ethical categories in political interpretation, Warren, in both plays, fuses ideological commitment and ethical conduct in an attempt to emphasize the absolute necessity of virtue and reason for the survival of the newly-born American republic:

Brutus

> He who in virtue's cause remain unmov'd,
> And nobly struggles for his country's good:
> Shall more than conquer—better days shall beam,
> And happier prospects croud again the scene (*AD* III, iii).

Especially, in *The Group*, Warren's dramatic indictment of the Tory politicians is significantly enhanced by the staging of the characters' introspective approach to their own thoughts, feelings, and motives:

Collateralis

> I almost wish I never had engaged
> To rob my country of her native rights,
> Nor strove to mount on justice's solemn bench,
> By mean submission cringing for a place.
> How great the pain, and yet how small the purchase!(II, iii)

In the last scene of *The Group*, a series of confessions confirm the Tories' representation as depersonalised figures of inherent vice:

Meagre

> I hated Brutus for his noble stand
> Against the oppressors of his injured country
> I hate the leaders of this restless factions,

For all their generous efforts to be free. . .
And from the rancor of my venomed mind,
I look askance on all the human race (II, iii).

Warren's argument becomes stronger through the Tories' realization and acceptance of the everlasting effect of the Patriots' dignified and glorious deeds:

Dupe

They fight for freedom, while we stab the breast
Of every man who is her friend professed.
They fight in virtue's ever-sacred cause,
While we tread on divine and human laws.
Glory and victory, and lasting fame
Will crown their arms and bless each hero's name! (II, iii)

Interestingly, however, what really gives the satire its bite are Warren's constant references to the wives of the Tories. By incorporating personal details into the representation of the Tories and by making misogyny one of the most repulsive vices displayed by them, she presents a far more complicated argument and increases the weight of the bitterness with which the Tories are portrayed. Simple's unquenchable thirst for glory makes him insensitive to his wife's predicament who "weeps, -and urges my return to rural peace and humble happiness, as my ambition beggars all her babes"(I,i). Furthermore, unscrupulous Hateall does not hesitate to sacrifice his wife in order to gratify his own ego: "I'll not recede to save from sweet perdition my wife, my country, family, or friends" (I,i):

Hateall

Pho—what's a woman's tears,
Or all the whistlings of that trifle sex?
I never felt one tender thought towards them.
When young, indeed, I wedded nut-brown Kate—
Blithe, buxom, dowager, the jockey's prey—
But all I wished was to secure her dower.
I broke her spirits when I'd won her purse,
For which I'll give a recipe most sure

> To every hen-pecked husband 'round the board.
> If crabbed words or surly looks won't tame
> The haughty shrew, nor bend the stubborn mind,
> Then the green hickory, or the willow twig
> Will prove a curse for each rebellious dame
> Who dare oppose her lord's superior will (II, iii).

The presentation of women as the victims of the Tories' inhumanity and brutality, on the one hand, connects political and historical events to women's specifically domestic interests, while, on the other, emphasizes the idea that only men as villainous and unscrupulous as the Tories' take advantage of women's weakness. Warren consolidates her belief that domestic happiness depends upon civil and political virtue, upon republican principles, by ending her play with a woman's perspective introducing a nameless 'lady' who voices patriot sentiments:

> Instead of the landscape's beauteous dies
> Must the stained field salute our weeping eyes,
> Must the green turf and all the mournful glades,
> Drenched in the stream, absord their dewy heads;
> Whilst the tall oak and quivering willow bends,
> To make a covert of for their country's friends
> Denied a grave amid they hurrying scene
> Of routed armies scouring o'er the plain,
> Till British troops shall to Columbia yield,
> And freedom's sons are masters of the field! (II, iii).

This anonymous female character exemplifies Warren's argument that women, too, are greatly affected by history and culture. Warren's increasingly clear perception of political and ethical decline due to corruption, as well as her growing sense of the equality of the sexes constitute the two sides of her attempt to identify the role of women with the preservation of democratic principles and practices. Probably frustrated by the impossibility of women engaging in direct political action, she presents an anonymous lady who stands for all American women and who actually becomes the bearer of republican history and the source of virtue and patriotism. Nina Baym explains that "the fact that it is only men of republican principle who support domesticity and therefore honor women is a virtual proof that republicanism is the divinely sanctioned form of government" (547). Warren's philosophical contemplation of the interrelation between private/public morality and political ideology justifies the compatibility of domestic values and republican principles in Revolutionary America. Gender representation in her plays is related to politics on two levels. Morality, political ideology, and women's sphere are successfully integrated into Warren's republican language as she highlights some of the female experiences of the Revolution.

The point is that Warren uses her pen and adopts the public language of republicanism in order to advance her democratic vision and her larger aspirations regarding women's political function. However, there is something ironic and unfortunate in Warren's realization of the personal and civic implications of republicanism, which, in fact, becomes more evident in her later tragedies, *The Sack of Rome* (1790) and *The Ladies of Castile* (1790).[21] Although her work appears to be consistent in the insistence upon republican virtue as a means of maintaining the fundamental unity of self, politics and ethics for the nations' prosperity, when it comes to the fusion of womanhood and politics into a single unified performance, then late-eighteenth-century social and political reality defeats Warren's aspirations.

However, to the extent that Warren's commitment to enunciating republican values reinforced her idea that women's lives depended upon the government under which they lived, it can be inferred that her view of women's position and status in society stressed the right of women to speak about and influence, if necessary, the political ideology. This brings us to the second level upon which Warren connects politics to gender. Her propaganda plays become the site where Warren exercises her patriotic and moral obligation to promote the ideals of democracy and freedom and contemplate upon a possible political role for the republican woman.

V: POST-REVOLUTIONARY DRAMA: WARREN'S *THE LADIES OF CASTILE* (1790) AND *THE SACK OF ROME* (1790), AND ROWSON'S *SLAVES IN ALGIERS* (1794).

It has been my endeavor to link the analysis of the plays to the larger social processes and ideological changes as these affected the status of women in American society. My approach to the plays written by

Warren and Rowson is mainly grounded in a critical assessment of the political, cultural, and ideological interests they articulate as well as in an investigation of the tensions between women's perceptions and experiences and the existing post-revolutionary framework. A close reading of Warren's and Rowson's plays reveals the playwrights' particular appropriation of republican ideology in an effort to skillfully interweave political consciousness and women's social status. Significantly, *The Sack of Rome, The Ladies of Castile*, and *Slaves in Algiers* engage in processes of reorganizing and reorienting post-revolutionary definitions of democracy, freedom, and equality. In each one of these plays, the presence of tyrannical rulers like Valentinian III in *The Sack of Rome*, Don Velasco in *The Ladies of Castile*, and the Dey of Algiers in *Slaves in Algiers*, allows a better understanding of the insidious workings of tyranny in general, while, at the same time, it provides insight into the invisible power of patriarchy, as we are made to observe more intently the interactions, the limitations and the inhibitions of the female characters.

Central to the questions of political freedom and social equality the plays tackle is the figure of the republican woman. Donna Maria, in *The Ladies of Castile*, stands as the embodiment of humanity, morality, righteousness and as the symbol of republican femininity. The wife of Don Juan, the leader of the revolutionaries, Maria powerfully projects the new model of American femininity shaped by the democratic tenets of the Revolution, by the belief in social and political equality for all people. Maria, like Susanna Rowson's Fetnah in *Slaves in Algiers*, provides a positive image for post-revolutionary American women to identify with. Interestingly, both Warren and Rowson develop this image in relation to concepts of duty and responsibility to one's country as well as around an overriding quest for self-definition and autonomy. From this image, the two playwrights craft dramas that challenge the relationship between national and sexual politics by symbolically connecting their exploration of women's status within American society with powerful revolts against monarchical dominion.

In studying the plays of Warren and Rowson, my emphasis shifted to the way existing discourses about the cultural construction of republican femininity are questioned, to the exploitation of male values and ideals for the benefit of women, and finally to the articulation of the possibility of an alternative feminine discourse. The republican rhetoric of the revolution as well as women's actual historical experiences of the various social, cultural and political transformations provided both Warren and Rowson with an alternative dramatic discourse which, to a great extent, reflected early American women's social and material conditions, their feelings and thoughts. Teresa de Lauretis clearly distinguishes between the notion of "woman" as a male-produced fictional construct and "real, historical women" (5-6). Within theater practice, the cultural construction of the female gender, the fictional "Woman," has consistently appeared on stage revealing and, at the same time, perpetuating deep-seated patriarchal biases concerning women. What is particularly interesting in the plays of Warren and Rowson is the fact that women's experiences are brought out of the recesses, the margins, and are placed center-stage as the archetypal distinction between public and private spheres is inherently minimized.

Warren's post-revolutionary historical tragedies were written in the late 1780s and published in 1790. Although she sent these plays to John Adams, while he was in London, in the hope that they would be produced there, they were never performed. *The Sack of Rome* and *The Ladies of Castile* are less technically-flawed than her earlier propaganda plays. Despite the fact that we still have instances of long monologues and the plays are less-spirited than her protest dramas, the characters are more completely-drawn and the structure, the plot, the conflicts, the tensions between the characters are more solidly presented. In her romantic tragedies, Warren continues to employ nature imagery, powerful monologues and dramatic confrontation scenes as her characters act and interact in a world of political and military conflicts. Although the plays are not obviously related to the American-British struggle, Warren reiterates her previous didacticism as she actually urges Americans to guard against corrupt leaders and protect their democratic institutions and lofty ideals:

> May their conduct never contradict the professions of the patriots who have asserted the rights of human nature; nor cause a blush to pervade the cheek of the children of the martyrs who have fallen in defence of the liberties of their country (*The Ladies of Castile* 101).

In the preface to her play *The Ladies of Castile*, Warren reveals once again her wish to foster the ideals of liberty, dignity, loyalty and integrity in post-war America:

> The history of Charles the fifth, the tyranny of his successors, and the exertions of the Spanish Cortes, will ever be interesting to an American ear, so long as they triumph in their independence, pride themselves in the principles that instigated their patriots and glory in the characters of their heroes, whose valour completed a revolution that will be the wonder of ages.

Similar in technique and theme, both *The Sack of Rome* and *The Ladies of Castile* reflect divided loyalties, duplicity, corruption, despotic rulers, and the unattainable ideals of freedom and democracy. Warren's preoccupation with right and wrong, virtue and vice, corruption and morality, is more forcefully depicted in her later tragedies than in her propaganda plays since she explicitly probes into issues of personal and political deception, violence, and sexual abuse. The opening scenes of both plays establish Warren's concern for freedom, her commitment to democratic principles and republican sentiments as well as her intention to warn free Americans against the corrupting influence of "luxury," "pride," "intemperance," and "lust" (*SOR*: I,i). In *The Sack of Rome*, the Emperor, Valentinian, has "supinely sunk in dreams of wanton bliss, ignoble pleasures of a splendid court," while his depravity and his morbid desire for Maximus' wife will eventually drive him to rape. In *The Ladies of Castile*, the main focus is upon the relentless crushing of Spain's last heroic struggle for liberty before the establishment of tyranny and despotism by the family of Ferdinand. The ending in both plays is essentially pessimistic. *The Sack of Rome* ends with most of the major characters dead and with Rome controlled by the invading army of barbarians led by Genseric and his evil son, Hunneric. In *The Ladies of Castile*, almost all the revolutionaries are killed, and the values of freedom and democracy are about to disappear as corruption quashes liberty and fosters deception and vice.

In her dramatic world, Warren systematically utilizes the construction of tremendous moral and political antitheses to enhance her inherent nationalism, while, at the same time, she shifts to an awareness of the complex implications of the issues involved in women's quest for social and political equality. The female characters in Warren's tragedies are deliberately placed within a complex socio-cultural context in order to show how politics and gender are implicated in the production of the female body as a site of domination and struggle. In *The Sack of Rome* as well as in *The Ladies of Castile*, Warren provides us with images of women's painful struggle for survival and re-definition. In the plays, the representations of death, of rape and victimization serve to criticise those cultural and political attitudes that reduce the female body to a position of dependency and passivity, to objectification and sexual abuse. Warren's critique of the constraints of patriarchy, as these are realized in the position culture grants femininity within society and in the oppression connected with the female body, constitutes part of her attempt to foreground a world marked by a democratic political system in which women's position would be re-defined and re-emphasized free from social, political and gender restrictions.[22]

In *The Sack of Rome*, Warren dramatizes women's contradictory relationship with the social, cultural and political context in which they live as she exposes the dangers and violations of the feminine body in a society which turns Woman into a commodity, into a passive object in any exchange. Throughout the play, the political setting of unrest and struggle for freedom most prominently intersects with the heroines' experience of loss and death. Ardelia's rape by Emperor Valentinian becomes the initiating force of the play's action. From the very beginning, Warren invites us to recognize the close connection between a corrupted political system and women's experience of commodification within patriarchal culture. Although Ardelia as a character is physically absent in the play, the incident of her rape and her eventual suicide extend throughout the first three acts. This technique produces a powerful effect in terms of the classical representation of gender roles in which men are active subjects and women are passive victims. Jill Dolan argues that "left passive in a narrative articulated by men who control its linguistic, social, political, and psychological power, women become objects pursued for the fulfillment of male desire" (49). The male control over the female discourse and the female image is evidenced in both the way the male characters repeatedly point to the public construction of Ardelia as a figure of virtue and innocence, thus ensuring that the tragic story of her violated femininity is documented and circulated among her society, and in Maximus' description of Ardelia's death scene:

> Dismay'd she held a dagger in her hand
> As half resolv'd to plunge it in her breast,
> Yet trembled at the purpose of her soul (III,i).

Like Richardson's Clarissa, and so many other heroines who had the same fate in world literature, Ardelia's rape means the complete destruction of any sense of esteem and value. In response to the violence of her rape, Ardelia turns to death, the most radical form of self-destruction. By giving up her life willingly, she actually sets an example for the triumph of virtue while, at the same time, all the characters address this "pure and spotless" matron with tenderness and admiration (II, i). The emphasis on her natural dignity and inner nobility assures Maximus and the other characters of the legitimacy of their pain in mourning her and endows them with a powerful sense of righteousness that allows them to place all the blame for her demise on Valentinian. Ardelia's silent body assumes two different attitudes: it exposes to critique the patriarchal political and sexual ideology and emerges as a source of regenerative modification as it actually effects a revitalizing upsurge that takes the form of revolution against corrupted and deprave tyrants like Valentinian and the political systems they represent:

Maximus

> But yet her wrongs may urge thy dauntless arm,
> And give full vigour to a bold design,
> To smite a scepter'd brow—yes—that is all—
> The man himself's a poltroon—
> Yet he's an emperor (III,i).

Throughout the first three acts of the play, the thematic dimensions of such a primordially repressed social taboo like rape merge with constant references to the necessity of morality and integrity for a nation's governing. Warren's drama simply shifts from Ardelia's tragic story to the oppressive impact of tyranny, thus establishing the unambiguous conjunction of the disturbing effects of this particular incident and the general atmosphere of tension and turmoil pervading the last two acts of the play. Rape, in *The Sack of Rome*, is treated as a male ritual, a property crime of men against men in which women become victims in the political and social exchange. Maximus, in order to avenge his wife's death, will eventually lead a successful assault against Valentinian and succeed him as Emperor.

Ardelia falls victim to male power as this is realized in both the primordial sexual desire of men towards women and the social, political, legal and economic overshadowing of women by men. Her tragic choice of suicide emerges as a form of assuagement in the first place, in that she imagines death not only as a source of relief, but also as a vindication of her primary image and privileged role in society as a virtuous and honorable matron:

Maximus

She breath'd a sob as if a seraph sigh'd,
Drop'd a kind tear, and smil'd a last adieu. . . .
The shining angel left this blasted world,
And now methinks, ineffably serene (III,i).

Realising her now irrevocable sense of her loss of honor, Ardelia turns to death in an attempt to gain authority and assert herself against the insidious influence of a disintegrating political system. Ardelia's elaborate dying, which takes place before Maximus' eyes, can be read as a ritual of deliberate disengagement from patriarchal and political society. Thinking that Maximus implicitly supported the Emperor's scheme to rape her, she forces him to watch the gradual obliteration of her body while, at the same time, she directly accuses him and her society for allowing the destruction of virtue:

Maximus (reports Ardelia's last words)

"Poor Maximus she cry'd—spite of thy guilt
My soul still pities thee—receive this pledge
To cheat some other soft, believing fool;
Blot from thy thought that e'er Ardelia liv'd
To be the sport of riot and debauch (III,i).

Ardelia deliberately positions herself as the object of Maximus' gaze in order to express her precarious and vulnerable position in a male-dominated political order that has violated her body and repressed her discourse. In order to counter the figurative "death" of rape, to break out of the snare of silence and regain her subjectivity, Ardelia takes the disruption of her body, engendered by the act of rape, to its full consequence and uses literal death to make a statement, to speak through her body. Even as she embraces death as the only way to reverse her deprivation of speech during the rape, she actually supersedes death as she continues to have effect and influence after her demise precisely because of her demise. In her interesting book about women and death, Elizabeth Bronfen argues that:

> suicide implies an authorship with one's own life, a form of writing the self and writing death that is ambivalently poised between self-construction and self-destruction. . . . . The choice of death emerges as a feminine strategy within which writing with the body is a way of getting rid of the oppression connected with the feminine body (142).

The precariousness of women's status within a male political system and social order is again emphasized in the play with the introduction of Edoxia, Valentinian's wife and queen of Rome. Although Edoxia is wronged by Valentinian in that he is blatantly unfaithful to her, she nevertheless appears to incorporate all those patriarchal values attached to the gender of "Woman" that suppress her actual feelings and thoughts. Representing the extremely good, self-sacrificing wife, Edoxia warns Valentinian of Maximus' plans to overthrow him and expresses her concern for his safety:

> My wrongs I here forgive—thy safety now
> Is all I have to wish—my soul is all alarm (II, i).

However, a closer reading of the scene of Valentinian's and Edoxia's encounter reveals in essence the archaic male fear of woman as the embodiment of the dangerous and the chaotic that threatens male order and control. The power and ambivalence of woman's position as Other is tacitly invoked in this scene as Valentinian is so fearful of his caring and righteous wife that connects her presence with death:

> But hah!—here comes my torment—
> My other conscience-to kill me with a look—
> The fair—the excellent—the wrong'd Edoxia;
> Her presence freezes all my powers of speech;

> I dare not lift my eye to meet her frown—
> I am all confusion—guilt—perdition—death (II,i).

Edoxia and death coalesce in Valentinian's discourse in that they both inspire fear in him, fear of an ultimate loss of control and power. Her presence is actually felt as more disruptive than supportive of his sense of omnipotence, of his illusion of wholeness. She, in fact, reflects his division, his inner conflict because she functions as his smiting conscience. The conjunction of femininity and death is also registered in Edoxia's language as she becomes a harbinger of death prophesying Valentinian's actual demise:

> Ill boding dreams and gloomy apparitions—
> Fresh bleeding ghosts, and shades of darkest hue,
> Haunt all my slumbers—some deep design,
> Of terrible import, in Maximus I saw (II, i).

It is evident, throughout the play, that Warren manipulates her dramatic material to create a curious amalgam of cultural, political and philosophical attitudes. Ideas, events, and people interpenetrate and give substance to a number of ideological points. Warren articulates exactly the emotional and moral split of human existence in an attempt to authenticate the truth of her implicit statement about the romantic delusion of ambition, fame, and glory. We are constantly presented with insights into the major contradiction between human experience and material reality, into the characters painful psychological confusion.

Consciously conveying her message through a recuperative lesson emphasizing the necessity of integrity, morality and stability for the welfare and prosperity of all nations, she explicitly turns to the abstract concept of political consciousness and explores its reality. The notion of political consciousness is constructed in relation to the close proximity between leadership and degeneration. The play warns people that the absence of judgment and morality will simply lead to an unremitting succession of corrupt rulers morbidly sealing the fate of any nation. The paradox inherent in the revolutionary ideal is that it can either purge the political system from corruption and deception or, if desecrated, mark its disintegration and demise. Ironically enough, this

final message is explicitly transmitted by Genseric, the barbarian king
who invaded and enslaved Rome:

> Empire decays when virtue's not the base,
> And doom'd to perish when the parts corrupt (V,iii).

The theme of female objectification, of a necessary 'exchange' in a
male social reality and political order is further enhanced in the play as
the passage from Valentinian's reign to that of Genseric's is effected
through the mediation of Edoxia. Here Edoxia is implicated as an
essentially passive object in the masculine struggle for power and
control. It is made quite clear that her status as queen of Rome and the
power this title entails are sharply undercut by her own gender.
Ornamented with a much-enviable crown, she, in fact, becomes
Maximus' prize to obtain for his successful revolution:

> Maximus
>
> And now, I have another game to play;
> Edoxia must be mine—her hand I'll seize—
> Her heart I leave till time may do its work.
> By a long line of ancestry, a queen,
> Her regal title to the imperial crown
> Must bind it fast on Maximus brow. . . .
> Yet ere tomorrow's son descends the vale,
> And hides behind yon western burnish'd hill
> Our hands are join'd by wedlock's sacred tie;
> It must be so, or I'm but half aveng'd (IV,i).

Attempting to escape the claustrophobic pressure of Maximus, who
wishes to unify Rome by marrying her, Edoxia turns for assistance to
Genseric and exposes her family and Rome to destruction. However, in
Edoxia's story the issue is more than simply the notion of a fatal
mistake. The major dramatic confrontation between Maximus and
Edoxia attests specifically to her refusal to sexually submit to Maximus
(IV,iii). However, Edoxia's tragic fate is sealed when, in her attempt to
escape objectification and victimization, she reaches a political and
sexual dead-end in an uncanny moment of betrayal and confinement. Its
effect is drawn mainly from her inability to turn necessity into power

and choice and act on her own account. In Edoxia's case, there seems to be a transparent relation between her political consciousness and her gender identity leading her to enfold Genseric's delusive promises to save her from Maximus. In the end, the impossibility of her taking on the position of agent of the action transforms her into the emblem of lost political status and violated femininity as she is no longer the queen of Rome but a slave woman carried off by Genseric's soldiers:

Edoxia

Enough of life and all life's idle pomp—
Nor by a tyrant's fiat will I live—
I leave the busy, vain, ambitious world
To cheat itself anew, and o'er and o'er
Tread the same ground their ancestors have trod,
In chase of thrones, of sceptres, or of crowns,
Till all these bubbles break in empty air,
Nor leave a trace of happiness behind(V,iii).

The fact that the play presents a woman, stripped of her political rights, who becomes the site of implicit sexual abuse, is crucial. Edoxia, as well as her daughters, become the image bearing the inscriptions imposed upon the female gender, the double restriction and denial of political and sexual rights. Placida has already been "borne away and made the mistress of a Gothic lord" (V,iii), while Eudocia stabs herself before she becomes the mistress of Hunneric, Gensric's son.

In *The Ladies of Castile*, the same pessimistic spirit continues to pervade the play as Mercy Warren focuses upon the conjunction of power/leadership with despotism, abuse and degeneration. Like *The Sack of Rome*, the play concerns a despotic ruler, Don Velasco, who manages to withstand a revolt led by Don Juan de Padilla and Don Francis. In a profound exploration of the ideals of the revolutionary cause, Warren continues to employ the dominant language of republicanism, while, at the same time, she emphatically concentrates on the significance of the role of women in periods of social and political upheaval.

Evident throughout the play is the imagery and metaphorical structure of a poetic language that reaches more philosophical notions of freedom as it concentrates upon the ideological encroachment of the ideal of freedom on human passions, desires, and weaknesses, and effectively conveys Warren's preoccupation with an in-depth analysis of human conscience, morality and integrity. It is my contention that, though Warren is still addressing most of her earlier ideological concerns in *The Ladies of Castile*, she has somehow ameliorated her disturbingly rigid attitude towards human nature which actually engendered the powerful dichotomy between right and wrong, vice and virtue, so prevalent in her earlier propaganda plays. Although the characters are also categorised as bad or good, moral or villainous, according to their political and ethical standing, an intended turn to the expression of the complexity of human emotions, desires and thoughts, is evident.

Conde Haro, Don Velasco's son and perhaps the most tragic character in the play, becomes the symbolic realization of the complexity of human nature. Throughout the play, he moves within an emotional plurality, inherent in any interpretation of human character, and articulates several aspects of the reality of human existence, especially at moments of tension and turmoil, which render the stability and wholeness of self impossible. When Conde Haro first appears in the play, it is made quite clear that the source of his inner split is the major conflict between his duty as soldier and his own sense of personal morality:

Conde Haro

> Inur'd to arms, my soul's estrang'd to fear;
> Yet I lament my fate;—my sire and prince,
> Point me to glory, combating my will,
> And make my duty lead to deeds I hate. . . . . . .
> Urg'd on by thee, by glory and renown,
> I'll serve my sov'reign as a soldier ought,
> And take the field against my former friends,
> But in the hero ne'er forget the man (I,ii).

Forced by duty and honor to obey his father, Conde Haro's 'tortur'd soul' (II,iii) in fact suggests the simultaneous co-existence and incongruity of conflicting feelings in human soul. Donna Maria is so astonished to hear that Conde Haro supported her husband in his last hours that she exclaims:

To what extremes is human nature wrought! Can dignity and real
greatness dwell, thus mix'd and blended, in a servile soul?(V,ii).

Probably experimenting with a more truthful portrait of human nature,
Warren seems to accentuate and reconfirm her initial meaning—the
superlative effects of freedom and democracy on the people—which is
mainly realized in Conde Haro's unlimited admiration for the
revolutionaries' high sense of morality and virtue, his secret love for
Donna Maria, as well as his contradicting his own father.

In *The Ladies of Castile*, the characters act and interact variously
and struggle against the claustrophobic pressures of a tyrannical
political system, while they experience a series of psychological,
emotional as well as political changes. However, the play's final
denouement of death, in which most of the major characters die or
commit suicide, attests specifically to Warren's intention to bring to
stage a frightening image of a political and social reality that objectifies
and victimizes its people. The reestablishment of despotism and
tyranny, which accedes in the end, allows only a tiny glimpse of hope
that Conde Haro himself provides as he utters the closing lines of the
play:

> Oh! thou whose word directs the pointed flame,
> When the blue lightnings curl about the clouds,
> And thunders roll across the ragged vault,
> Let down thy benediction from the skies!—
> To virtue bend the wayward mind of man—
> Let not the father blast his children's peace
> By rancour—pride—and cursed party rage;—
> Let civil feuds no more distract the soul—
> Blast the dark fiends who wake mankind to war,
> And make the world a counterpart to hell (V,iv).

As in *The Sack of Rome*, Warren employs feminine sacrifice to criticize
those cultural and political attitudes that construct Woman as an image
ruled and violated by others. The tyrannical political system of Don
Velasco serves as the setting for the enactment of women's double
disempowering experience within society, their confinement to a
subordinate position and their denial of both political and sexual rights.
Again, the theme of female victimization is powerfully interwoven with

the play's general atmosphere of revolt and male violence. These poetic representations of death in both Warren's tragedies constitute a dramatic strategy for legitimating her argument about the necessity of political morality and integrity and collapse into the plays' overall resurgence of republican and democratic sentiments.

Like Ardelia, Louisa, Conde Haro's sister and Don Velasco's daughter, finds herself inextricably implicated in power structures that actually confine her and make an autonomous existence impossible. From the very beginning, Warren presents Louisa's existence as that of a lengthy process of suffering. Her personal odyssey stems from her wavering between the love for her brother and Don Francis, a member of the revolutionaries, as well as the realization of her own emotional incompatibility within the normative political order her father represents:

Louisa

Oh! what a bubble 'tis, ye glory call—
Mistaken name—a phantom of the brain,
That leads the hero on to leap the bounds
Of every social tie—till blood—till death,
Spreads horror over nature's frighted face (III, i).

Louisa's language connects her own romantic desires and passions with images of pain, destruction, and death (II, ii). Her dissatisfaction with life is expressed in profound thoughts about the logic of the masculine struggle for power, the dialectic of death and violence that men are forced to repeat in society. Her encounters with her brother (III, i) and Don Francis (II, ii) introduce her confusion and inability to accept the codes and laws of the male order, and actually reveal her awareness and fear that the normative order they belong to threatens to destroy them. Louisa's subconscious melancholic desire for death—"My heart's too full—it bends me to the grave"—emphasises her own separation from the male social laws and politics, which will eventually culminate in her actual choice of suicide (III, i).

Throughout the play, Louisa symbolically functions as the site where not just political but also socio-economic and gender issues are raised. Even though Louisa is denied the role of instigating agent within the world of male politics, she is nevertheless involuntarily implicated in the process of female objectification and depersonalization. Like Edoxia, Louisa painfully realises that by some fateful logic she herself has become the price to pay for the preservation of the distinctions and laws of male political order. Her father, obeying the principle recommending the commodification of women, has chosen her as the privileged object of exchange in a transaction of political expediency:

Velasco

Then will I now bestow thee caste and pure,
And bless the noble Pedro with thy hand;
Thou art his bride—bound by my solemn oath,
A just reward for loyalty and faith (IV, iii).

However, Louisa manages to stage the power feminine disruption has to dismantle the laws of the male order on two occasions. First of all, her deliberate disengagement from parental power, which is materialized in her choice to disobey her father by secretly marrying Don Francis, proves to be potentially wounding to the stability of the male-defined familial and social order:

Louisa

Then am I thine!—witness ye heavenly powers!—
This is the signet of thy wedded wife; [Gives him a ring]
(II, ii).

Because of her decision, Don Velasco experiences a momentary dissolution of the law he represents and in his attempt to maintain the continuation of this law, to have power over his daughter again, he becomes abusive and violent and actually orders her and Don Francis to death:

Velasco

Then take my sword, and use it as ye list;
Thy paramour this moment meets the death
Thy perfidy extorts and his deserves (IV, iii).

In Louisa's decision to kill herself, the distinction between active agent and passive receiver is somehow blurred as her death is ambivalently poised between a conscious choice of setting a final mark and a self-defeating escape from "this mazy world," from life's tensions, anxieties, pains and perturbations:

> I cannot live—to see Don Francis die—
> Yet worse to live, and be Don Pedro's wife—
> I must not live—my father bids me die.—(V,iv)

As in the case of Ardelia, however, Louisa openly accuses her father and the political and social order he represents. It can be argued that Louisa's tragic death mainly signifies her deliberate and absolute refusal to support those social structures that deny her an independence of will. Self-defeating though it seems, her suicide, as a potential form of self-dissolution, makes a double statement: first, it serves as the site at which cultural norms and political ideology are debated, and, second, it enacts the complex disempowering experience of women within the normative male order.

Although Louisa turns to death, the most supreme form of self-destruction after her experience of deprivation within the familial law and political society in general, her counterpart, Donna Maria, in a way obliterates the gap between political power and women's social status. Maria can be seen as Louisa's dormant double, as her secret rebellious self who finds outlet in her acts of disobedience and suicide. However, in contrast to Louisa's self-renunciation before cultural laws, Maria's excessively passionate nature, her courage and patriotism become the sources of her power within the social order. Maria resists male power, as this is realized in the political as well as sexual oppression of women, by developing a high sense of political consciousness:

Maria

> But for myself—though famine, chains, and death
> Should all combine—nay, should Don Juan fall—
> Which Heav'n forbid—I ne'er will yield,
> Nor own myself a slave (II,i).

It is made quite clear that Warren deliberately introduces Maria as an essentially political being, who moves within the public world of politics and is acutely aware of the social conditions under which she lives. In the conversation with her brother, Don Francis, Maria consciously externalises her defiance of her culturally-imposed gender limitations:

Francis

Thy soul was form'd to animate the arm
Of some illustrious, bold, heroic chief,
And not to waste its glorious fire away,
Beneath the weakness of a female form.

Maria

Men rail at weaknesses themselves create,
And boldly stigmatize the female mind,
As though kind nature's just impartial hand
Had form'd its features in a baser mould (I, v)

Throughout the play, Maria functions as a kind of hero, in the broader sense of the word, since her primary value in society is determined in relation to her patriotism, her courage, and her self-supporting sense of honor and duty. Maria manages to escape the most conventional representations of femininity—the passive, fading woman or the dangerous Other—by becoming the spokesperson of a new set of values, by drawing a safe boundary between herself and the normative male order as she formulates the important connection between femininity and a totally renewed social and political destiny of responsibility, autonomy and equality. Maria's participation in the world of politics is so effectively presented that it actually displays an alternative image of femininity, articulating the belief in women's greater control over their fate as well as the fate of their own country. Maria's authority reaches its highest point of public recognition when she addresses the citizens and soldiers of Spain in an attempt to avenge her husband's death and rally the troops against Don Velasco:

Maria

Come, shew on sample of heroic worth,
Ere ancient Spain, the glory of the west,
Bends abject down—by all the nations scorn'd:—
Secure the city—barricade the gates,
And meet me arm'd with all the faithful bands:
I'll head the troops, and mount the prancing steed;
The courser guide, and vengeance pour along
Amidst the ranks, and teach the slaves of Charles
Not Semiramis' or Zenobia's fame
Outstrips the glory of Maria's name (V, i).

A fierce republican, Maria would not hesitate to go to great lengths to secure victory and freedom for the revolutionaries. Even at the end of the play, when everything is lost, when Conde Haro arranges for her and her son to escape, she continues to exert control and affirm her power by adhering to the principles of democracy and freedom.

Susanna H. Rowson's contribution to the American theater should not be underestimated. The first woman playwright to be produced in America, she was one of the most resourceful, witty, intelligent, and versatile women in early American letters. Born in Portsmouth, England, in 1762, she was raised in America after 1768.[23] While for most eighteenth-century girls educational options were extremely limited, Rowson benefited from the resources of her father's library and studied Greek and Latin, the works of Aristophanes, Euripidis, Shakespeare and other Elizabethan dramatists. According to Langdon L. Faust, "by the age twelve, she was considered remarkably well-read in the Classics" (199). Throughout her adolescence, Rowson was aided in her literary quest by James Otis, Mercy Otis Warren's brother, who frequented the Haswell residence and actually took an interest in Susanna's intellectual abilities. This connection certainly bears evidence that the two women, though separated by age, were acquainted. As Elias Nason, her biographer, points out, it was James Otis who "instilled into her inquisitive mind those principles of liberty, of which he was one of the most eloquent advocates" (15).

Rowson's career in the theater began in 1792, when she and her husband, William Rowson, joined an English theatrical troupe, and were brought to America by Thomas Wignell to act in his company in the new Chestnut Street Theater in Philadelphia. Edward T. James argues that "although not a gifted actress. Mrs. Rowson had a warm personality and versatile talents; she could dance, sing, play the harpsichord and guitar, write plays, and compose both lyrics and librettos"(202-3). She became really popular as a writer of song lyrics and was in constant demand by such musicians as Reinagle, Hewitt, Van Hagen and Carr (Mates 190). It has been argued that Susanna Rowson claims the distinction of being "the mother of that uniquely American art form—the Broadway musical" (Turner 13). Although *Slaves in Algiers* is Rowson's only extant drama, she, nevertheless, wrote two other plays, *The Volunteers* (1795), of which only the songs and the vocal score are extant, and *Americans in England* (1797). Alexander Reinagle composed the music for both *Slaves in Algiers* and *The Volunteers*, a "musical entertainment based on Pennsylvania's recent Whiskey Rebellion, in January 1795. President and Mrs. Washington apparently attended its second performance" (Pollock 239). *Slaves in Algiers,* however, was the first and most important American play dealing with the Barbary Coast pirates. Consisting of a number of subplots, the play revolves around a most pressing political issue: the enslavement of American citizens by the pirates of the North African States.[24] It was performed on December 22, 1794 at the Chestnut Street Theater in Philadelphia, and during the next few years it was also presented in Baltimore, New York, Hartford, and Charleston.

In 1797, however, Rowson, after an extensive career in the theater, decided to retire from the stage and open a school for young ladies in Boston. Although the academy began with only one pupil, Rowson's rectitude as well as the amazing results of her school prompted parents to ignore the rumors about her past life in the theater and trust their girls under her tutelage.[25] Rowson proved to be a progressive and effective teacher, introducing her young women to elocution and dramatics. She also wrote a series of textbooks on geography, history, mathematics, literature, spelling and science, "at first only for the use of her own students, but they were so excellent and there was such a dearth of similar material, that they were soon published and used all over the Northeast for 50 years or more" (Turner 170).

Susanna Haswell Rowson died on March 24, 1824, having paved the way for a number of free-thinking women who would follow her

literary steps, women like Anna Cora Mowatt and Julia Ward Howe.
Rowson's achievements suggest an exceptional personality, an
unconventional eighteenth-century middle-class lady who contravened
the traditional constraints of her private sphere by becoming actress and
playwright. She was one of the first American female writers to express
through her work a subtle protest against the subordinate status of
women in her day.[26]

The belief in a new model of American femininity free from sexual and
political oppression is also given resonance in Rowson's *Slaves in
Algiers* through the aesthetically staged exotic harem of the Dey of
Algiers. Throughout the play, the rhetoric of republicanism and equal
rights harmoniously blends with the sentimentally melodramatic scenes
of recognition, captures, disguises, and escapes. As I have already
stated in my introduction, post-revolutionary politics provided the
setting within which American women invested radical ambitions for
social change and encompassed demands for legal, political and
economic parity with men. Stimulated by the egalitarian spirit of
republicanism and, at the same time, thwarted by their eventual
exclusion from it, American women were led to a growing awareness
of their common condition and experiences as well as their increasing
isolation from the political developments of their society.

Susanna Rowson chooses to place the action of her play in the
submissive harem of the Dey of Algiers where women's experiences
and self-perceptions take a more collective form. The cultural
connotations of the harem imply those power relations in which males
wield absolute control and influence over females. Relegated to the
status of slaves, the women in the harem lose their personal identity and
become politically, legally, and sexually dependent on men. Although
the play was inspired by the predicament of the enslaved American
officers and shippers, the major characters are all women.[27] Placing her
female characters within a context of explicit social, political and
sexual constraints, Rowson elaborates on the complex implications of
republican ideology claiming, at the same time, a privileged role for
women in a highly-politicized social reality. By refusing to endorse the
cultural processes of female victimization, she exposes to critique the
sanctions, taboos and prescriptions of the normative masculine order.
Rowson's oriental stage world, which in fact functions as a microcosm
for the larger real world, enables her to move beyond the confines or

external boundaries of American society and provides her with the power to project freely her own understanding of the paradoxical relation between women's actual experiences and all those social and cultural norms that have traditionally defined and circumscribed female reality.

There is no doubt that Rowson's vision and perspective are uniquely feminine, that she offers unique images of women of all races and classes in their struggle for survival and re-definition. Borrowing from republican ideology, Rowson articulates a vision of equality and independence for all women and actually challenges other people to imagine a new set of sexual relations:

Fetnah

woman was never formed to be the abject slave of man. Nature made us equal with them, and gave us the power to render ourselves superior (I,i).

She introduces Fetnah, a young spirited Moriscan woman, who becomes the spokesperson of her most radical ideas, who functions as a force disruptive of the patriarchal coherence of the harem while, at the same time, her desire to escape and be free is directed against the arbitrary laws of the masculine order. Fetnah openly and forcefully decries male power over women as this is sanctioned by law and custom:

Fetnah

. . .that word slave does so stick in my throat—I wonder how any woman of spirit can gulp it down.

Selima

We are accustomed to it.

Fetnah

The more's the pity: for how sadly depressed must the soul be, to whom custom has rendered bondage supportable (II,ii).

Fetnah's words clearly denounce women's acquiescence to their own subjection and reveal Rowson's counter-ideological strategy that resists the ideology of passive and commodified womanhood, female sexual repression and the masculinization of desire. Earlier in the play, Rowson employed the powerful imagery of the bird in the cage to symbolically represent female experience and reality and reconfirm women's need for autonomy and independence:

Selima

Yet, surely, you have no reason to complain; chosen favourite of the Dey, what can you wish for more.

Fetnah

O, a great many things—In the first place, I wish for liberty. Why do you talk of my being a favourite; is the poor bird that is confined in a cage (because a favourite with its enslaver) consoled for the loss of Freedom. No! tho' its prison is of golden wire, its food delicious, and it is overwhelm'd with caresses, its little heart still pants for liberty: gladly would it seek the fields of air, and even perched upon a naked bough, exulting, carrol forth its song, nor once regret the splendid house of bondage (I,i).

The rest of the play functions as a direct expression of women's demand for equal rights focusing specifically upon the construction of an authentic feminine model of regained autonomy. This effect is primarily drawn from the ideological conjoining of politics and gender into a celebration of women's break from their political and sexual confinement, and the high-spirited satire which is directed against male chauvinistic postures. In the course of the play, the female characters' resistance to patriarchal power takes a double form of rebellion which involves the need to overthrow monarchical tyranny and everything it stands for, as well as the supplementary invalidation of sexual masculinist presumptions. As women's demand for independence, autonomy, and self-assertion gradually gains power, the arbitrary authority of the masculine culture and social order is sufficiently undermined. The fierce over-sexed Dey of Algiers is ridiculed in Fetnah's mocking description as she exposes the absurdity of the male illusion of control and power:

-he is old and ugly, then he wears such tremendous whiskers; and
when he makes love, he looks so grave and stately, that I declare, if it
was not for fear of his huge scymetar, I shou'd burst out a laughing in
his face (I,i).

Later in the play, in a most amusing scene of perfect reversal of
attitudes and roles, a potential wound to the representation of the
stereotypical sexual relations between men and women is effected when
Frederic, an American who longs to become Fetnah's noble savior,
ends up himself having to be rescued by Fetnah's "invention," and
"ready wit"(II,ii).

By placing American characters, especially women, in the
oppressive context of the harem, Rowson consciously aims at drawing
a comparison between the self-annihilating state of slavery in Algerian
society and the revitalizing laws and customs of democratic America.
This crude representation of difference, which serves to expose and
criticize an excessive state of female degradation, enhances Rowson's
effort to undermine deep-seated patriarchal myths and stereotypes
about women and remind Americans that the doctrine of equality and
freedom should embrace women as well. *Slaves in Algiers* emphatically
suggests that the starting point for women to bring politics to bear on
the conditions of their sex is the social and political experiences they
share with each other. With respect to its impact on women, the
American revolution not only helped to break down the barriers which
separated women from the public world of men, but also gave
considerable impetus to the emergence of a common social awareness
and emotional proximity:

Fetnah

I have a dear friend, who is a captive at my father's; she must be
released, or Fetnah cannot be happy even with the man she loves (*SIA*
III,i).

The significance of the play lies in the fact that it transcends national,
racial and class boundaries and brings all women, American, Moriscan,
free and slave women, together in a context of female solidarity and
collective activity. The merging of American and Moriscan women
within the harem emphasises the universality of women's culturally-

imposed social reality in which they are forbidden to aspire to independence and self-determination. The centrality of the female characters' experiences and thoughts as well as the preponderance of women-only scenes constitutes a dramatic strategy for the clever re-examination of the roles allotted to women in society. Fetnah, Rebecca, Zoriana, and Olivia all find themselves positioned in a context that demands total subjugation before cultural laws. However, they soon realize that the potential for change resides in the acknowledgment of their power to assume authorship and responsibility for their own destiny. The dramatization of women's struggle for freedom helps Rowson juxtapose the republican concepts of liberty and egalitarianism against a number of gender issues. Trapped within two different cultures and ideologies, the women in the play begin to question their position in man's world, their status in society, the family, and their roles as wives and mothers. Although the fixed social and cultural boundaries between Algeria and America are blurred as the women are implicated in common experiences and exchanges within the harem, it is made quite clear that Rowson aims at celebrating America as the land of democracy and equality between the sexes:

Fetnah

> She [Rebecca] came from that land, where virtue in either sex is the
> only mark of superiority—She was an American (I, i).

The destruction of any sense of human decency that Fetnah experiences when she is sold by her family to the Dey of Algiers and she is forced to accept his affections is sharply contrasted to Rebecca's own experience of fulfillment at her freedom of choosing to marry the man she loves (I, i/ii). Furthermore, throughout the play the republican conception of matrimony based on mutual love and respect as well as a redefined image of American motherhood are consistently emphasized (III, ii). It is my contention that Rowson elaborates on this direct contrast between the two different cultures in an attempt to make a statement, to secure a fundamentally different social reality for all women.

Freedom from any kind of bondage emerges as the only viable form of personal and political existence. For Fetnah as well as for the other female characters in the play, escape from the harem, experienced as a kind of redemption, means the complete retrieval of any sense of self-esteem, value, and personal integrity. In the immensely optimistic last scene of the play, when all the characters are free again, Rebecca articulates the republican concepts of liberty and egalitarianism for all people:

> By the Christian law, no man should be a slave; it is a word to abject, that, but to speak it dyes the cheek with crimson. Let us assert our own prerogative, be free ourselves, but let us not throw on another's neck, the chains we scorn to wear (III,iii).

The Sack of Rome, The Ladies of Castile as well as *Slaves in Algiers* successfully enact the association of femininity with politics through the depiction of the stifling impact of a tyrannical government upon the female citizens. Their representations of the struggle for independence and freedom contain meanings that are equally personal and political. Warren's tragedies as well as Rowson's play embody this duality. Both playwrights attempt to reassess the position of their respective female characters against the backdrop of monarchy and the traditional patriarchal order. The plays are not only coterminous with American women's actual historical experience, but they also foreground female reality within a complex socio-political and sexual context in an attempt to explore femininity as a site of oppression and struggle. By staging the reciprocity between national and sexual politics, the plays attempt to construct an alternative image of assertive femininity and actually articulate the need for a radical break from both political and sexual oppression.

NOTES

1. For information concerning early American drama, see Coad, 1918: 190-7; Meserve, 1977, 1965; Moody, 1977; Moses, 1964; Odell, 1927-49; Quinn,1944; Seilhamer, 1889-91; Taubman, 1965; Vaughn, 1981; Wilson, 1973.

2. For details concerning the ideological and behavioral principles of the Puritan way of life, see Bercovitch, 1974; P. Miller, 1956, 1963; Morgan, 1963; Simpson, 1955; Slotkin, 1973.

3. In the 1730s and 1740s, an explosion of religious fervor, known as the Great Awakening, swept through the colonies creating many problems for acting companies. It must be noted that the Awakening was ignited in response to certain liberal ideas which had begun to challenge the old-time religion by proclaiming that human beings were not necessarily predestined to damnation but could save themselves by good works. The impact of the Great Awakening upon the American church was to seriously undermine the authority of the older clergy and set off schisms in many denominations. Seeing, however, from a broader social and cultural perspective, we can infer that the Awakening started out as a reaction to the fact that "New Englanders were abandoning a strict Christian morality for the code of the American businessman" (Meserve 1977: 24). In New England, the tendency towards a secularization of life partially liberated cultural activities as the increasing prosperity of the colonists made pleasurable entertainment possible. As far as drama is concerned, attitudes towards the theater changed considerably, as this is manifested in the various controversies over drama which appeared in publications.

4. The first play printed in the United States was Robert Hunter's three-act satire, *Androboros* (1715). Other plays written before the 1770s were, *The Paxton Boys*(anonymous,1764) which was based on events in western Pennsylvania, Thomas Godfrey's five-act tragedy, *The Prince of Parthia* (1765), Robert Rogers' *Ponteach; or, The Savages of America* (1766)—the first play to treat a native subject seriously-, Robert Munford's *The Candidates, or the Humours of a Virginia Election* (1770 or 1771), and finally, *The Disappointment* (1767), a comic opera in three acts by Colonel Thomas Forrest.

5. For historical information regarding the American War of Independence, see Bailey, 1987; Bailyn, 1967; Carroll, 1977; Ellis, 1979; Silverman, 1976.

6. Vernon L. Parrington has rightly described the battle of words that began to wage fiercely in the Revolutionary period, by which Loyalists and Patriots attempted to defend and persuade their readers to their own social and political positions, as the 'War of Belles Lettres.' More specifically Parrington argues that "a civil war of belles lettres broke out, that exceeded in animosity any other known to our literary history. Attack and counter-attack were slashing and acrimonious. Gentlemen forgot their manners and indulged fiercely in tall language. Satire ran about the streets seeking new victims to impale; slander lay in wait for every passer-by (357).

7. Part IV of this chapter deals in great detail with the propaganda plays of Mercy Otis Warren.

8. Best examples of Patriot political satires are Mercy Otis Warren's plays *The Adulateur* (1773) and *The Group* (1775). She also wrote a third one, *The Defeat* (1773), which, unfortunately is an incomplete and fragmentary dramatic work. It appears that Warren did not finish composing it. Furthermore, some scholars have credited her with two more satires, *The Blockheads; or, The Afffrighted Officers* (1776) and *The Motley Assembly*(1779), but Warren's authorship of both these plays has been seriously questioned since there is no proof that she wrote either of them. Quite a few male dramatists followed her example and employed the satirical farce as a dramatic mode for propaganda purposes. The most-well known protest plays are Hugh H. Brackenridge's *The Battle of Bunkers-Hill* (1776) and *The Death of General Montgomery* (1777), and John Leacock's *The Fall of British Tyranny*(1776). On the other hand, Tory writers seemed less inclined to engage in literary warfare than their Patriot counterparts. Some of the best examples of Tory propaganda are Mary V.V.'s *A Dialogue Between a Southern Delegate and his Spouse* (1774), Jonathan Sewell's *The Americans Roused in a Cure for the Spleen; or, Amusement for a Winter's Evening* (1775), and the anonymous *The Battle of Brooklyn* (1776). Finally, Robert Munford's comedy, *The Patriots* (written sometime between 1777 and 1779), is the only play which did not deal directly with the British-American conflict, but rather concentrated upon the events that took place in Virginia, far from the maelstrom of war, and actually commented on the political attitude of the American Patriots.

9. In her most interesting book about women and early American society, Kerber goes further to examine some of the basic tenets of Enlightenment literature by focusing upon the work of John Locke, Montesquieu, Condorcet, and J.J. Rousseau. For women in early American society, see also Lewis, 1987: 689-721; Ryan, 1990; Stansell, 1987.

10. For details concerning the education of early American women, see Benson, 1935; Farello,1970; Kerber, 1980: 189-231; Norton, 1980: 256-94.

11. For information about the legal rights of women in early American society, see Cott, 1976: 586-614; Foster, 1913; Grossberg, 1985; Gundersen, 1982: 114-34.

12. As Gerald Argetsinger points out, "the lofty tragedies and the extravagant comedies popular at the time became the models for the first American playwrights"(62). It must be remembered, however, that the plays written by American dramatists occupied an exceedingly small part of the theatrical offerings of the time. It was the English and the European plays which greatly pleased American audiences. The plays of Shakespeare, Farquhar, Dryden, Fielding, Addison, and Congreve dominated the American

theatrical scene for many years. Even when native dramas were being increasingly accepted, American plays were not entirely free from foreign influence, which manifested itself in the plays' form rather than in their subject matter.

13.   For biographical information regarding the women playwrights briefly discussed in this chapter, see Bacon, 1888; Benson, 1935; Elliott, 1984; Field, 1931; James, 1971; Kunitz, 1966; Mainiero, 1977.

14.   Quite a few works have been published on Mercy Otis Warren, see Anthony, 1958; Baym, 1990: 531-54; Brown, 1896; Cohen, 1983: 481-98, 1980: 200-18; Fritz, 1972; James, 1971: 545-6; Marble, 1903: 163-80; Nicolay, 1995: 33-63; Richards, 1995; Richardson, 1993; Robinson, 1981: 131-7,1989: 897-901; W.R. Smith, 1971: 203-25, 1966:73-119; Weales, 1979: 881-94; Zagarri, 1995.

15.   Although Warren's plays are excellent examples of the patriotic writing done in the period of the American Revolution, they never reached the stage. The truth is that these plays were intended primarily for reading and are not at all dramatic. Paul L. Ford argues about *The Adulateur* and *The Group* that "in neither is there any plot; the scenes are shifted without rhyme or reason, and there are no women in the cast" (680).

16.   Bearing in mind Chris Weedon's observation that in women's writing "the concern is more often with sexual and family relationships than with areas which are thought to constitute public life," Warren's undertaking to deal with political matters seems to be quite unbelievable (153).

17.   In their very interesting book, *The Madwoman in the Attic,* Sandra M. Gilbert and Susan Gubar explain that "like most women in patriarchal society, the woman writer does experience her gender as a painful obstacle, or even a debilitating inadequacy" (50).

18.   As in her propaganda plays, Warren provides striking models of virtue and abhorrent images of vice in her *History of the Rise, Progress, and Termination of the American Revolution*(1805). Lester H. Cohen argues that Warren's *History* is a "work of moral art: a self-consciously created instrument of ideology and ethics that simultaneously expressed the Revolutionaries' commitment to republicanism and served as a beacon shining back upon the exemplary forebears"(1980: 203-4). The study of human character, so evident in both *The Adulateur* and *The Group*, is best expressed in her *History* as Warren surveys the historical events of the American Revolution in an ostensibly straightforward way, and reveals her anxiety and apprehension about the future of the republic because of people's the increasing unwillingness to

fulfill the promise of the Revolution. In historical narrative, Warren epitomizes the significance of individual virtue and morality in societal and political terms:

> The study of the human character opens at once a beautiful and a deformed picture of the soul. We there find a noble principle implanted in the nature of man, that pants for distinction. This principle operates in every bosom, and when kept under the control of reason, and the influence of humanity, it produces the most benevolent effects. But when the checks of conscience are thrown aside, or the moral sense weakened by the sudden acquisition of wealth or power, humanity is obscured, and if a favorable coincidence of circumstances permits, the love of distinction often exhibits the most mortifying instances of profligacy, tyranny, and the wanton exercise of arbitrary sway (3).

19. As I have already pointed out in the introductory part of this chapter, the republican ideology of the late-eighteenth century emphasized the importance of women as the teachers of morality and virtue. It became absolutely essential for the welfare and survival of the young republic that its citizenry would be trained to political virtue. Therefore, it was assumed that women, certainly not politically active citizens, could exercise a salutary influence upon their husbands and sons. 'Virtue,' as Mary Kelley explains, "was defined most broadly as a selflessness in which individual desires and interest were secondary to the welfare of the body politic"(60).

20. The Boston Massacre was the upshot of a series of brawls between British soldiers and colonial citizens incited by the Americans' protest against the right of Parliament to tax the colonists in matters of trade. On March 5, 1770, British troops fired on the agitated crowd and killed five civilians.

21. In the study of Warren's tragedies, one cannot fail to detect her growing awareness of the possible political role of the republican woman as well as a decided alteration in attitude towards the conventions of femininity. It's worth mentioning that Warren's romantic tragedies appeared for the first and only time in Benjamin V. Franklin, *The Plays and Poems of Mercy Otis Warren* (New York: Scholar's Fascimiles and Reprints, 1980).

22. Investigating a politics of the female body has always been paramount for feminist theorists and critics. De Beauvoir has demonstrated that" one is not born, but rather becomes, a Woman" (267). Feminists on both sides of the world have insisted on an awareness of the complex set of social and historical systems that shape women's lives, while, the study of the cultural

"representations" of the female body has flourished. Women playwrights and film directors have regarded the female body as a locus to dramatically challenge the images of women determined in dominant discourses. See, for example, Butler, 1988: 519-31; Forte, 1988: 217-35, 1992: 248-62; Hart, 1989: 1-21; Kaplan, 1988; Jacobus, 1990.

23. For biographical information, see Brandt, 1975; Faust, 1983: 199-201; Freibert, 1985; James, 1971: 202-4; Kornfeld, 1983:56-62; Kunitz, 1966: 663; Nason, 1870;Robinson, 1989: 757-61; Turner, 1990: 5-18; Weil, 1976.

24. From 1785 to 1816, America was involved in a continual struggle with the pirates of the Barbary States. According to information provided by George O. Seilhamer, about "fifteen American vessels had been captured, and one hundred and eighty American officers and seamen made slaves by the Algerines before the close of 1793" (155). A number of plays were written at that time dramatizing the romantic adventures of American sailors captured and enslaved in the mysterious, exotic land of Algeria. The first play on this subject was Rowson's *Slaves in Algiers*. Other plays about the struggle with the pirates were James Ellison's *American Captive; or, The Siege of Tripoli*(1812), John Howard Payne's *The Fall of Algeria* (1825).

25. Rowson's contribution to education for women was invaluable. As Mary Turner argues, "her young ladies were well-educated, polished, graceful and charming, ready to enter society with conversation and accomplishments, rather than simpers and silences"(17).

26. Susanna Rowson was also well-known as a novelist. Within a relatively short time, she published three novels: *Victoria* (1786), *The Inquisitor; or, Invisible Rambler*(1788), and *Mary; or, The Test of Honor*(1788). She continued to write and in 1791 she published her major novel, *Charlotte Temple, A Tale of Truth.* The book was reprinted in American three years later and actually became America's first best-selling novel. According to Dorothy Weil, Susanna's *Charlotte Temple* "conquered the American market in 1794 and has since been printed in nearly two hundred editions" (1). It was definitely the most popular book in America before the appearance of *Uncle Tom's Cabin*(1852). During her years as an educator, Rowson edited one magazine, *The Boston Weekly,* she wrote poetry, songs, and novels, and she also participated in several charitable organizations. A number of her poems were published in Susanna Rowson, *Miscellaneous Poems* (Boston, Gilbert and Dean, 1804). It must be noted that Rowson's literary and dramatic efforts were attacked by William Cobbett, a contemporary critic writing under the pseudonym Peter Porcupine:

The inestimable works that she has showered (not to say poured, you know) upon us, mend not only our hearts, but if properly administered, our constitutions also: at least I speak for myself. They are my Materia Medica, in a literal sense. A liquorish page from the *Fille de Chambre* serves me by way of a philtre, the *Inquisitor* is my opium, and I have ever found the *Slaves in Algiers* a most excellent emetic. As to *Mentoria* and *Charlotte*, it is hardly necessary to say what use they are put to in the chamber of a valetudinarian (27).

Nevertheless, a word of comfort was written to Mrs. Rowson by the anonymous "Citizen Snub" who forcefully accused Cobbett of most offensive criticism: "such an attempt to stab the reputation of a woman, who never gave you any cause of provocation, resembles the indiscriminate fury of desperadoes in the dark, who are unkennelled for the dreary purposes of assassination"(77). Furthermore, Citizen Snub recognized the limiting social and cultural circumstances under which women lived:

In consequence of the customs and manners now prevalent in the world, there must be an essential distinction between the sexes, and man's pride and arrogance make him the most ostensible character in our creation; but can you prove that a male education would not qualify a woman for all the duties of a man? (76).

27. As maintained by Walter J. Meserve, "national themes figure prominently in [Rowson's] plays, where women characters dominate or direct the action. She was an imaginative if sometimes too compassionate writer, and the courage and resourcefulness with which she endowed her heroines are representative of her own life" (1977: 115).

CHAPTER 3

Industrial Capitalism and the Status of Middle-class Women in the Mid-Nineteenth-Century American Family

Anna Cora Mowatt's *Fashion (1845)* and
Sidney F. Bateman's *Self (1856)*

> Drama is an expression of community, feeling the pulse of an age or
> of a moment in time like no other art. A play is a social event or it is
> nothing (Styan 11).

I: SOCIETY AND CULTURE IN EARLY-NINETEENTH-CENTURY AMERICAN SOCIETY

Moving into the nineteenth century, the people of the United States
experienced a number of social, economic and political changes which
asserted their feelings of independence and nationalism, while, at the
same time, led them to an age of individualism, self-interest and
capitalist economy. The defeat of federalists and the election of Thomas
Jefferson in 1800 paved the way towards democracy and liberalism.
Furthermore, a rising tide of nation-consciousness was primarily
inspired by the War of 1812. Although the United States did not attain
the military objects for which war was declared, "in an economic sense,
as well as in a diplomatic sense, the War of 1812 may be regarded as
the Second War for American Independence"(Bailey 209). For one
thing, the War revived a fresh spirit of nationalism, while, at the same
time, intensified bitterness towards England.[1] A vibrant feeling of self-
confidence sprang mainly from the lessening of economic and political
dependence on the mother-country as well as from an exulting belief in

the future of the nation. Moreover, in the aftermath of the war, the Federalists declined rapidly as a political party and, for the first time, Americans began to enjoy a feeling of national unity.

Presumably, this heightened spirit of nationalism actually took on a new kind of emotional validity as it became closely associated with the American doctrine of progress. The achievements of the American people—their successful revolution, their political and economic independence, the establishment of a democratic government—as well as the unlimited opportunities offered by the vast American continent all helped substantially to integrate the idea of progress into the broader context of nationalism and democratic idealism. For the Americans of the first half of the nineteenth century, the idea of progress was not simply a philosophical abstraction, but rather a visible dynamic reality which could be "hastened by science, government, education, technology, and by the efforts of individuals and groups in combination" (Nye 16). After all, the construction of transportation facilities, the introduction of new machinery, the invention of the steam engine, the printing press, and the telegraph, lent further proof to the idea of progress and to the belief in man's advancement.

To a certain extent, this kind of social and cultural transformation freed Americans from the theological determinism of the eighteenth century and introduced them to the idea of a more worldly order controlled by human achievement. As a matter of fact, the early nineteenth-century American was no longer a "helpless sinner in the hands of a Calvinist God, but a self-reliant, free-standing individual, capable of making choices to his own benefit" (Nye 9). On the other hand, however, the destruction of the communal values of the colonial period and the transformation of the economic pattern of American society into capitalist economy had a profound impact on the social and emotional life of the Americans. The assumption of unlimited progress in a boundless society that promised immense material advantages for all men encouraged the creation of a new individualistic credo and the celebration of self-interest.[2] As Eric John Dingwall observes, "it was an age of buoyant individualism in the sense that the ordinary American citizen wanted to rise ever higher in the social scale, and, to attain his end, did not hesitate to enter into harsh and ruthless competition with those around him' (67). Selfishness and an obsessive pursuit of wealth and high social status became the salient values of the new materialistic ethic. Wealth was everywhere recognized as a sign of power and individual success. Industrial expansion offered unlimited opportunities and brought increasing wealth and luxury to a number of adventurous Americans who already possessed some capital and were ready to invest it. Therefore, a fairly prosperous middle-class, composed of skilled artisans, professionals and innovative merchants, began to emerge. The ideological framework of the rising middle-class' claim to higher social status was carefully circumscribed within the rhetoric of the self-made man. According to a nineteenth-century Whig journalist:

> Ours is a country where men start from an humble origin, and from small beginnings rise gradually in the world, as the reward of merit and industry, and where they can attain to the most elevated positions, or acquire a large amount of wealth, according to the pursuits they elect for themselves (Carroll 155).

However, in the theoretically fluid American society, the rapid progress, the persistent social changes as well as the hazardous speculative economic activity caused feelings of uncertainty, anxiety and fear among the more conservative American citizens. The various rags-to-riches success stories proved to be largely illusory since the greater part of the population in the big cities suffered by industrialization, lived in poverty and actually had very little chance of advancement. Nevertheless, with the presidency of Andrew Jackson, a new period in American history began which promised a resurgence of the patriotic and democratic principles of the American Revolution and actually centered thoughtful attention on the rights and liberties of the common man. Jackson owed his election to the fact that he "appealed to a growing sense of helplessness before the vicissitudes of a vast and unpredictable market" (Halttunen 19). Jackson's government by the people, his concern for economic equality, and his faith in the wisdom of the common man managed to reshape America's life and thought. In an age of rapid economic and social change, Jackson's democratic party articulated the philosophy of frugality, simplicity and virtue, condemned the economic institutions—chartered corporations and banks—of the new capitalism, and proclaimed the power of the people to govern themselves. With the election of Andrew Jackson, the common man was at last moving to the center of the national political stage:

the sturdy American who donned plain trousers rather than silver-buckled breeches, who besported a plain haircut and a coonskin cap rather than a powdered wig, and who wore no man's collar, often not even one of his own. Instead of the old divine right of kings, America was now witnessing the divine right of people (Bailey 232).

The democratic spirit of Jackson's government promoted education and reform. Education was considered a most powerful force for social progress and moral improvement. In an essentially democratic nation, like the United States, free public education was deemed vitally important for the creation of intelligent citizenry capable of decisive, progressive thinking and action. Consequently, instruction was greatly improved by better teachers and texts, state-supported schools for children multiplied, while, at the same time, academies and colleges grew swiftly in number.[3] Furthermore, during the age of Jacksonian Democracy, the United States experienced a number of reform movements ranging from temperance and prison reform movements to abolitionist and organized women's movements.

II: WOMEN'S STATUS AND ROLES IN AMERICA DURING THE FIRST HALF OF THE NINETEENTH-CENTURY

The major shifts in the American economic and social patterns following the development of industrial capitalism had a dramatic effect on women's lives. For one thing, the rise of the factory system contributed significantly to the separation of the dwelling place from the work place, constructing separate spheres of activity and social life for men and women. As it has already been stated, in the masculine world of economic competition, the accumulation of wealth became a sign of individual success. Under capitalism, therefore, the predominant masculine ethos of fierce competition and economic advancement resulted in profound changes in American family relations. The division of labor within the family brought the development of homemaking as women's vocation, while men, as participants in the capitalist economy, acquired the characteristics of competition, restlessness, self-seeking and self-interest.

The constitution of homemaking as a profession for women actually involved the subordination of women to the needs of the family and reinforced the notion of woman as a figure associated with virtue and morality. Julie A. Matthaei argues that "it was up to women, as vocational homemakers, to articulate the needs of their families, and then to fill them. To the extent that social institutions prevented healthy family life, it was up to women to fight for their transformation" (112). Isolated from the world of finance and industry, the American middle-class woman devoted herself to the domestic realm, provided emotional comfort and support for her family members, upheld moral values and inculcated religious principles. As a matter of fact, the influence or "authority" the middle-class woman gained within her household was, to a great extent, justified by an ideological framework—the cult of domesticity—which celebrated the home as a refuge from materialism.

Not surprisingly, the participation of men and women in different spheres of social activity made them complementary to each other. The competitive man needed a woman to create a home for him, a reassuring abode where he could relax and be rejuvenated on returning from the competitive world of the market economy. On the other hand, the home-centered woman depended upon a man to support her and her children financially. Therefore, in the nineteenth-century American society, two different but complementary ideologies emerged regarding men and women: the masculine individualistic ethos of economic self-advancement and the cult of domesticity which celebrated women as guardians of the family, creators of home. However, the class and race division inherent in industrial America differentiated both the life of men as well as the requirements of homemaking for women. Among the lower classes of society, in particular, woman's elevated status in the family proved to be simply a cultural myth as financial necessity, combined with limited economic opportunities, hindered the development of the cult of domesticity. What's more, the conflict between myth and reality concerning woman's social role was most apparent in the case of black women. As Catherine Clinton rightly maintains, "in or out of slavery, black women were confronted by the irony of their status within a culture which celebrated a feminine model of domestic gentility"(33). Although black and working-class women were blatantly denied any vestiges of ladyhood, upper- and middle-class females who aspired to the idealized status of lady soon realized that the ideology of domesticity and female moral superiority served to compensate for the severe restrictions and inhibitions placed upon them.[4]

It seems that in the early nineteenth century, the notion of equality—generally accepted as equal chance of advancement—carried different connotations when applied to women. Even the promotion of education and the building of various female academies did not essentially contribute to the cultivation of female intellect or the preparation of women to enter the public world of professions. Rather, wealthy urban families provided their daughters with a more refined education which actually prepared the girls for a favorable marriage. A smattering of

> French, a bit of religious reading, the ability to write a fine hand and recite some uplifting verse, embroidery, sketching, a little dancing, and enough skill on the piano to entertain family and guests with a few selections—these were considered sufficient "accomplishments" for a young lady. Once married a lady had to follow the fashions, adorn her home so as to display her husband's wealth to the best advantage, and help raise her family's cultural standards (Lerner 32).

The division into distinct areas of responsibility between men and women was reinforced by an enormous didactic literature which served to define every aspect of women's domestic life. This outflowing of didactic literature, which included child-rearing manuals, housekeeping guides, and etiquette books, reached an unprecedented audience and shaped the behavior and manners of a vast number of American middle-class women.[5] Most of these periodicals addressed questions "of domestic economy as well as motherhood, treating the subject of health as well as recreation, morality and religion, reform, and indeed most subjects imaginable, with the notable exception of politics" (Clinton 47). Thousands of women were socialized to the unattainable ideal of the bourgeois lady. The majority of them, however, failed to realize that instead of equality and freedom, restriction and oppression were drummed into their lives.[6] None of these advice manuals ever hinted at the essentially oppressive condition of women, at the social and legal circumscription of their activities and responsibilities. In essence, the various ladies' conduct and etiquette books aimed at shaping the personal manners of the middle-class ladies and served to solidify, on the one hand, the image of the domestic woman, and, on the other, that of the fashionable lady who sought to demonstrate her gentility.

However, the various economic shifts in American society, coupled with the widespread belief in individual ability and progress, gave considerable impetus to a number of perceptive and well-educated middle-class women who began to question their social status, explore their own economic and educational opportunities, and actually envision new social roles for themselves. Once segregated from men and the public world of business and politics, women set out to turn their liabilities into assets. More specifically, women's experience of the nineteenth-century ethos of individualism mainly concentrated on their greater freedom in choosing their marital partners and on their indispensable functions as supervisors of the education of the children and tenders of the hearth. However, in the early decades of the century quite a few women realized that their significant role as preservers of the moral, spiritual, and physical well-being of the family could be extended into the larger social arena. White, middle-class women began to form associations to achieve temperance and prison reform as well as abolition. Women's reform movements not only filled a significant gap in American social life but also gave "disenfranchised women a degree of public authority" (Kerber 1995: 171).

III: WOMEN AND AMERICAN DRAMA IN EARLY NINETEENTH CENTURY

As wars were fought and rapid changes occurred in American society, the fervent feeling of nationalism, so powerfully expressed in the propaganda plays of the late-eighteenth century, was revived in an attempt to remind Americans of their nationalistic and democratic tradition. The tendency of American dramatists to focus on historical events and insert nationalistic sentiments and a strong patriotic feeling in their plays continued well into the first decades of the nineteenth century. A number of plays were written appealing directly to the national feeling of the Americans and focusing upon the political incidents of the Revolution, the battles with the Barbary Coast pirates, and the War of 1812. Although the nationalistic plays written at the time do not rank among high quality dramas, a number of significant playwrights—like James Nelson Barker, Mordecai M. Noah, Richard Penn Smith, and George Washington Parke Custis—saw nationalism as the first step towards the creation of a national dramatic literature.[7]

Caught within this fresh spirit of nationalism, American women playwrights continued to use historical events and republican values as the background for their exploration of how women could maintain or lose their identity and integrity in a male social and political order. Although Sarah Pogson Smith's *The Female Enthusiast* (1807) does not elaborate on any particular historical event of the American War of Independence, it nevertheless focuses on the patriotic ideals and democratic principles for which the French fought in 1789, and which were beginning to filter into American society. The theme of the play offers a different version of the assassination of the demagogue Jean Paul Marat by Charlotte Corday during the French Revolution. What is really remarkable about *The Female Enthusiast* is that, although it basically conforms to the rules of romantic tragedy—it is written in stilted blank verse and aims at moral instruction,—it presents a female character of human dimensions whose passionate nature and independence of spirit do not evaporate in the midst of rhetorical speeches. The play offers a really sympathetic portrait of Charlotte Corday as a thoughtful, intelligent, and dynamic young woman, while, at the same time, it explores the moral reasons that impelled an upper-middle-class girl from a respectable family to commit a political assassination. It is made quite clear throughout the play that Charlotte's action is spurred only by her patriotic feelings, by her love for her country, by her humanitarian ideals in spite of the expected cost to her. In the gothic atmosphere of the French prison where Charlotte is locked up awaiting her execution, she courageously reveals to her brother Henry that "I feel the strong conviction that I bleed—For the benefit of my poor country—And should the demon of carnage present—Another fiend, as murd'rous as Marat,—May he soon share the horrid monster's fate; And the true patriot who dares cut him off,—Find in his country's gratitude- reward" (V, i).

The rebellious flame kindled by the American Revolution is also reflected in Delia Bacon's *The Bride of Fort Edward* (1839), published in the early part of the nineteenth century and elaborating on a particular incident of the Revolution: the story of Jane McCrea, the hapless victim of an Indian slaughter. The play is a closet drama and, as the dramatist herself explains in the preface, "it is not a Play. It was not intended for the stage, and properly is not capable of representation. I have chosen the form of the *DIALOGUE* as best suited to my purpose in presenting anew the passions and events of a day long buried in the past." *The Bride of Fort Edward* is not divided in acts and scenes but in parts and dialogues. Bacon utilizes the American War of Independence as the background for a simple romantic love story. Interspersed are allusions to the great natural beauty of the new country, the evils of war and the celebration of democracy and freedom. The play treats the love of Everard Maitland, an officer in the British army, for Helen Grey, a supporter of the revolution. The dramatic setting of the couple's separation occupies the entire play. Just a couple of days before their weeding, war broke out and they were forced to separate. He took the king's part while Helen with her family sided with the revolutionaries. Bacon effectively elaborates on the theme of divided loyalties, of personal struggle resulting from opposing allegiances. However, when two years later, Maitland's regiment camps near Fort Edward, not very far from Helen's house, a sequence of events is triggered off that makes the lovers' reunion possible. Helen exhibits an unparalleled courage and strength as she refuses to follow her family to Albany. In a truly melodramatic fashion, she stays behind waiting for Maitland defying danger and the impending warfare. But the tragic power of fate guides her destiny; she is killed in an Indian fight. When Maitland discovers her dead body, he begins raving as he gradually deteriorates into madness. The play ends in the accepted manner of revolutionary plays praising freedom and patriotic sentiments. It is interesting to note that Helen, the play's heroine, is introduced as an essentially political being who moves within the public world of politics and exhibits unparalleled courage, strength, and determination.

However, not only the Revolutionary War of Independence but other military engagements of the United States were also reflected in the plays by American women. For example, the War of 1812 served to enhance the patriotic spirit of the Revolution, the ever-growing faith in the power of the people to shape their destiny, in human rights and democracy. Mary Clarke Carr chooses the War of 1812 as the battleground of her five-act comedy, *The Fair Americans* (1815). Replete with patriotic speeches, songs, and pageantry, the play is an essentially melodramatic piece. As the title itself implies, the story focuses on young women, 'the fair Americans,' and explores in a fascinating and sometimes comic manner the way their lives are affected by the war. In the preface to her play, Carr points out that she attempts to draw the portrait of a 'national female character,' a model American woman whose laudable qualities include "strength of mind, purity of heart, magnanimity of soul, sweetness of temper and domestic virtues." Although the plot of the play is rather weak and scattered and there is little concern for character, Carr manages to provide with romantic fervor and brightness of style a fusion of ardent patriotism and humanitarian impulses. The play opens with a view on the romantic surroundings of Lake Erie where the American farmers' serene daily routine contrasts with the news of the impending war. The farmers, the Fairfields and the Harleys, become apprehensive as the American military tries to recruit soldiers to invade Canada. However, they all display a great degree of courage and are prepared to fight for their country. Spirits become elated as the news comes that the British fleet is defeated in Lake Erie and that the Americans are planning to "make a grand attack on York" (III, i). At the same time, the young ladies of Erie embroider the American flag which they offer to the American officers with the wish to "return it triumphant" (IV, i). Into the nationalistic and patriotic sentiments of the story, Carr injects melodramatic elements of suspense when the two heroines are seized by Indians in a most spectacular scene. Luckily, the girls are saved by Captain Belford and Major Clifford, two British officers, who are then captured by the Americans. However, the general humane quality of the play precludes any animosity toward the British and the play ends with one of the officers free to go and the other in love and ready to marry the girl he rescued.

During the first decades of the nineteenth century, more and better theaters were built and managers tried hard to cater for the excitement the American audiences craved for by providing them with famous actors and spectacular entertainment. Theater managers were forced to be extravagantly inventive and often "found success by reflecting the topics of the day—political problems, social issues and fads, newspaper headlines, or current interests in patriotism, reform and the latest popular fiction" (Meserve 1986: 118).

But, who were the people who constituted the American audience in the first half of the nineteenth century? Without question, a variety of people, ranging from the social elite to the growing middle-class to the urban workers, attended the theater. The classes of spectators to be found in playhouses and their seating arrangements roughly represented the structures of power in American society. Wealthy merchants, brokers and professional men generally occupied the box seats, some of the better-off workers sat in the pit, while, male apprentices and servants were gathered in the gallery and the rear balcony. Apart from the prostitutes who continued to inhabit the third tier until the 1840s, very few respectable women attended the theater. When they did so, they mainly sat with their husbands or fathers in the boxes.

According to the customary behavior at the playhouse, audiences felt that they were entitled to express themselves freely. First of all, they arrived at the theater and left their seats whenever they wished, they chatted away during the performance, they distracted the actors with frequent applause, they rudely hissed inferior actors, and sometimes even pelted them with fruit. The renowned English visitor, Mrs. Frances Trollope, graphically describes instances of the behavior of American audiences:

> One man in the pit was seized with a violent fit of vomiting, which appeared not in the least to annoy or surprise his neighbours. . . The spitting was incessant; and not one in ten of the male part of the illustrious legislative audience sat according to the usual custom of human beings; the legs were thrown sometimes over the front of the box, sometimes over the side of it; here and there a senator stretched his entire length along a bench, and in many instances the front rail was preferred as a seat (234).

However, as American theater approached mid-century, it broke into segments along class and ethnic lines. Working class attendance at fashionable theaters began to decline in the 1830s and 1840s as workers shifted their attention to the museum theaters, or the Mose plays, in an attempt to find something that mirrored their lives and appealed to their social values. Furthermore, a number of theaters that catered to Irish or German audiences sprang, and entertainment like minstrelsy and burlesque was particularly popular at least in the first decades of the nineteenth century.

Although Shakespearean dramas, restoration comedies, and French and German melodramas continued to dominate the theatrical scene of the time, American dramatists strove hard, on the one hand, to create a distinctly American drama, and on the other, to please the divergent social groups that comprised their audience. The major interests of early nineteenth-century American playwrights focused upon a variety of themes and dramatic forms. Their plays elaborated on politics, current social events and issues and ancient scenes, while they generally reflected the prevalent spirit of nationalism and the belief in the progress of the common man. American playwrights wrote poetic dramas, political and patriotic plays, light farces and comedies, adaptations of successful European plays, and more importantly, melodrama. From William Dunlap's adaptations of the plays by Kotzebue in the late eighteenth century, to the sensationalism of Dion Boucicault, the techniques and devices of melodrama were prominent in the majority of plays produced during that period, whether these plays were written in poetry or were concerned with native characters and social issues.[8]

One of the most successful contributors to spectacular melodrama in Jacksonian America, Louisa Medina, a professional playwright, exhibited outstanding talent in embellishing her plays with those elements of melodrama—adventure, disguises, mystery, romantic love,—that greatly appealed to nineteenth-century theatergoers. Without question, Medina created some of the most popular melodramas of the 1830s, which actually held the American stage for many years after her death. However, only eleven of her plays have been documented from stage histories and only three of these appear to have survived.[9] Medina began to write plays working almost exclusively with Hamblin during his management of the Bowery Theater and made an astonishing career by dramatizing popular novels of the time. Shortly after the opening of *Ernest Maltravers* (1838), *The New York Mirror* observed that Medina's "power of composition is said to be astonishingly rapid. She is partial to startling and terrible catastrophes. Her knowledge of stage effects is very great, and there is an impassioned ardour in her poetry, which enhances the thrilling interest of her pieces" (April 28, 1838).

It was clearly an age of melodrama, and it seems that Americans "worked through their political anxieties and desires at the melodramatic theater, not by listening to speeches on political philosophy but by applauding heroes, scapegoating villains, and weeping for victims" (McConachie 68). The transcendental quality of the melodramatic plot closely resembled a fairy tale where everything was possible, while the "melodramatic rhetoric implicitly insist[ed] that the world [could] be equal to our most feverish expectations about it" (Brooks 40). Fostering the values of Jacksonian democracy in an increasingly mobile American society, melodramas offered a romantic escape into the land of fantasy, while at the same time, they centered upon cherished middle-class values like self-reliance, manly independence, social respectability, and female domesticity. Furthermore, melodrama appealed essentially to working-class audiences since it was "full of aristocratic, greedy villains and praise for the simple laborer. Working-class audience members viewed the stories as a protest against the impositions of the rich and the cruelties of an acquisitive class society" (Dudden 71).

Equally successful, however, were the plays dealing with American character types, like the Yankee, the Indian, the Negro, the Irish.[10] From Robert Roger's *Ponteach* (1766) to Charlotte M. S. Barnes' *The Forest Princess; or, Two Centuries Ago* (1848), the Indian play remained a favorite among American audiences. Barnes' *The Forest Princess* was first performed in Liverpool, England, in 1844, while its American premiere was a few years later on February 16, 1848, at Burton's Arch Street Theater in Philadelphia. The play is simply another dramatization of the story of Pocahontas, the young Indian maiden who played a vital part in the English settlement of Jamestown. *The Forest Princess* greatly resembles James Nelson Barker's *The Indian Princess* (1808) and George Washington Parke Custis *Pocahontas; or, The Settlers of Virginia* (1830). Like its predecessors, the romantic quality of the play mainly rests on its constant allusions to the magnificence and sublimity of the new country's natural surroundings as well as the portrayal of the Indians in their most glorified aspect. What is remarkable about the play is that it offers a more unbiased view of the white man's cruel treatment of the Indian and the seizing of his land. It should be mentioned that Barnes tries to present the entire Pocahontas legend in a manner that insists upon historical accuracy, which at times stifles theatricality and the dramatic presentation of the story. The play is written in a rather dull blank verse while its action is essentially melodramatic and the characters fit the accepted classifications of hero, heroine, and villain. Compared to Custis' and Barker's versions of Pocahontas, however, *The Forest Princess* introduces a white man, Volday, as the villain of the play rather than an evil Indian, like Miami or Matacoran. Furthermore, it extends the story to include episodes in England following Pocahontas' marriage to Lieutenant John Rolfe. There, in a most romantically spectacular scene, Pocahontas dies after Rolfe has been cleared of a charge of treason.

   Interestingly enough, A. B. Lindsley presents an amusing amalgam
of conventionalized stage-types in her three-act comedy *Love and
Friendship; or, The Yankee Notions* (1809). The play was produced at
Park Theater, where Lindsley was a member of the company during the
season of 1807-8. As the playwright herself explains in the Preface, the
piece was originally "designed for a farce, but being considered too
long has been printed as a comedy." It takes place in Charleston, South
Carolina, and the basic story-line involves the Bostonian, Algernon
Seldreer, who is desperately in love with Augusta Marcene but who is
forced by her father to marry the man of his choice. Dick Dashaway, a
very rich but dissipated fellow, is to become Augusta's husband. It is
interesting to note that throughout the whole play the notions of love
and friendship are continually put to the test. For example, Dick's
father, Mr. Dashaway, a cunning businessman who admits that he got
his "fortune by cheating and lying," was once a close friend of
Seldreer's father. However, at the right moment, he did not hesitate to
ruin his 'friend' financially. Also, Miss Lightlove, out of jealousy and
revenge, presents Augusta with a false marriage contract claiming that
she and Seldreer were secretly married. Of course, at the end of the
play, in a truly melodramatic fashion, the good are rewarded with the
truth and the bad repent and reform. Like most plays written at that
time in America, *Love and Friendship* presents a most amusing Yankee
character, Jonathan, who greatly resembles Tyler's Jonathan in *The
Contrast* (1787) and actually provides comic relief in the play. In true
'Jonathan' fashion, Lindsley's Yankee employs a most picturesque
colloquial language, renders a few verses of "Yankee Doodle," and has
a weakness for the ladies. Lindsley also introduces the first college type
to be satirized in the play. Dick Dashaway flaunts his college education
which, in fact, is responsible for all the 'useful' things he has learnt,
that is to drink, talk politics, play billiards, and sport with the girls (II,
iii). Finally, a major distinction in *Love and Friendship* is the
introduction of Harry, the black servant. Although Harry exhibits some
of the typical stage-Negro characteristics, he is nevertheless, the first
black character who longs for his native land and feels homesick.
Embedded with a strong sentimental quality, he became a forerunner
for black characters in later abolitionist plays.
   For the most part, American playwrights expressed opinions about
social and political issues with an inclination towards satire and a
nationalistic attitude towards American people. For a playwright with a

certain degree of wit and sophistication, the developing American social landscape provided incomparable opportunity for social commentary. Various aspects of American social life, American manners and mores as well as the American business world and fashionable life were caricatured in a number of farce-comedies. In particular, the eagerness of the fashion-conscious middle-class to rise in the social scale by imitating European manners and practicing ceremonial etiquette captured the attention of certain nineteenth-century American dramatists who felt particularly uneasy about the welfare of the American republic.[11] Starting with Royall Tyler's *The Contrast* (1787), the impulse to satirize fashionable manners seems to have been present throughout the nineteenth century. Some of the most well-known American social comedies focusing on the ambitious parvenu and dealing critically with fashionable life, were James Nelson Barker's *Tears and Smiles* (1807), Joseph Hutton's *Fashionable Follies* (1809), James K. Paulding's *The Bucktails; or, American in England* (1815), Edward S. Gould's *The Very Age* (1850), Thomas Blaydon de Walden's *The Upper Ten and the Lower Twenty* (1854), Sidney F. Bateman's *Self* (1856), E.G.P. Wilkins' *Young New York* (1856), and, of course, Anna Cora Mowatt's *Fashion* (1845).

My interest in both Mowatt's *Fashion* and Sidney F. Bateman's *Self* is primarily grounded on the plays' significance as the site where a most powerful social criticism of the new material structure of American society meets with the playwrights' acute frustration regarding woman's lack of political power and her purely ornamental role as status symbol. Their plays elaborate satirically on the new industrial ethos of material success and individual progress in society, while, at the same time, they trenchantly lament the blatant exclusion of women from the whole ideological framework of personal advancement. Having made a career in the public world of the theater as both playwrights and actresses and having been financially rewarded for their efforts, Mowatt and Bateman began to realize, more clearly than anyone, that the "public realm was where economic resources were divided and decisions about social policy were made: the penalty for failure to present oneself in public was powerlessness, poverty or dependency"(Dudden 3).

The powerful ideal of lady, and the ambivalent status it entailed for women, encouraged a clash of definitions and interpretations in

American antebellum society. The interplay between the cultural myth
of ladyhood and the reality of women's restrictive roles and limited
political status was largely emphasized when a number of middle-class
'ladies' increasingly incorporated new interests in their domestic realm
and actually challenged their confinement and imprisonment. It is
precisely this realization of the highly circumscribed roles American
women were forced to assume, as well as their blatant discouragement
from venturing into the male public sphere of activity that Mowatt and
Bateman attempt to project in their plays.

Written within the context of the rapidly changing American
society and economy, both *Fashion* and *Self* center around the nature of
fashionable American culture in mid-nineteenth-century New York,
and question the new industrial value system and the behavioral codes
of the fairly prosperous middle-class. The plays' effect is partly drawn
from the structural conjoining of elements of melodrama, farce and
social comedy and partly from the thematic reciprocity between the
various social and economic processes and the stifling ideal of
femininity. The plays, through their powerful satire of the false
standards imposed upon men and women in industrialized America,
reveal a real sense of social consciousness as well as a knowledge of
cultural conventions. *Fashion* and *Self* clearly exhibit a reforming spirit
and moral seriousness as they satirize folly and contemporary social
problems. Without minimizing sentiment and moral judgment, the
plays satirically approach the various codes of behavior founded upon
prevailing social values and actually strive to project the traditional
republican pieties.

From the very beginning, both plays elaborate on the centrality of
fashion and actually attempt to construct a set of exaggerated images
that serve to widen the gap between the characters' imaginary notions
of self and their social reality. An issue intensely debated within the
plays' critical approach to the two prevalent functions of American
middle-class women, as republican mothers and wives and as
fashionable ladies, involves the degree of women's willing consent and
their internalization of those ideological processes that have
manipulated female consciousness and sense of self. If we bear in mind
Nancy K. Miller's argument that "when we tear the web of women's
texts we discover in the representations of writing itself the marks of
the grossly material, the sometimes brutal traces of the culture of
gender; the inscriptions of its political structures," it is easy to

understand how the two plays revolve round a mindful process of reinterpreting a cultural reality laden with prescriptions and social rules and roles.

Both Mowatt and Bateman contravened the nineteenth-century culturally-established principles and expressions of domesticity by making a highly successful career in the 'disreputable' world of the theater as both actresses and playwrights. It was really uncommon for an upper middle-class lady like Mowatt, a descendant of one of the most distinguished American families, and a member of the literary aristocracy, to launch into a theatrical career.[12] When Mowatt decided to embark upon a career as an actress, she was made particularly aware of the fact that she "would never find a home within the class into which she had been born,. . . [that] she had betrayed her social class by forming an alliance with the theater" (Johnson 130). Nevertheless, Mowatt proved to be a really talented actress and actually held, for eight years, a place among the most notable actresses in America and in England. As a matter of fact, when she appeared in London starring in her own play *Armand* (1847), she was so favorably received by the British audiences and critics that the *Manchester Guardian* wrote that "she is the most refined American actor whom we have yet seen" (Barnes 247).

The ninth of fourteen children, Anna Cora Mowatt was born in 1819, in Bordeaux, where her father was living temporarily with his family on business. When Mowatt was seven, they returned to New York City where she was educated primarily at home and at private girls' schools. As a child, she exhibited a talent for acting and a precocious interest in Shakespeare. Her large family was devoted to amateur theatricals and Anna Cora became the adapter, producer, and leading actress in their private productions. In 1834, at the age of fifteen, she eloped with James Mowatt, a well-to-do New York attorney thirteen years her senior. She continued her studies under the supervision of her husband and began to write verse, various articles for popular women's magazines and essays contrasting the manners of Europeans and Americans.

A closer look at Mowatt's dramatic works reveals a broad spectrum of dramatic forms ranging from social comedy to melodrama to romantic tragedy. In 1836, inspired by her reading of poetry and history, she wrote *Pelayo, or The Cavern of Covadonga,* a romantic epic poem in five cantos, which she published under the name of

'Isabel.' *Pelayo* is set in Spain and its theme is primarily founded upon
the life and history of the first king of Asturias. Unfortunately, the
poem was not favorably received by the critics, and, in Mowatt's own
words, "as readily exterminated by the critics as a butterfly could be
crushed, it died an easy death" (66). A year later, more mature,
determined, but still bitter because of *Pelayo*'s failure, she wrote a
clever satiric essay on criticism which she deliberately named
Reviewers Reviewed.[13] Soon, however, her first serious attempt as a
dramatist was bound to follow with *The Gypsy Wanderer, or The Stolen
Child*, an operetta which was performed before a circle of relatives and
friends. Written in blank verse and interspersed with a number of songs,
the play is essentially melodramatic and actually reveals Mowatt's
versatility and talent. In the midst of various scenes of recognition and
a highly mystical atmosphere which adds to the suspense of the play,
the plot centers around the story of a young widow whose infant child
is stolen by gypsies.

    In 1837, Mowatt developed symptoms of tuberculosis and a sea
voyage was recommended. During the time she spent in Europe, she
composed a verse drama in six acts entitled *Gulzara, or The Persian
Slave*, which was intended for private performance to celebrate their
return to America. Since the play was to be enacted only by Mowatt
herself and her sisters, it was particularly designed for an all-female
cast. As a matter of fact, the only male character in the play, Amurath, a
ten-year old boy, was represented by one of Mowatt's younger sisters.
The play is set in the exotic palace of the Sultan Suliman, but, as the
Sultan along with the rest of the male population have gone away to
fight against their enemies, attention is focused upon the enclosed space
of the harem where women's relationships and feelings towards one
another take shape. Although there is a preponderance of long
monologues in the play and Mowatt actually fails to provide powerful
insights into her female characters, there are various passages of noble
poetry which best illustrate Mowatt's dramatic talent. The entire play
was published in *The New World* newspaper and actually received
some very complimentary comments. More specifically, the editor of
the newspaper remarked that:

> The drama of *Gulzara, or The Persian Slave*, was written by a young
> lady lovely and accomplished. There is a unity and simplicity in its
> design and execution which cannot fail to give sincere pleasure. It is

pervaded by rare and delicate thought; many passages are strikingly beautiful; and the impartial critic will think, with us, that the drama could do credit to a much more experienced writer.[14]

However, it is *Fashion*, Mowatt's bright satire on American fashionable life that secured her a place in the canon of American dramatic literature. As Epes Sargent points out, the play "met with a success which certainly has not attended any other American comedy" (iii). *Fashion* is considered the most significant social comedy in the history of American drama, and it is without question the most frequently anthologized play by a nineteenth-century female playwright. The play was favorably received by the critics and the public as a thoroughly American social comedy depicting contemporary New York society. Edgar Allan Poe, one of Mowatt's sternest critics, reviewed *Fashion* twice in *The Broadway Journal*. At first, he observed that the play was a bad imitation of *The School for Scandal*, but, when he compared it to other American plays, he realized that "in many respects it [was] superior to any other American play" (61). Also, in his second review, he moderated his first observation that the play lacked originality as he admitted that "in one respect, perhaps, we have done Mrs. Mowatt unintentional injustice" (63).[15]

Furthermore, *The Spirit of the Times*, the newspaper which literally reflected the spirit of American society and generally expressed profound distrust against native dramatic creations, wrote:

> The announcement of a new comedy, *Fashion*, by Mrs. Mowatt has awakened some little interest with regard to the ultimate fate of American comic writing. . . American dramatic literature is, at present an unploughed field for genius. . . The reason why so little has been written for the stage is first, the want of ability, and secondly, the lack of reward, should the ability be discovered (32).[16]

The Spirit of the Times quite explicitly projected the pervasive belief in women's inability to create literary and dramatic works of high quality:

> A Native Comedy, by a Mrs. Mowatt, is rumored to be in rehearsal at the Park. We have little confidence in female dramatic productions of the present time, but we wish the lady a happy debut although it may be in five long acts (33).

Nevertheless, a few years later and after having witnessed the immense success of *Fashion* in both the United States and in England, the same newspaper wrote:

> The American Comedy of *Fashion; or, Life in New York* in five acts, from the graceful and polished pen of Anna Cora Mowatt, was produced for the first time in England at the Olympic theater, on Wednesday evening last, to a crowded, fashionable and critical audience. . . . . . . The 'Times' says, that the American tone given to all the characters endows the work with a freshness, which distinguishes it from the many comedies produced on the British stage. The 'Daily News' says it is an exceedingly clever work, and conveys a lively but good-humored satire on the foibles of American society. The 'Sun' of last evening says that America has not hitherto produced any play that would stand the test of representation before a London audience, rough and ranting melodrama being the staple of what she has sent across the Atlantic; but the reproach has been wiped out by the appearance of *Fashion,* which will take its place by the side of the best English comedies (600-1).[17]

Following the success of *Fashion,* Mowatt created *Armand; or, the Child of the People* (1847), a romantic drama in blank verse set in the time of Louis XV. Although the play is intrinsically conventional, it actually represents a popular trend in American theater. As will be shown in the fourth chapter of this book, from 1820 to 1850 a romantic atmosphere pervaded all artistic creation in America reflecting the democratic spirit of the nation as well as the need to crush all institutions that suppressed the will of the common man.[18] After its initial production at the Park Theater, *Armand* also appeared in Boston and afterwards in London, where the play ran to full houses for twenty-one nights. The play was reasonably successful and it was described by *The Spirit of the Times* as having

> living and suggestive outlines of character, scenes of pathos whose power is testified by the emotions of the audience, and a pervading simplicity, truth and loveliness, both of thought and language which act as a charm and are full of fascination (2).[19]

When her husband died in 1851, Anna Cora Mowatt returned to New York where she began writing her lively *Autobiography of an Actress* (1854). The same year her book was published, Mowatt married William F. Ritchie, a prominent Virginian and editor of *The Richmond Enquirer*. Her second marriage proved an unhappy one and she left her husband seven years later on the grounds of irreconcilable political and personal differences. Mowatt died in 1870 having proved to the still Puritan American society that a woman of breeding and social standing could succeed on the stage and yet remain untainted by the 'evils' of theater.

FASHION

What makes Mowatt's play a landmark in the history of American theater and drama is, first of all, the unprecedented reception that it had; second, its undisputed quality as a spirited social satire, and, finally, the social background of its author. Eric Barnes remarks that "it is probably quite safe to say that no play ever written by an American is comparable to *Fashion* in the immediate sensation which it created or its long-range effects on the course of American drama" (142). Arthur Hobson Quinn also explains that "*Fashion* deserved its success. It is that rare thing, a social satire based on real knowledge of the life it depicts, but painting it without bitterness, without nastiness, and without affectation. It is true to the manners of the time and place, but it is based on human motives and failings that are universal" (312). Another very important reason for the play's significance is the fact that it "encouraged that necessary cooperation between professional theater people and the literati" (Meserve 1986: 129). According to the *Herald Tribune*, on the opening night of *Fashion*, the "boxes, pit, and gallery were crowded; all of the literati of the city were present, with a tolerable sprinkle of the elite" (Hutton 59). A social aristocrat herself, Mowatt made her debut as a professional playwright by shrewdly presenting currently popular themes, characters and situations, in a manner that appealed to the more sophisticated part of the audience.

Fashion aims primarily at exposing social pretension and extravagance, while, at the same time, seriously examines the economic foundations of fashionable American culture. The manner in which American society is satirized as well as the relation of the individual to an immensely mobile society clearly reveal that Mowatt was highly aware of the various social, economic, and cultural changes that were taking place in America at that time. Exhibiting great social knowledge, cultural maturity and perceptiveness, Mowatt, however, extends her vision beyond fashionable manners and affectation to include a pointed satire on a number of social and cultural phenomena, characteristic of mid-nineteenth-century American society. Daniel F. Havens identifies some of these phenomena with certain real problems in American society, such as "parvenu values, heiress-hunting foreigners, and filial obedience" (4).

The play imparts the story of Mrs. Tiffany, an uneducated former milliner, whose marriage to Mr. Tiffany, a New York wealthy merchant, opened her way into fashionable society. Mrs. Tiffany, who apes foreign manners and despises everything that is American, is sharply contrasted to Gertrude, the play's heroine, who actually becomes the embodiment of native worth and American virtues. Though mainly caricatures, the characters' witty conversation and exaggerated gestures add a great deal of charm and humor in the play. The opening scene of Mowatt's *Fashion*, repeatedly establishes a sense of disorientation as Mrs. Tiffany fails to realize the vanity of her illusory self-assurance that she is an accomplished and respectable lady of fashion. Her obsession with establishing a social elite within New York as well as the self-deluding vanity of a woman with upwardly mobile aspirations betray her total lack of self awareness and make her comic downfall almost certain. The satire directed against Mrs. Tiffany, the representative of a large number of American middle-class women, and her 'major' social responsibility as arbiter of fashion, is inherently benevolent and good-humored and actually exemplifies what was only implied in the various conduct books of the time.

Mrs. Tiffany's inadequate education, which can only be imperfectly veiled by a smattering of French, her admiration for everything European and her disgust at the "vulgarity of the Americans," as well as her inability to see the true nature of things beneath the veneer of fashion, all serve to construct her as a fearful product of the new materialistic ethic of American society. Although Mrs. Tiffany's insistence that she dotes on titled nobility, and that she is part of the American 'ee-light' are delineated with unmerciful delight, Mowatt's audience can recognize the political and cultural groundings of such representation. Functioning as the painful reminder of a 'disgraceful' past—a plebeian background,—Mrs. Tiffany's sister,

Prudence, momentarily forces her to face her previous image and social status:

> Pru. Who would have thought, when you and I were sitting behind that little mahogany-colored counter, in Canal Street, making up flashy hats and caps-. . .
>
> Mrs. Tif. Prudence! never let me hear you mention this subject again. Forget what we have been, it is enough to remember that we are of the upper ten thousand (I,i).

Mrs. Tiffany's distorted values and misguided aspirations are clearly revealed in her insistence on changing the name of the Black servant from Zeke to the more fashionable Adolph, in her desire to marry her daughter, Seraphina, to Count Jolimaitre, "the most fashionable foreigner in town," as well as in her exaggerated epigrammatic lines:

> . . . A woman of fashion never grows old!
> Age is always out of fashion (I,i).

Although foreign affectation defines Mrs. Tiffany's character and actually provides the major situation for satire, Mowatt also directs her good-natured criticism against a number of intrinsically American social types. For one thing, Zeke, the stereotype of the contented, docile black American servant, has so much internalized the false standards of the white people he works for that he willingly renounces his own identity. The language he speaks, the clothes he wears, the fact that he tries to look important, all suggest a hidden desire to adopt the materialistic values and manners of the bourgeoisie.[20] In order to attain a certain degree of dignity in this artificial, fashionable society, Zeke happily acquiesces to the devaluation of his own cultural values. So, when, later in the play, Mr. Tiffany calls him Zeke, his reply is highly predictable:

> Mr. Tif. Zeke.
> Zeke. Don't know any such nigga, Boss (III,i).

Through the portrayal of various American types, Mowatt projects her own impressions, and, perhaps, ambivalences towards contemporary urban life and towards class roles and distinctions. The representation of "the ornamental appendages to the drawing room" in the character of Mr. Twinkle, the poet, and Mr. Augustus Fogg, scion "of one of our oldest families," allows Mowatt to attack literary and social superficiality and pretentiousness as well as expose the pervasiveness of the fashionable codes of behavior, which have opened the way to a number of abusers of the 'drawing room' society (I,i).

Mowatt's incisive criticism of the fashionable home of the Tiffanys' arises from the fact that it actually allows people like Count Jolimaitre and Snobson—the representatives of vain affectation and moral decadence—to enter. Count Jolimaitre continues the American native tradition of stage rake-fops. His predecessors can certainly be traced back to Dimple, the English fashionable fop, in Royall Tyler's comedy *The Contrast* (1787), Fluttermore in James N. Barker's *Tears and Smiles* (1808), Captain Pendragon in Mordecai M. Noah's *She Would Be a Soldier* (1819), and Bellamy in Samuel Woodworth's *The Forest Rose* (1825). His main difference as a rake, however, is the fact that, although he retains his foreign affectation and exaggerated manners, dress, and speech, Count Jolimaitre is only portrayed as an essentially comic figure. His aristocratic affectation is not maliciously presented and he bears no resemblance to the cynical fortune-hunter and dangerous womanizer of the previous plays. As a matter of fact, his clever asides comically reveal his awareness of his own ridiculous situation:

Count. Ah! I find but one redeeming charm in America—the superlative loveliness of the feminine portion of creation,—and the wealth of their obliging papas. (Aside). . . . .

Mrs. Tif. Count, I am so much ashamed, -pray excuse me! Although a lady of large fortune, and one, Count, who can boast of the highest connections, I blush to confess that I have never travelled,—while you, Count, I presume are at home in all the courts of Europe.

Count. Courts? Eh? Oh, yes, Madam, very true. I believe I am pretty well known in some of the courts of Europe—police courts. (Aside crossing) (I,i).

On the other hand, however, Snobson, Mr. Tiffany's lower middle-class clerk is comically portrayed as the representative of the decadent extreme of the industrial ethos of individual progress. As Mr. Tiffany reveals, Snobson, in his desire to rise financially and socially, has become a ruthless man who wouldn't hesitate to blackmail him in order to attain his goal:

> . . . . .To rise himself he mounts upon my shoulders, and unless I can shake him off he must crush me! (II,i)

The metaphor of the American dream for all men as social ascent and financial achievement is criticized in the play through Snobson whose dream is to marry his boss's daughter, Seraphina, and, thus, rise in society:

> Snob. Six months from to-day if I ain't driving my two footmen tandem, down Broadway—and as fashionable as Mrs. Tiffany herself, then I ain't the trump I thought I was (II,i).

In Snobson, Mowatt has managed to capture the ambivalence that characterized most nineteenth-century lower middle-class men who wavered between self-righteous egalitarian and republican sentiments for social advancement and a smoldering morbid desire to enter fashionable society and enjoy all the advantages wealth would bring them. Demonstrating great competence with dialogue, special dialects and slang, Mowatt constructs Snobson's language in such a way so as to distinctively reveal his social identity, his greed for money and the material objects of luxury, as well as his silliness when attempting to observe etiquette:

> Snob. How dye do, Marm? (Crosses.) How are you? Mr. Tiffany, your most!—
>
> Mrs.Tif. (Formally.) Bung jure. Comment vow porte vow, Monsur Snobson?
>
> Snob. Oh, to be sure—very good of you—fine day.
>
> Mrs.Tif. (Pointing to a chair with great dignity.)

Sassoyez vow, Monsur Snobson.

Snob. I wonder what she's driving at! I ain't up to the fashionable
lingo yet! (aside.) Eh? What? Speak a little louder, Marm? (III,i).

Cutting deep into the various social layers, Mowatt's play, in many
ways, satirizes not the 'true' values of 'refined' middle and upper-class
American society, but those who abuse those values and, even more
important, aspire undeservedly to that society. It appears that Mowatt
uses satire as the most appropriate medium to express an intended
meaning and, thus, reach the superlative degree of intended effect on
her audience. It could be argued that the 'literati of the city' and 'the
tolerable sprinkle of the elite' who attended the opening performance of
Fashion did so not only to laugh (refinedly, of course) at themselves,
but to laugh even more at pretenders to their class, and probably, in
their laughing, have their own materially and socially very comfortable
way of life confirmed. Snobson, Count Jolimaitre, Mr. Twinkle, Mr.
Fogg, and, of course, Mrs. Tiffany were recognizable figures in mid-
nineteenth-century American society.

The satire of the affectations, of the misdirected views and illusory
ambitions of the characters, reveals Mowatt's profound concern for the
Americans' obsession with financial success, a social problem rooted
far beneath the surface of fashionable foibles and follies. It is the
problem of the disintegrating American dream of individual progress
and prosperity, whose luster is beginning to fade away. The realization
of the self-alienating power of the new market economy can be clearly
seen in Mowatt's sarcasm towards Mr. Tiffany, representative of the
new American type of man of business affairs. Although the rest of the
characters receive an essentially good-natured satire, Mowatt's
approach of Mr. Tiffany is quite different; she is critical of his folly in
an extremely blunt and non-comical way. For Mr. Tiffany, the new
ideology of industrial economy entails the complete destruction of any
sense of self-esteem and dignity and actually results in a threatening
emotional void. The paradox that repeatedly emerges in the
representation of the masculine materialistic ethos is the presence of a
degenerating self. Adam Trueman, Mr. Tiffany's old friend and
representative of such solid virtues as industriousness and thrift,
explicitly articulates the profound impact that the growing ethos of
individualism and the money-making ideology have upon Mr. Tiffany:

.....You look as if you'd melted down your flesh into dollars, and mortgaged your soul in the bargain! Your warm heart has grown cold over your ledger—your light spirits heavy with calculation! You have traded away your youth—your hopes—your tastes, for wealth! And now you have the wealth you coveted, what does it profit you? Pleasure it cannot buy; for you have lost your capacity for enjoyment—Ease it will not bring; for the love of gain is never satisfied (II,i).

These powerful images of alienation, which remain till the final scene of the play, serve to highlight precisely those values that Mowatt seeks to negate. In Mr. Tiffany's case, the desire for social ascendancy and wealth engenders a significant conflation of loss of self and the disruption of the illusion of wholeness constructed in relation to family, the love and obligation to his wife and child. Certainly, Trueman's words inject a sub-human dimension to Mr. Tiffany's personal characteristics and strongly link him to the monstrous figure towards the end of the play who wouldn't hesitate to force Seraphina to marry Snobson in order to save himself:

Mr. Tif. . . . Seraphina, my child, you will not see me disgraced— ruined! I have been a kind father to you—at least I have tried to be one—although your mother's extravagance made a madman of me! The Count is an impostor—you seemed to like him—(pointing to Snobson). Heaven forgive me! Marry him and save me.

Mr. Tiffany's selfishness generates feelings of disgust in Adam Trueman who forcefully reproaches him:

Shame on you, Antony! Put a price on your own flesh and blood! Shame on such foul traffic! (V,i).

The main difference, however, between Mr. and Mrs. Tiffany's attitude towards Seraphina's marriage is grounded on the fact that, although Mrs. Tiffany's desire to raise her daughter's social status by having her marry the Count is induced solely by her foolishness and ignorance, Mr. Tiffany is revoltingly conscious of the far-reaching repercussions of such a self-centered decision upon his child.

Significantly, in the home of the Tiffany's, the notion of an emotional and moral wholeness of the family, which, according to the nineteenth-century middle-class ideology had to be constructed against the wound of material values, collapses when the conventional relation between husband and wife is shattered. The belief in the harmonious expression of the unity and conventional function of the middle-class household appears as a specifically romantic delusion since it fails to remain intact from the dehumanizing power of money and the nineteenth-century materialistic ethic. Ironically, at stake here is the simultaneous interpretation of the American middle-class home as a haven protected from the material public world and as a most vulnerable site where fashionable values, codes and manners are built. The depiction of the ambivalent status of the nineteenth-century middle-class household as the place most remote from the economic sphere of competition and self-interest, and, yet, inevitably and essentially affected by it, is really crucial. The question of understanding and respect inherent in the notion of any successful conjugal union is challenged in the play through a number of comic, yet disturbing, arguments between husband and wife. As a matter of fact, Mr. and Mrs. Tiffany's marriage appears to be part of the overall material structure of *Fashion*. The facticity of their relationship coincides perfectly with the general atmosphere of false standards, fashionable behavior and outward appearances. The true schism between husband and wife is exposed in carefully constructed dialogues where the lack of understanding and the absence of any real communication become evident:

> Mrs Tif. Mr. Tiffany, I desire that you will purchase Count d' Orsay's "Science of Etiquette," and learn how to conduct yourself— especially before you appear at the grand ball, which I shall give on Friday!

> Tif. . . . A pretty time to give a ball when you know that I am on the very brink of bankruptcy!

> Mrs. Tif. So much the greater reason that nobody should suspect your circumstances, or you would lose your credit at once. Just at this crisis a ball is necessary to save your reputation! Then there was Mrs. Honeywood—

Tif. Gave a ball the night before her husband shot himself—perhaps
you wish to drive me to follow his example?

Mrs. Tif. Good gracious! Mr. Tiffany, how you talk! I beg you won't
mention anything of the kind. I consider black the most unbecoming
color (III,i).

Fashion revolves around the encroachment of fashionable artificiality
upon people's lives, their manners, feelings and expressions. At the
same time, the play rises above the inevitable chauvinistic prejudice of
an older nationalism and actually elaborates on the central dual notion
of materialistic values and senseless fashion as a wound inflicted upon
all expressions of human existence. Adam Trueman, the seventy-two-
year-old Catteraugus farmer, articulates the essence of fashionable
conduct:

Fashion! And pray what is fashion, madam? An agreement between
certain persons to live without using their souls! to substitute etiquette
for virtue—decorum for purity—manners for morals! to affect a
shame for the works of their Creator! and expend all their rapture
upon the works of their tailors and dressmakers!(IV,i).

From the very beginning, the play's positive values of individual merit
and dignity regardless of social class, honest labor, simplicity and
common sense, are embodied in Adam Trueman and Gertrude,
Seraphina's governess. Trueman, who, throughout the play, emphasizes
pastoral virtue while chiding the Tiffanys' way of behaving, is an
inherently comic character reminiscent of Royall Tyler's Jonathan in
The Contrast. As a latter-day Yankee, Trueman incorporates an
exaggerated combination of rural virtues and values; he is a little more
sophisticated than Jonathan, but equally shrewd and clownish,
especially when he waves his stick about in his attempt to strike moral
corruption (II,ii).[21] Adam Trueman's bluntness and honesty proved to
be really appealing to American audiences, and, as Mowatt explains in
her *Autobiography,*

The only character in the play which was sketched from life was that
of the blunt, warmhearted old farmer. I was told that the original was

seen in the pit vociferously applauding Adam Trueman's strictures on fashionable society (203).

In studying Trueman, one cannot overlook the fact that, although he functions as a character fully aware of the seriousness of the decadent materialistic ethic underlying fashionable behavior, he, as well, is a caricature. Brusquely critical of the gross foolishness, vanity, and greedy opportunism of Mr. and Mrs. Tiffany's circle, Trueman exhibits an exaggerated degree of conservatism and sentimentalism. He is, nevertheless, the representative of democratic values and republican principles that the Tiffanys oppose, and by the end of the play he succeeds in establishing the connection between democracy and moral probity as well as the reinstitution of the traditional American values. Gary A. Richardson declares that "Trueman's names, age, rural background, and direct speech identify him with the revolutionary war era, and he strides through the play like a Founding Father purging cultural enslavement as he had earlier expelled political bondage" (101).

Following the pattern of the majority of Yankee plays, Trueman's romantic conception of the recuperative impact of a pastoral setting on people's lives leads him to a largely sentimental solution by urging the Tiffanys to return to their virtuous pastoral origins in an attempt to learn how to combine republican virtues with their prosperity, and never again let themselves be led astray by dreams of wealth and false fashions:

> You must sell your house and all these gew gaws, and bundle your wife and daughter off to the country. There let them learn economy, true independence and home virtues, instead of foreign follies. As for yourself, continue your business—but let moderation, in future, be your counsellor, and let honesty be your confidential clerk (V,i).

In this artificial world of moral corruption, Gertrude's presence serves as a revitalizing power which effects a possible reconstitution of the former pastoral virtues of simplicity, honesty, and social conservatism. Typical of a sentimental heroine, Gertrude embodies the stock sentimental qualities of patience, virtue, and filial obedience. Nevertheless, she is endowed with a capacity for independent, decisive action, with intelligence and a bright sense of humor. One of Gertrude's wittiest displays comes in the scene with Colonel Howard in which he struggles to express his love for her. Although she loves Howard as well and is secretly pleased with what he is about to say, she, nevertheless, takes advantage of every man's vulnerability at the moment of wooing and with a remarkable brightness of spirit she makes Howard stammer:

> Ger. I think I informed you that Mrs. Tiffany only received visitors on her reception day—she is therefore not prepared to see you. Zeke—Oh! I beg his pardon—Adolph, made some mistake in admitting you.
>
> How. Nay, Gertrude, it was not Mrs. Tiffany, nor Miss Tiffany, whom I came to see; it—it was—
>
> Ger. The conservatory perhaps? I will leave you to examine the flowers at leisure!
>
> How. Gertrude—listen to me. If only I dared to give utterance to what is hovering upon my lips! (Aside.)
>
> Gertrude!
>
> Ger. Colonel Howard!
>
> How. Gertrude, I must—must—
>
> Ger. Yes, indeed you must, must leave me! I think I hear somebody coming—(II,ii).[22]

In the dramatic line of heroines of spirit, Gertrude is the only one who rallies her wit and intelligence, not for the purpose of gaining the man she loves, but rather for a more objective goal, that of exposing an impostor, thereby protecting the people she works for. Her strong sense of duty and loyalty coupled with an authentic sense of obligation to see justice done, as well as her shrewdness and sophistication transform her into the autonomous image of agent of the action. Gertrude's uniqueness as a character is realized in the fact that she can exert the freedom to decide which cultural conventions are most adequate to her self-expression. The supreme form of her autonomy is inscribed in her choice to leave Geneva, where she had been brought up, and move to the United States. She herself explains to Colonel Howard that

> I have my mania,—as some wise person declares that all mankind have,—and mine is a love of independence! In Geneva, my wants were supplied by two kind old maiden ladies, upon whom I know not that I have any claim. I had abilities and desired to use them. I came here at my own request; for here I am no longer dependent! (II,ii).

As I have already pointed out in the second part of this chapter, within the context of the increasingly commercialized American economy, a number of women were determined to explore the limited possibilities of change for themselves, to gain control over their own lives, to acquire skills and self-confidence, and to work towards female achievement. In *Fashion*, Gertrude is the representative of this new breed of women who were anxious to break free from their disadvantaged position and demanded equal social, political, economic and educational rights with men. Kathleen L. Nichols observes that she is "perhaps the first self-supporting heroine in American drama"(134).

Though Gertrude's status in the home of the Tiffanys' is considered essentially vulnerable—"a species of upper servant—an orphan—no friends" (II,ii)—she manages to gain authority and rise from her subordinate position in society by repeatedly establishing her sense of independence, will, and merit. Far from posing as a disenchanted, despondent young woman in a world of folly, Gertrude constructs her public self as a figure of virtue making a separate innocent and autonomous existence possible while releasing herself from those social structures that deny her an independence of will and relegate her to a purely ornamental status. At the end of the play, and in a truly melodramatic fashion, Gertrude is rewarded when her social status is elevated to that of a wealthy heiress as she proves to be Trueman's long-lost grandchild.

Gertrude's independent, almost fierce spirit becomes the source of the major complication in the play as she devises a bold plan to expose Count Jolimaitre in time to prevent his marriage to Seraphina. Unfortunately, however, her scheme fails and she is discovered in a dark room with the Count. Her public construction of herself as a figure of conscious merit and applauded virtue is strongly undermined as everybody believes that she is secretly involved with Count Jolimaitre. Although Gertrude repeatedly attempts to disperse the story of her loss of honor and of her failure to remain pure and perfect, she finds herself inextricably implicated in power structures that demand her punishment without even listening to her version of the story:

> Ger. Mr. Trueman, I beseech you—I insist upon being heard,—I claim it as a right!
>
> True. Right? How dare you have the face, girl, to talk of rights? You had more rights than you thought for, but you have forfeited them all! All right to love, respect, protection, and to not a little else that you don't dream of. Go, go! I'll start for Catteraugus to-morrow,—I've seen enough of what fashion can do! (IV,ii).

Disacknowledged by Trueman and Howard, the people she loved and respected, Gertrude is forced to face the social, cultural, and personal repercussions for supposedly losing the primary value that marked her position in society. Her action is regarded as a transgression potentially wounding to the stability and integrity of her social image as well as the stability of the social order in general. Ironically enough, in this comic moral outrage, it is Mrs. Tiffany herself who orders Gertrude to leave the house at once as she now constitutes a most sinister threat against the ideological and moral codes of her household:

> Get out of my house, you owdacious—you ruined—you abime young woman! You will corrupt all my family. Good gracious! Don't touch me,—don't come near me. Never let me see your face after to-morrow. Pack (IV,ii).

In the final act of the play, Mowatt stages a grand finale in which solid moral and social structures are established through a number of admonitions against fashionable behavior and pretense. In the highly melodramatic ending of the play, the virtuous are rewarded, while the villains are exposed and forced to reform. Employing the dramatic techniques of melodrama and comedy of manners, Mowatt manages to highlight the risible in human affairs through comically constructed complications and spirited dialogue. Furthermore, she succeeds in placing her characters in a complex socio-economic and cultural context marked by constant changes, confusion, and a crisis of ethics and identity. In *Fashion,* we can trace the characters' loss of a truthful self-presence as we probe into their personal relations, their family ties, their principles and code of values. Underneath their illusory social images and caricatured actions, the characters are torn between the ravages of fashion and materialism.

The theme of *Fashion* was soon imitated by another successful, but less distinguished actress-playwright, Sidney F. Bateman. Born in New York, in 1823, Bateman's association with the world of theater began at a very early age.[23] Her father was Joseph Cowell, an English actor who performed both in England and the United States, and her husband was Hezekiah L. Bateman, an actor-manager in St. Louis, Mo. Unfortunately, our knowledge of Bateman's life and background is limited and her plays, most of which have failed of record, are hardly ever mentioned in American theater books. She must have made her professional debut at the age of fourteen in New Orleans during the season 1837-38. Although she was not really a great actress, her extensive knowledge of theatrical technique as well as her ability in playwriting and stage management secured her a small place among nineteenth-century American dramatists.

Her most successful play, *Self* (1856), seems to have enjoyed a large number of performances both in New York and Boston. Although *Self* lacks the artistic finesse of *Fashion,* it was "received with great praise, and it took its place in popular favor by the side of Mrs. Mowatt's comedy" (Hutton 79). The play has been characterized by George C.D. Odell as "a work of some significance in the American drama"(520). *Self* follows closely the plot of *Fashion* and concentrates on the story of Mrs. Apex, the extravagant and irresponsible wife of a New York merchant, who persuades her son, Charles, to forge a cheque for $15,000 dollars in order to get her stepdaughter's money and pay off her own debts. Modeled after Mowatt's comedy, *Self* is a combination of aspects of farce and melodrama laced with local references while satirically exhibiting the follies of fashionable life in New York. Like *Fashion,* the play involves patriotic sentiments, moral commentary, a melodramatic villain, a Yankee character, and a Black servant, elements very popular in the American drama of the time.

A year later, in 1857, Bateman wrote a three-act social comedy called *The Golden Calf; or, Marriage a la Mode.* The play is set in

England and in Paris and actually comments on the insiduous power of
money on the individual as it satirizes snobbery through a number of
entertaining situations and problems. The characters are mainly social
caricatures and the mood of the play is explicitly didactic and
melodramatic.

In 1863, the Bateman family moved to England where Sidney and
her husband became joint-managers of the Lyceum Theater in London.
Even after her husband's death in 1875, Mateman continued to manage
it with remarkable acumen.

SELF

My discussion of Bateman's *Self* will again focus on the play's
examination of the relationship between middle-class fashionable
culture and economics in mid-nineteenth-century American society. In
Self, the issue is once more the double wound of fashion and
materialism which is depicted through the presentation of self-
disintegrating characters and the destruction of sound republican
principles. The satire of fashionable affectations, some obviously
imported while others clearly indigenous to the new American society,
explicitly marks Bateman's attempt to express the desire for the
regaining of full and truthful self—and social presence. *Self* essentially
reiterates Mowatt's theme of native republican worth as this is
contrasted to the decadent extreme of the Jacksonian American dream
of individual progress.

The play opens with the establishment of the fashionable practice
of conspicuous consumption as the widespread folly in New York
society. The setting in the first scene is a "fashionable Dry Goods Store,
in Broadway," the meeting place for a number of middle-class ladies. In
support of the disintegrating impact of the new fashionable materialistic
ethic, a number of images are projected which actually serve to disrupt
women's imaginary self-constructions and social personalities. The
'privileged' role of women as emblems of their husbands' wealth and
social status is undermined in the play through the unremitting use of
powerful adjectives and metaphors that equate women with the vile
side of fashion and material luxury. Scathing asides repeatedly
construct an irrevocable public image of women that actually becomes
the site of all possible degeneracy:

Prompt. [Aside at his desk.] I knew she would kiss her! What
hypocrites these women are!

Mrs Apex. .... [Aside.] Deceitful monster!—but she is too
fashionable to quarrel with!

Mrs. Radius. [Aside.] Artificial creature! I am resolved to mortify
her!
. . . .
Charles. [Aside.] Tell them both how well they look! That's the way I
always manage to please mother, and the other dragon is just as vain!
(I,i)

Caught into the explicitly pretentious web of bourgeois etiquette, the
female characters' social relations as well as their personal expressions
of feeling and thought are split into a form of self-alienation and a form
of ambivalent self-articulation. To emphasize the distinct angle of her
vision regarding middle-class women's misdirected personal aims and
aspirations, Bateman creates a social and familial context that
challenges both men's and women's traditional definitions of
appropriateness and cultural conditioning. By staging a world of
pretense and superficiality, the play is bent upon transmitting a
threatening image of disintegrating values and principles. The
dramatization of Mrs. Apex's and the other 'fashionable' ladies'
confusion and hopelessness as they live their lives in a social milieu,
forced to play a game whose rules they did not invent is really crucial.
The same misguided aspirations seen in Mrs. Tiffany are satirically
mirrored in all the female characters' dream of social ascendancy.
However, the play lacks the true comic spirit of Mowatt's *Fashion* as it
deliberately intends both pity and scorn for the representatives of
fashionable foibles. In the grotesquely expressed images of bourgeois
femininity, *Self* fails to rise above bitterness and nastiness, and,
although it employs a sufficient amount of wit and humor, it mainly
focuses upon the characters' potential for vileness. The satire directed
against Mrs. Apex is far from being good-natured as she is repeatedly
portrayed as a figure capable of evil-doing. Mrs. Apex's destruction of
any sense of honor and dignity is gradually completed by her emotional
disintegration. Her attitude towards her stepdaughter, Mary, when the

latter refuses to lend her the 15,000 dollars she needs to pay off her debts, reveals her consciously unscrupulous character:

> Mrs. Apex. [Looks a moment astonished.—Aside.] Is it possible! This pliant child, whom I have been able at will to exile from her father's affections, and whose very thoughts I have constrained to serve my interests, has rebelled against me! Mary, I have requested this money—I now implore it of you! I cannot tell what may be the result of your refusal!
>
> Mary. Indeed it gives me great pain to deny your request, but my father's wish is paramount.
>
> Mrs. Apex. Cold-hearted girl, this hypocrisy will not serve you. Your selfish heart bids you deny my request because you fear you may never again be repaid your paltry fortune! I leave you to the enjoyment of your generous reflections!(I,ii).

Mrs. Apex's vileness, which stems primarily from her extravagance and greed, culminates in her perverse decision to force her son Charles to forge Mary's signature in order to get the money. The arguments she uses in order to convince Charles are absolutely despicable:

> Charles. Oh, mother!—a forgery!!
>
> Mrs. Apex. Nonsense, Charles! do you suppose I think there is any sin in such an act as this? Would your mother counsel you to commit forgery? These over-nice scruples are ridiculous!
>
> Charles. But, mother, I,—is there no other way?
>
> Mrs. Apex. Why seek for another, when this is so simple and apparent? Come, come, be a man and not a child, frightened at a spectre of your own creation! I wish to borrow some money of your sister, for a few days, and you call it forgery!—such baby-fears are only fit for the nursery (II,i).

For Mrs. Apex, fashionable folly constitutes an incursion into her character integrity as well as her ideal self-image and her existence in social reality. Mrs. Apex's image of vileness is softened only through her emotional changes registered in her long conscience-smitten monologues. From the very beginning of the play, Mrs. Apex hovers between her contradictory self-conception as fashionable lady and as wife and mother whose primary role is the promulgation of solid moral values and principles. What is less clear and more troubling in the play is that Mrs. Apex, like a large number of real-life middle-class women, is trapped within an apparently immutable social structure. Both Mrs. Apex and Mrs. Tiffany are caught in elemental confusion about their own identity. Mrs. Apex herself articulates the essential facticity of her own existence as she realizes that she is forced to conform to two highly conflicting roles, as custodian of secular morality and as symbol of male wealth and power:

> . . . but no one loves me—not even my husband, or my own child! I lead a false life among thousands as false as myself. With superficial accomplishments, I assume to be patroness of the arts, and, though of low extraction, I affect in the position of leader of the ton, the pride and importance of a duchess (I,ii).

Although Mrs. Tiffany is, essentially, a social caricature, here, Mrs. Apex's emotional conflict, her scruples and fears as well as the realization of her own misguided choices and aspirations, bring insight into her character. Produced and inhibited by contradictory cultural and ideological practices, she is, in fact, blamed for supporting those social structures that make an autonomous existence impossible. Her husband accuses her of having failed to play out the role of the dutiful and supportive wife successfully:

> . . . Will you assist me?—or must I regard as my most dangerous enemy, the woman who, did she realize the importance of her marriage obligation, would prove now my truest friend? (I,ii).

In this ambivalent hovering between her two roles, she is severely criticized by her own son for allowing the destruction of virtue in her family, for not being able to instill in him a sense of value and dignity:

> . . . What useful thing have you taught me? What am I? What can I do? Look at my hands—what are they fit for, but to be encased in kid

gloves, or to handle a billiard cue, or a pack of cards? I will not reproach you; your conscience will do that sufficiently hereafter. But I tell, you, you have brought me up badly, and the result will be disgrace to us both (II,i).

The effect of these painful accusations is the grim realization of the illusory construction of her own self-image. Although Mr. Unit calls her an "unscrupulous woman" near the end of the play, it is quite obvious that Mrs. Apex has already entered a process of corrective remaking of her own existence. Her folly disappears in her panic-stricken, almost hysterical, reaction when she realizes that her son, Charles, will take full responsibility for the act of forgery:

> No, no, no! do not believe him!—you cannot believe him—he is so young—his soul is free from guilt! It was me alone—me—to gain an empty triumph—to gall my hated rivals!—I bartered my peace of mind for ever—and now they laugh at me! Ha! ha! ha! (III,iii).

While the dramatis personae of *Fashion* are an assemblage of delightful comic social types, most of the major characters in *Self* are figures tragically involved in a threatening process of self-alienation. The precision of Bateman's language bites, and there is never a moment that we are not made aware of social hypocrisies. Of course, there are instances of comic relief, provided mainly by Mr. Unit, the Yankee character in the play, which display a fair amount of humor and wit. Although in *Fashion* the situation itself is basically amusing, here, the characters revolve around a rather frightening social reality. Failing to realize the vanity of their self-assured social presence, they alienate themselves even as they construct their public image. The effect of the distorted materialistic values on Mr. Apex is presented in such an exaggerated manner that he appears to be a far more inhuman creature than Mr. Tiffany himself. For one thing, Mr. Apex has irrevocably lost any sense of self-respect as he has become a slave to the insidious power of money:

> And money, my child, is that all-powerful agent, that unites, that separates, that creates, that destroys, that yields a rod of mysterious power to sway the destinies of humanity (I,iii).

Furthermore, the attitude of Mr. Apex towards his daughter, Mary, is absolutely repulsive. In order to protect her stepmother and Charles, Mary refuses to tell her father what happened to the money, thus leading him to believe that she has used it for her own purpose. Therefore, his daughter's supposed refusal to aid him financially causes Mr. Apex to explode in violent anger:

> Apex. Cold-hearted, selfish wretch! Henceforth this house is no home for you! Take all you have; and when, to-morrow, you hear of my bankruptcy, remember my worst foe was my own child! . . . .
>
> Mary. [Kneeling at his feet.] My heart will break! Father, only hear me. I cannot now explain my seeming guilt—but, believe me, I am innocent of any design.
>
> Apex. You are all design! Your apparent readiness to aid me, all was art, cunning, and hypocrisy! Out of my sight, viper that you are! (II, ii).

It is probably with this threatening image of dissolution of the familial order that the play attempts to point at the vulnerability of American society. Weakened family ties, lack of emotional support and understanding among husband, wife, and children, all sharply expose the erosive influence of industrial values on the harmony and unity of the American middle-class home. However, as in *Fashion*, the play's positive values of dignity, common sense and individual honor and merit, are embodied in Mr. Unit and Mary. Like Adam Trueman, Mr. Unit appears to be fully aware of the seriousness of the corrupted ethics underlying fashions in American society. Constantly repeating his favorite phrase, "won't pay," he is extremely straightforward and honest with all the characters and exposes folly bluntly wherever he sees it. Explicitly critical of the artificial manners and superciliousness of the fashionable ladies, he shows his unmitigated admiration for everything that Mary represents:

> Unit. Good girl!—good heart—sound head—. . .
>
> Mary. Indeed, you praise me much more than I deserve.

Unit. Not a bit!—you have a good sense—common sense. . . If you
had come here to-night and gone into hysterics, like the heroine of a
novel or a melodrama, I should have sent you away with a scolding;
but you came like a girl of sense, poured out my tea, told a straightforward story, and only showed, by emotion you could not repress,
the deep interest you felt in getting my aid (III,ii).

Although part of the satire, here, is directed against the stereotypical
qualities of stock sentimental heroines, Mary herself incorporates some
of these qualities as she stands out as the symbol of virtue, filial
obedience, patience and suffering. Unlike Mowatt's Gertrude, however,
Mary does not exhibit the same degree of independence and autonomy;
she is intelligent, but not as witty and vital as Gertrude, and she resorts
to some rather stilted and inherently melodramatic speeches in order to
express her feelings of love and anguish. Nevertheless, Mary, too,
represents an alternative image of femininity as she demonstrates an
admirable capacity for adjustment to her new social reality:

I must endeavour immediately to get some employment that will pay
our expenses. Perhaps my former music teacher may be able to
recommend me to some pupils (III,i).

Although in both *Fashion* and *Self* the satire is primarily directed
against fashionable excesses, the central trajectory of the plays is
determined by the telling contrast between the two types of American
woman which emerged out of the various social and economic
transformations that were taking place in American society in the first
half of the nineteenth century. Mary and Gertrude both gain their
authority from their independent thinking and autonomous existence
and actually fit into the Ideal of Real Womanhood which offered
American women a "vision of themselves as biologically equal
(rationally as well as emotionally) and in many cases markedly superior
in intellect to what passed for male business sense, scholarship,
theological understanding (Cogan 5). In her very interesting study of
middle-class women's roles and status in mid-nineteenth-century
America, Frances B. Cogan juxtaposes an alternative ideal of middle-
class womanhood to the notion of women as "mindless consumers and
drudges of a male-dominated capitalist world" (3). According to Cogan,
this ideal advocated "intelligence, physical fitness and health, self-

sufficiency, economic self-reliance, and careful marriage" (4). Mary
and Gertrude exhibit a considerable degree of sophistication and culture
and exemplify the all-American virtues of integrity, dignity, and hard-
work, qualities that encourage the emergence of a self-supporting sense
of value and esteem.

On the other hand, however, Mrs. Tiffany and Mrs. Apex are
satirically portrayed as extravagant and senseless fashionable ladies,
whose marriage to wealthy men have turned them into idle, nouveau
riche status symbols. They both represent the tremendous idiocy of
middle-class women who strove really hard to fit into the ideal of 'Lady
of Leisure.' Their social ambitions and pretensions, their misdirected
energy and various shortcomings establish Mrs. Tiffany as an
especially ludicrous character and Mrs. Apex, who has expanded her
role beyond the comic presentation of a social type, as a dangerous
character.

In the plays, the process of reproducing hyperbolic images of
bourgeois femininity undermine the credibility of these representations
as well as the traditional definitions of "naturalized" womanhood. As
Roland Barthes maintains, "the best weapon against myth is perhaps to
mythify it in its turn, and to produce an artificial myth" (135). Mrs.
Tiffany and Mrs. Apex effectively parody themselves by pretending to
be even more exaggeratedly embarrassing mothers, wives, and ladies of
fashion. The excessiveness of their roles is clearly visible as they
exhibit their garishness and lack of taste through their dress, manners
and language. Mowatt's and Bateman's dramatic strategy, which aims
at reenacting the roles and gestures of a patriarchal version of
femininity in an exaggerated way, brings to mind the strategy of
mimicry advocated by Luce Irigaray:

> One must assume the feminine role deliberately. Which means
> already to convert a form of subordination into an affirmation, and
> thus to begin to thwart it. . . . To play with mimesis is thus, for a
> woman, to try to recover the place of her exploitation by discourse,
> without allowing herself to be simply reduced to it (1985: 76).

Both *Fashion* and *Self* center around the existing economic system
in American society in the nineteenth century and actually elaborate
on the effect of the parvenu values of aggressive industriousness
and fashionable behavior on the members of the rising middle-class.

Mowatt and Bateman frame the theme of their plays within the middle-class nuclear family in an attempt to expose the constraints and limitations it imposes on women as well as urge American women to recognize and reject their social and cultural conditioning. Women are drawn out of the recesses and are placed center-stage, in their own homes, in an attempt to initiate a powerful debate over the rights and liberties of women in Jacksonian America. Mrs. Tiffany and Mrs. Apex are frightening products of the emerging ideology of industrialism, extremely vulnerable to the insidiousness of material luxury. However, in the last scene of both plays, a spirit of reformation pervades Mrs. Tiffany and Mrs. Apex as they both realize the facticity of their previous behavior and existence. Their turning themselves into figures of virtue and reason, at the end of the plays, is based on the revitalizing assumption that they will somehow be able to shake off their 'ladylike' role as consumers of luxury goods and devotees of fashion. The playwrights' intrinsic understanding of culture and signification is best reflected in their ability to thwart the illusion of cultural encoding. The disintegrating state of Mrs. Tiffany's and Mrs. Apex's households seems to be used as a strategy to simultaneously undermine the new material values and principles and the construction of femininity within the existing economic and ideological framework.

In *Fashion* and *Self*, the fragmentation and instability of the middle-class family unit are closely associated with the image of a problematic father. For Mr. Tiffany and Mr. Apex the pursuit of wealth in industrialized America has inflicted a self-alienating wound to their humanity, which is primarily reflected in their nearly 'monstrous' behavior and emotional numbness. On the other hand, however, trapped within the cultural connotations of this economic system, Mrs. Tiffany and Mrs. Apex experience their separation from the public world of money and decision-making and their relegation to a purely ornamental status, as an emotional and behavioral split since they are deprived of the possibility of an autonomous existence and of the freedom to shake off the disempowering construction of their own social image of femininity. What women need in order to rise above the false standards and values imposed upon them, is a resistance to those power structures that victimize them and prevent them from creating a self-assuring image of autonomy and wholeness.

Focusing upon the American middle-class household, both playwrights take the decomposition of republican values and principles as well as the pervasiveness of the new materialistic ethic to their full consequence and expose the threatening image of dissolution in society and human and gender relations. However, on an optimistic note, *Fashion* and *Self* manage to signify the emergence of a new system of egalitarian values, embracing American women as well, which would successfully supersede the disintegration of the new industrial ethos that leads men to self-alienation and women to confinement and disorientation.

NOTES

1. Ray A. Billington explains that the war allowed the United States to enter upon a long period of uninterrupted development by: 1) convincing Europe that it was no longer a third-rate power whose interests could be ignored; and 2) initiating a period of peace on the continent which lessened the temptation of other powers to meddle in American affairs (115).

2. It must be noted, however, that for the working classes this optimistic belief in onward progress proved to be rather illusory. Furthermore, the black slaves who labored in the southern states suffered a great deal from the new capitalist ethos.

3. It is also worth mentioning that the nationalistic upsurge following the War of 1812 and the high idealism of the age of the common man reinforced by Jacksonian Democracy gave considerable impetus to a genuinely American literature. Washington Irving and James Fenimore Cooper were the first American literary figures to win international fame. However, the golden age of American literature dawned in the second quarter of the nineteenth century with the flowering of transcendentalism. The most well-known of the transcendentalists were Ralph Waldo Emerson, Henry David Thoreau and Walt Whitman. Their literary works stressed self—reliance, self-confidence and freedom from the authority of formal institutions.

4. Michele Barrett clearly explains that one of the processes for reproducing gender ideology in society is compensation, which "refers to the presentation of imagery and ideas that tend to elevate the `moral worth' of femininity" (109).

15   It is really interesting to read some of the advice manuals which embodied the cult of domesticity. See, for example, Alcott, 1838, 1855; Arthur, 1848; Aster, 1878; Coxe, 1839; Farrar, 1853; Leslie, 1854; Tuthill, 1839.

6.   For information regarding the legal rights of American women, see Basch, 1982; Foster, 1913.

7.   The best examples of nineteenth-century Revolutionary War plays were Mordecai M. Noah's *Marion; or, The Hero of Lake George* (1821) and Oliver Bell Bunce's *Love in '76* (1857). Apart from Susanna H. Rowson's *Slaves in Algiers* (1794), which was actually the first play to dramatize the struggle of Americans with the Barbary States, frequent allusions to the issue can be found in James Nelson Barker's *Tears and Smiles* (1807), James Ellison's *American Captive; or, The Siege of Tripoli* (1812), John Howard Payne's *The Fall of Algeria* (1825). Finally, the best of the plays written dealing with the War of 1812 were M.M. Noah's *She Would Be A Soldier* (1819) and Richard Penn Smith's *Eighth of January* (1829).

8.   Some of the melodramatic plays most enjoyed by American audiences were, *Mazeppa; or, the Wild Horse of Tartary* (1825), *Putnam, the Iron Son of '76* (1844), *The Poor of New York* (1857), and *The Octoroon* (1859).

9.   Only three of Medina's plays have survived: *The Last Days of Pompeii* (1835), *Ernest Maltravers* (1838), and *Nick of the Woods* (1838).

10.   The American dramatists of the nineteenth century explored in farce and melodrama the potential of American scenery, custom, character, and ideas. Plays like *Uncle Tom's Cabin* (1852) and Dion Boucicault's *The Octoroon* (1859) concentrated upon the Black man as hero, while, James N. Barker's *The Indian Princess; or, La Belle Sauvage* (1808), John A. Stone's *Metamora; or, The Last of the Wampanoags* (1829), and George W. P. Custis' *Pocahontas; or, The Settlers of Virginia* (1830) elaborated on the romanticized theme of the noble red man. Finally, plays like Benjamin A. Baker's *A Glance at New York* (1848), Dion Boucicault's *The Poor of New York* (1857), and Timothy S. Arthur's *Ten Nights in a Bar Room* (1858) focused upon various aspects of America social life.

11.   Once the revolution and the vociferous spirit of egalitarianism had abolished the distinctions of birth as legitimate social barriers, the increasing mobility in American urban society forced the members of the rising middle-class to adopt fashion as a means to segregate themselves from the democratic mob. As Alexis de Tocqueville cleverly observed, "in democracies, where there is never much difference between one citizen and another and where in the nature of things they are so close that there is always a chance of their all

getting merged in a common mass, a multitude of artificial and arbitrary classifications are established to protect each man from the danger of being swept along in spite of himself with the crowd" (605).

12. For biographical information, see Barnes, 1954; Faust, 1983: 185-87; James, 1971: 596-98; Kunitz, 1966: 549-50; Mowatt, 1980; Robinson, 1989: 678-83; Van Doren, 1974: 749.

13. *Reviewers Reviewed* is included in Mowatt's *Autobiography*, 67-9.

14. See *The New World* 2 (1841): 259-62.

15. For both Edgar Allan Poe's reviews, see Moses, 1934: 59-66.

16. *The Spirit of the Times* (March 15, 1845).

17. *The Spirit of the Times* (Feb. 2, 1850).

18. The early part of the nineteenth century was a period of poetry and romantic themes. A number of American dramatists, like James N. Barker, Nathaniel P. Willis, Robert M. Bird, George H. Boker, chose to escape from the familiar by placing their characters in a foreign atmosphere and investing their themes with an exotic spirit, while, at the same time, they remained faithful to the greatness and universality of the ideals of freedom and democracy.

19. *The Spirit of the Times* (Feb. 24, 1849).

20. The theatrical representation of the black man in early American drama was clearly affected by the strong prejudice that persisted against black people. Without social status, political and economic power in real life, that black man never became an important stage figure. He remained a low-comedy character whose humorous qualities largely derived from his attempt to emulate his white master. The loyal, good-hearted, devoted servant was the popular stage-type of the American black. See, for example, James K. Paulding's *The Lion of the West* (1831), and, later, in the nineteenth century, William Gillette's *Held by the Enemy* (1886).

21. A great number of American playwrights found the Yankee an appropriate character through whom to express their nationalistic and democratic sentiments. Following the Jonathan tradition, William Dunlap created William, an honest, patriotic Yankee in *The Glory of Columbia* (1803) and J. N. Barker presented Nathan Yank in *Tears* and *Smiles* (1807). Also, Samuel Woodworth, in *The Forest Rose* (1825), introduced one of the most well-drawn Yankee characters in American drama, while, later in the nineteenth century, J. S. Jones' *The People's Lawyer* (1839) was favorite Yankee play

22. Gertrude continues the tradition of the girl-of-spirit heroine, which emerged as a native type in a large number of American plays, mostly melodramas. More specifically, Louisa Campdon in Barker's *Tears and Smiles* exhibits a comparatively high degree of individuality as she is determined to

follow the man she loves despite her father's objections. In M.M. Noah's *She Would Be a Soldier* (1819), Christine, in order to avoid an unwanted marriage and to find her beloved one, disguises herself as a man and enlists as a soldier. Although the picture of an independent, decisive woman was carefully circumscribed within her acknowledged sphere of action, instances of the tendency to present heroines of extraordinary intelligence and courage pervaded a number of later nineteenth—century American plays. See, for example, Oliver Bunce's *Love in '76* (1857), Augustine Daly's *Under the Gaslight* (18670, William Gillette's *Held by the Enemy* (1886) and *Secret Service* (1895).

23. See, Kunitz, 1966: 62-3; Malone, 1929/1957: 45; Robinson, 1989: 58-62.

CHAPTER 4

Gender Perspective and Ideology in Frances Wright's *Altorf* (1819) and Julia Ward Howe's *Leonora* (1857)

The theater's cultural role as image-layer and image definer in shaping society's outlook is particularly tied to the dominant culture's ideology and particularly liable to reinforce it(Davis 71).

I: POETIC DRAMAS IN EARLY NINETEENTH-CENTURY AMERICAN THEATER

In examining the dramatic development in the United States in the first half of the nineteenth century, one cannot fail to notice the preponderance of a number of poetic plays with romantic themes, which exhibit a considerable degree of dramatic quality. From Thomas Godfrey's *Prince of Parthia*(1765) to George Henry Boker's *Francesca da Rimini*(1855), poetic plays occupied a significant niche in the history of American drama. Although they were prevalent during the early half of the nineteenth century, their popularity diminished with the rise of the realistic movement in the last part of the century. The popular acceptance of poetic plays can be traced in the assumption that poetry, as the highest form of expression, had its roots in the English dramatic tradition.[1] Thus, imitative of Shakespearean plays and the neoclassical dramas of the eighteenth century, American poetic plays appealed to the more sophisticated part of the nineteenth-century American audience—those people who had a cultural background in England and Europe. As Walter J. Meserve explains, "it would be a fair

generalization to say that any American playwright with ambitions to write a play on a serious theme or one with literary pretensions would create a play imitative of foreign models and written in verse" (1977: 269).
Generally, the majority of verse plays in the early decades of the nineteenth century were tragedies. They focused upon distant places in older times, provided the American audiences with a political theme of noble rebellion against tyranny, and reflected the growing democratic spirit of the Americans. The historical setting, the heroic style, the poetic speeches as well as the treatment of the universal passions of love, jealousy, and hatred, infused moral instruction and a sense of greatness and universality into the romantic themes of poetic dramas. Furthermore, these plays successfully provided the audiences with the mystic and splendor they so much enjoyed. The American theater historian, Richard Moody, argues that three types of conventional poetic drama were popular in the American theater during the nineteenth century:

> Probably the most prevalent, presented a dramatis personae of quasi-historical characters against a colorful romantic background of some distant locale. The second type differed from the first in that it treated historical figures. The third group consisted of gloomy gothic presentations of the mysterious and sinister adventures of medieval nobility (187-8).

With very few exceptions, the characters in poetic dramas revealed little psychological insight on the part of the playwright, while, in fact, they represented the moral antithesis typical of melodramatic plays. The characters became personifications of virtue and vice and were rewarded or punished respectively. Showing no internal conflict, the hero was simply virtuous, honorable and essentially democratic and patriotic. On the other hand, the villain, who was portrayed as evil, unscrupulous and ambitious, scoffed at democracy. Against this backdrop of stereotypes, the female characters were, in their vast majority, portrayed as faithful wives, obedient daughters, virtuous and modest women.[2] However, the most interesting portrait of a poetic drama heroine was that of the temperamental, emotional woman, who, at the end of the play was destroyed by her own passionate nature. Examples of the most vivid and original heroines of nineteenth-century poetic dramas can be found in the character of Rosina in Frances Wright's *Altorf*, in George Henry Boker's *Francesca* and in Julia W. Howe's *Leonora*.[3]

Studying a great number of poetic plays written by American dramatists in the nineteenth century, it is my contention that these were the most daring characterizations of dramatic heroines. For one thing, all three of them appear to have human dimensions, they are systematically cut off from the traditional canons of behavior, and they are all tragically deceived in the world of men. How did the playwrights, however, manage to compromise their willful and passionate heroines with the sympathies of a Victorian audience? As I intend to show in my analysis later on in this chapter, all three dramatists relied upon the poetic drama technique of distant place and time. What's more significant, however, is the fact that the emotional and psychological transformation of their non-American heroines— which was gradually manifested in their assertive and autonomous self-expression—was staged through a series of betrayals and disappointments.

The demands of theater managers, actors, and audiences upon the poet-dramatist created a distinct effect upon the plays' form and subject matter. Following the traditions of English tragedy, poetic dramas responded, in varying degrees, to the need for moral instruction and focused upon themes that combined political and private virtue and actually dealt with the struggle of love with duty and honor. As the patterns of the nineteenth-century American poetic plays indicate, the characters and their actions actually disappeared in the midst of verbosity, stilted and lifeless blank verse, as well as excessive imagery. For the managers and the actors of the time a successful poetic drama included long rhetorical speeches and exaggerated poetic diction that conveyed the passions and suffering, the emotional turmoil and intense conflict of the characters. The greatest actors of the nineteenth century—Forrest, Booth, Cushman and Barrett—adopted verse plays in their repertories in an attempt to establish a fiery and vigorous acting style. The majority of the leading romantic dramatists of the period wrote their plays in response to the demands made upon them by the famous American actors.

In the first half of the nineteenth century, actors and not plays were the chief attraction for the American audiences. American playwrights soon began to realize that they had to write for particular actors and actresses if they wanted to see their plays performed. As Walter J. Meserve points out "it was an actor's theater in Jacksonian America" (1986: 15). Actors certainly won fame and public approval by identifying with such noble figures like Metamora, Spartacus, Brutus, Jack Cade, and they were fervently applauded for delivering highly emotional passages of poetry.

On the whole, the works of a number of American playwrights notably aided American drama in its progress during the nineteenth century. John Howard Payne, Mordecai M. Noah, Robert Montgomery Bird, John Augustus Stone, Nathaniel Parker Willis contributed a number of significant plays to the American stage. Some of them were performed as part of Edwin Forrest's prize plays, like Stone's *Metamora* (1829), Bird's *The Gladiator* (1831) and *The Broker of Bogota* (1834), testifying to the great influence American actors exercised on the promotion and development of American drama.

II: ROMANTIC PLAYS BY AMERICAN WOMEN DRAMATISTS

Following the romantic trend of the time, while, at the same time, augmenting the female tradition initiated by Warren and Faugeres, American women dramatists wrote plays that emphasized the power of the common man, the concept of universal freedom, and the heroic qualities that all Americans admired. As the number of women playwrights began to increase in the nineteenth century, the theme of female victimization began to appear with growing frequency. This can be attributed to the fact that the various economic shifts in American society following the War of Independence and the dawning of industrial revolution, coupled with the widespread belief in individual progress, impelled a number of women to question their social status and explore their own economic and educational opportunities. American women dramatists began to explore the image of women as victims of patriarchal power and expose the social and sexual injustices against women. Female powerlessness, male violence, seduction, madness, and suicide figure prominently in the romantic plays written in the first decades of the nineteenth century. Social as well as sexual oppression became a favorite theme among American women dramatists.

Similar in technique and theme, Frances Ann Kemble's romantic tragedies, *Francis the First* (1832) and *The Star of Seville* (1837), focus on the universal issues of corruption, freedom and tyranny, love and sexual passion. The dramatic element in both plays is built around a web of incidents of revenge, conspiracy, treason, and intrigue from which we get no relief. From the very beginning, however, Kemble invites us to recognize the close connection between a corrupted political system and women's experience of commodification within patriarchal culture. The plays dramatize women's contradictory relationship with the social and political context in which they live and expose the dangers and violations of the feminine body in a society that turns Woman into a commodity, into a passive object in any exchange. Kemble's female characters find themselves inextricably implicated in power structures that confine them and make an autonomous existence impossible. Francoise in *Francis the First* and Estrella in *The Star of Seville*, both figures of virtue and innocence, symbolically function as the site where not just political but also gender issues are raised.

In *Teresa Contarini* (1835), Elizabeth Fries Lummis Ellet probes into issues of public virtue and patriotism, tyranny, corruption and treason as she creates a female character who is eventually destroyed by the political and cultural codes that promulgate the social oppression of women. We must not forget that Ellet was a social reformer, the first historian of American women, and one of the first American feminists who questioned the status of women in American society. The story of *Teresa Contarini* is founded on incidents in Venetian history and actually focuses on political and private morality and the struggle of love with duty and honor. It is interesting to note that Ellet creates a really claustrophobic situation for her heroine from which there is no escape. Although Teresa appears as extremely powerful and dynamic, she dies at the end of the play, weary of all the injustice and corruption, while the citizens of Venice rise in rebellion.

A similar atmosphere prevails in *De Lara; or, The Moorish Bride* (1843), a tragedy in five acts by Caroline Lee Whiting Hentz. The play won the five hundred-dollar prize that was offered by William Pelby, a Boston actor and the manager of Tremont Theater, for the best original tragedy. *De Lara* bears a striking resemblance to Wright's *Altorf*. It, too, focuses on a theme that deals with the universal struggle of love with duty and honor and dramatizes the male protagonist's tremendous psychological conflict. The action takes place in a Spanish castle on the frontier of Granada, and elaborates on the hero's implacable dilemma: Fernando de Lara, like any man of honor, must avenge his father's death. But, the person who killed his father is also the father of his beloved one. Reminiscent of Shakespeare's Hamlet, Fernando has visions of his dead father's ghost demanding revenge. Torn between his duty and his love for Zoraya, he finds himself within a reality which is inevitable and offers no possibility of escape other than madness and death. His inability to resolve his inner conflict injects a frantic, neurotic dimension to his behavior that really frightens Zoraya. However, the ending of the play exposes the fundamental futility of the revenge code and is in accordance with the Christian injunction to forgive one's enemies. As in Hamlet, the final denouement of death resolves nothing that really matters. It is evident throughout the play that Fernando has fallen victim to society's definitions of what is appropriate and acceptable. As in *Altorf*, the significance of the concepts of honor and duty in men's lives comes into question. Zoryana, like Rosina, moves within a social and political order that victimizes her and controls her love, an order that shuts out her experiences, feelings and thoughts as a woman.

In *Octavia Bragaldi; or, The Confession* (1837), Charlotte Mary Sanford Barnes dramatizes a real incident of honor which attracted wide attention at the time. More specifically, in Frankfort, Kentucky, in 1825, Colonel Beauchamp murdered Colonel Sharpe when he discovered that the latter had seduced his wife before they got married. He was arrested, convicted of murder and sentenced to death. A couple of days before the execution, Colonel Beauchamp and his wife attempted suicide in his cell. The attempt was unsuccessful and the Colonel was eventually hanged. In Barnes' play, the action is transferred to Milan in the late fifteenth century. According to Barnes' story, Octavia disobeyed her father and eloped with Count Castelli, who deceived her by a false marriage, cruelly abandoned her and disappeared. Believing him dead, Octavia marries Bragaldi five years later. However, Castelli returns and slanders Octavia who is made to appear as a wanton. Bragaldi, as a man of dignity and honor, attempts to clear Octavia's name by challenging Castelli to a duel. Castelli refuses and Octavia confronts him and demands that he take back the slander, which he refuses to do. She, then, urges Bragaldi to kill him, in a most powerful scene. He is accused of the murder, confesses it and stabs himself before he is sent to prison. Octavia, realizing what she has done, takes poison and dies. What is particularly interesting about the play is that Barnes creates in Octavia the picture of a young woman who struggles for autonomy against a male-oriented system of sexual relations. Seduced, abandoned and slandered by Castelli, Octavia is finally driven to revenge and suicide. Barnes vision and perspective are essentially society-conscious and feminine. Employing the techniques of romantic tragedy, she manages to reveal her own awareness of the complex implications of political and sexual ideology in women's struggle for independence and self-definition.

My interest in Wright's and Howe's romantic tragedies is mainly grounded in the plays' significance as the site where a most 'poetical' social criticism meets with the playwrights' simmering feminist sentiments. Like the rest of romantic tragedies written in America in the nineteenth century, the conception of *Altorf* and *Leonora*, their development, their movement and their catastrophes are essentially dramatic. Although Howe's and Wright's plays are intensely poetical, they are not overweighed with poetry and verbosity. Emotional and powerful, their language is intensely figurative, and their blank verse exposes dignity and power. However, the great differences in *Altorf* and *Leonora*, when compared to the other poetic plays of the time, especially those written by male dramatists, lie in their subject-matter and character delineation, and not so much in their form and sentiment. For one thing, both dramatic compositions revolve round well-developed characters whose passionate nature and independence of spirit do not evaporate in the midst of rhetorical and exclamatory poetic speeches.

Furthermore, both Wright and Howe introduce a more radical discourse in their work and are certainly very outspoken on issues of gender equality and women's rights. The plays' attempt at the expression of feminist concerns substantially differentiates them from the romantic tragedies written at that time. Although both *Altorf* and *Leonora* basically conform to the accepted pattern of romantic tragedy, they, nevertheless, challenge the dominant dramatic gender conventions of the time. Taking into consideration Jacobus' statement that "though necessarily working within 'male' discourse, women's writing would work ceaselessly to deconstruct it", it appears that both plays elaborate on the possibility of a powerful reversal of the expected gender roles (13). They represent more than a romantic view of historical events in faraway places and times. Unlike the majority of verse dramas, the themes Wright and Howe tackle in their plays do not focus solely on the universal issues of freedom and patriotism, romantic love, duty and honor. Howe follows the rules of romantic tragedy in order to demonstrate the universality of the double standard as a powerful institution that promulgates the social oppression of women.[4] Wright's *Altorf* deals with the universal theme of the destructive impact of politics on the individual, while, at the same time, it reveals the playwright's gender awareness as it probes into a number of controversial issues like divorce and the viability of the patriarchal ideals of honor, courage and dignity.

We must not forget that both Wright and Howe were social reformers and among the first American feminists who championed the rights of women and demanded political, economic, and educational parity with men. The feminist concerns they expressed in their plays were contingent upon the social and political energies that began to take place among middle-class women in the early decades of the nineteenth century. As I have already pointed out in my previous chapter, with the growth of industrial capitalism, American women found themselves firmly excluded from public office and electoral politics. On the other hand, however, they were also attracted, like the men of their time, to the promise of individual progress and the political faith in the creation of a truly democratic society. Until the development of women's rights and woman suffrage movements, the social and political consciousness of women was sufficiently channeled into an ideological framework that supported the expansion of women's uplifted role into the public realm.[5] As a matter of fact, women began to make new claims to power in the name of their domestic role and moral influence, and actually entered the public world as militant orators, indefatigable travelers, and, later on, as determined suffragists.

Beginning in the first decades of the nineteenth century, women's associations were formed for a variety of purposes: to support the frontier ministry, to distribute Bibles and sell religious tracts, to educate poor children, to assist widows and orphans, and generally to combat the increasing ills of poverty, disease, social displacement and slavery.[6] Mary P. Ryan explains that "all these associations occupied a distinctive place in the social order of the community, somewhere along a muted boundary between private and public life" (69). Through a network of moral reform societies, nineteenth-century American middle-class women began to explore the theme of female victimization as they attempted to cross the sexually-defined barrier that marked the public world of men off from the private world of women.

In the decades preceding the Civil War, many female organizations protested against alcohol consumption and ministered not only to alcoholics but also to those wives and children who suffered at the hands of drunken husbands. The temperance movement had a strong feminist component. After all, alcoholic husbands were the main violators of family sanctity and unity, and actually posed a serious threat to individual wives and mothers and generally to women as a social group. Not only did inebriated men deprive their families of necessary income, but they also beat their wives and abused their children.

In the 1830s and 40s, the American Female Reform Society further expanded its activities throughout New England and the Middle-Atlantic States in an attempt to reform standards of sexual behavior. Women assailed the double standard of morality and forcefully exposed licentious men, while, at the same time, significantly assisted and protected seduced women and reformed prostitutes. Carroll Smith-Rosenberg argues that "American women could no longer willingly tolerate that traditional—and role-defining—masculine ethos which allotted respect to the hearty drinker and the sexual athlete" (115). Led and initiated by women, female moral reform was a collective, organized effort to give voice to the female consciousness of isolation and the sense of status inferiority. Women saw themselves as having few defenses against men, while, the double standard of morality came to embody the social and sexual injustices against women. In this instance, women played a vital role in reshaping aspects of the American sex/gender system.[7] So active were the female moral reformers that they began to publish a weekly journal, *The Advocate*, which grew into one of the most widely read newspapers in the United States.

In fact, antebellum reform-minded women were among the very first American women to undermine the image of the passive, submissive female and to explicitly articulate the need for a national union of women. Stepping out of the concentric structure of the American family, a number of women advocates of moral reform—like, Lucretia Mott, Emma Willard, Elizabeth Blackwell—later became active in the women's rights movement and actually challenged the relationship of women's domestic sphere to the rest of society.[8] Borrowing from the abolitionist ideology, they started to articulate a vision of equality and independence for women as well as criticize publicly the male-established values of the larger society. The antislavery campaign was significantly strengthened by the participation of thousands of women, who, through the fight to free slaves were propelled into an equally long and vigorous fight for their own liberation. Although not all abolitionists believed in equal rights for women, the founders of the women's rights movement were all abolitionists. By linking feminism to the fundamental principles of American democracy, Lucretia Mott, Elizabeth Cady Stanton and others met in Seneca Falls, New York, in 1848, and drew up the first public protest in America against women's political, economic, and social inferiority, the "Declaration of Sentiments."

The overwhelming majority of women who participated in the all-female collective organizations in antebellum America consisted primarily of educated middle—and upper-class ladies. The ideological framework of their protest was essentially republican, since the political ideology of the revolutionary war had, for the first time, afforded women an opportunity to define themselves as political beings. Glenna Matthews observes that " a few women had begun to refer to themselves as `politicians' in the early Republic, and now hundreds were marching onto the public stage to defend their interests in the name of the same tradition" (99). As women started to make new claims to power and influence, a handful of them proved to be brave enough to pioneer as public speakers and actually stand up before an audience. Frances Wright, a highly-determined flamboyant public woman, was the first one to give lectures on controversial subjects. Born in Dundee, Scotland, in 1795, Wright was a woman of extraordinary intellect and moral courage who "devoted her entire life to her vision of a cooperative society in which all people would share equal political, social, and economic rights" (Martin 273). An enthusiastic admirer of American people and American republican ideals, she eventually made the United States her home and became one of the best-known social reformers in the country. She championed the rights of women and demanded equal education as well as equal legal rights and liberal divorce laws for married women. A radical freethinker, she advocated the emancipation of the slaves, she denounced religious prejudice and attacked the church as the chief obstacle to social progress and human happiness. She also condemned capital punishment and protested against imprisonment for debt.[9]

In 1821, after her three-year visit to the United States, Frances Wright published her highly enthusiastic *Views of Society and Manners in America*, one of the most widely-read travel memoirs in the early nineteenth century. Returning to the United States in 1824, she became a public lecturer focusing her social criticism upon a number of major problems, like religion, slavery, women's status, for which she suggested reforms. She was a powerful, eloquent, and effective speaker who, according to Frances Trollope, had a strikingly dramatic beauty:

> it is impossible to imagine anything more striking than her appearance. Her tall and majestic figure, the deep and almost solemn expression of her eyes, the simple contour of her finely formed head, unadorned, excepting by its own natural ringlets; her garment of plain white muslin, which hung around her in folds that recalled the drapery of a Grecian statue, all contributed to produce an effect, unlike anything I had ever seen before, or ever expect to see again (73).

Her lectures were always crowded and, very often, she needed the protection of a bodyguard to ward off hostile members of the public. Wright was severely criticized for her audacity to compromise her virtue and reputation as a lady by appearing in public as well as for her extremely radical views that clearly shook up much of what Americans held sacred. Wright's radical ideas concerning women's marital rights, divorce laws, and birth control, infuriated Catharine Beecher so much that she called her a "strange excrescence of female character" (Boydston 236).[7] Although her lectures were always crowded, she often needed the protection of a bodyguard to ward off hostile members of the public. Wright was severely criticised for her audacity to compromise her virtue and reputation as a lady by appearing in public as well as for her extremely radical views that clearly shook up much of what Americans held sacred. Wright's radical ideas concerning women's marital rights, divorce laws, and birth control, infuriated Catharine Beecher so much that she called her a "strange excrescence of female character" (Boydston 236).[10]

Increasingly concerned with the abolition of slavery, Wright decided, in 1825, to materialize her project concerning the establishment of an experimental interracial community for the gradual emancipation of black people. Although her dream of solving the Negro problem failed, she, nevertheless, continued to criticize certain aspects of American society in her journal, *Free Enquirer*. In 1831, she married Phiquepal D' Arusmont, a Frenchman sixteen years her senior. The marriage, however, was not a success and it was eventually dissolved by divorce. Frances Wright died in Cincinnati on December 13, 1852. She stands as one of the most important social reformers in American history. Helen B. Woodward rightly observes that Wright's coming to the United States "was to fix the course of her erratic life and incidentally to provide the American people with their first exciting sample of the New Woman"(26).

Altorf

Although Wright was extremeley active as a social reformer, she was not, at all, prolific as a playwright. Her only dramatic attempt was *Altorf* (1819), a five-act romantic tragedy produced at the Park Theater with James Wallack in the title role. In her preface to the play, Wright makes a conscious gesture of affixing her name to a previously anonymous dramatic work, which had already been warmly received in New York, and actually offers a clear image of her democratic beliefs and optimistic idealism:

> I cannot offer this tragedy, with my name affixed to it, to the people of America, without saying a few words that may, in some degree, express my sense of the generous manner in which it has been already received by the inhabitants of this city. . . . . . . it will perhaps also occur to them that that foreigner [Wright herself] has sought their country uninvited, from sincere admiration of their government, a heart-felt love of its freedom, a generous pride and sympathy in its rising greatness (iii).

Altorf is built upon the theme of the Swiss struggle for independence against Austria in the early fourteenth century and dramatizes the inner struggle of the hero, Eberard de Altorf, former Austrian and now leader of the Swiss revolutionaries. Forced into a marriage of political expediency, Altorf betrays his much-beloved girlfriend, Rosina, by marrying the sister of one of the patriots, Giovanna, whom he does not love. In the meantime, Count de Rossberg, Rosina's father and representative of the old aristocratic order, tries to restore Altorf to his first allegiance. Rosina also sneaks into the rebel camp and meets with Altorf in an attempt to regain him. Torn between his duty as the brave soldier who led his people "to victory and freedom" (I,i), and his love for the fair Rosina, Altorf is finally forced to desert the patriot ranks and run off with Rosina when they are discovered together. Such an act of apparent treason draws upon him the curse of his aged father and a final denouement of death.

Wright shows considerable dramatic skill in the delineation of Altorf as well as a tremendous ability to capture and project the abuse of patriarchal power which eventually engulfs the main characters. Interestingly enough, the two women in the play, Giovanna and Rosina, represent the two sides of Altorf's inner conflict between honor and love. However, at no point in the play do they relinquish their right to self-determination, but rather, they derive their power from their ability to make conscious decisions and refuse to let politics conflict with their personal feelings. Although, as Kathleen L. Nichols argues, the play "has all the staple ingredients for a victimized-woman drama"(134), it is the hero who becomes the victim of patriarchal values and politics and eventually deteriorates into madness and suicide. Altorf's inner conflict as well as his tremendous psychological torment raise the play to a high level of dramatic intensity from which we get no relief.

Historically analogous to the American War of Independence, the theme of the play transmits a political message praising patriotic sentiments, heroic spirit, and republican liberty. Wright's drama, however, reaches beyond the revolutionary ideals of democracy and freedom. *Altorf* probes into philosophical issues, such as human nature, war, love, as it explores in a highly dramatic way the forceful clash between high ideals and personal feelings. The value of the play lies precisely in its radical approach to the institution of marriage, the right to divorce, as well as the attempt to undermine the stifling patriarchal ideals of duty and honor. The issue of political and personal freedom, so prevalent in Mordecai M. Noah's *The Grecian Captive* (1822), Robert Montgomery Bird's *The Gladiator* (1831) and John Howard Payne's *Brutus* (1820), takes on different connotations in *Altorf*. While the play, on the one hand, brilliantly integrates the conventional pattern of poetic drama into a theme of intense enthusiasm for political liberty, on the other, provides a tremendously incisive criticism of the destructive impact of male politics on the individual, and actually attempts to redefine political ideology challenging the male-constructed ideological assumptions imbedded in most early American romantic tragedies. The struggle for liberty, the value of the individual fighting against an overwhelming force is successfully blended in the play with the major contradiction in women's relationship to society. Unlike the majority of poetic drama heroines, the women in Wright's play begin a process of interpreting male politics and masculine values bringing into focus their awareness of their own exclusion from the enterprise of creating political systems, social ideologies and philosophies.

Although *Altorf* enjoyed only three performances, it was quite favorably received by the American audience, primarily for its republican message. At first, Wright did not reveal her authorship, but later, she had the play published under her name. The press treated the play with kindness, due, perhaps, to the impression that *Altorf* was the work of an American. The critic in the *New York Columbian* marveled at:

> the simplicity of the plot and action, the interest of the story, the elegant boldness of the style, never sinking into familiar mediocrity— nor soaring into bombast, the warm and true delineation of natural passions; and above all, the purity and generosity of the principles and sentiments, may challenge competition with the best productions of the British stage (Feb. 18, 1819).[11]

Altorf opens with the appearance of a dark figure, Count de Rossberg, Rosina's father and representative of the old nobility, whose disruptive presence will determine the events of the play. The purpose of the Count is to sow the seeds of discord in the camp of the "shepherd mountaineers," and win back young Altorf, the "courtly cavalier" of Austria. Sending his loyal servant, Eustace, to spy on Altorf, Rossberg reveals that he plans to succeed "by art or bribe" (I,ii). Almost like in a Shakespearean tragedy, the power of Rossberg lies upon the fact that he is a very good judge of human character and, thus, able to manipulate human passions:

> I'll tamper with the son; work on his pride;

> Waken his jealousy; stir up disputes;
> Or else resume his now forgotten passion
> For his betrothed Rosina (I,ii).

From the very beginning, there is a tendency to reduce Rosina's love for Altorf to the base function of passive pawn in political maneuvers. Rossberg's orders to Eustace imply that the power of the normative masculine order of politics and social codes lies precisely in its ability to preserve itself at any human cost:

> . . . . Take your pipe,
> 'T will gain you easy passport 'mong the
> rebels. And, I remember me, de Altorf loved
> To list the wild notes of our mountain airs
> When my fair daughter played them. Try
> your skill; Observe if you can move him. I
> esteem He hath not yet forgot his trothed
> love, But yields it only to a father's will (I, ii).

Early in the play, the powerful verbal juxtaposition between Rossberg and Erlach, Altorf's father, establishes Wright's commitment to democratic principles and republican sentiments while, at the same time, the use of similes, metaphors, and poetic expressions reveals Wright's tremendous eloquence and enunciatory skills. In the immensely philosophical style that characterizes *Altorf,* the forceful dialogue between the two men, spokesmen of opposing ideologies, underlines Frances Wright's acute social conscience as well as her awareness that "times are sore changed,. .—times and manners" (I,ii). Altorf's father stresses the new social and political ideas of democracy and freedom as he summarizes the failure of the old aristocratic system:

> Rossberg! Thou, who prefer'st the interest of
> one man,
> And that a base, and mean, and sordid
> interest, Unto the weal of thousands. Thou,
> who stoop'st
> A servile knee unto a thirsty tyrant,
> Whose hands are dropping with thy country's
> gore, And his vile coffers fill'd with plunder

of its poor (I,iii).

The general opposition between Erlach's and Rossberg's political beliefs takes on a fatal aspect, revealing a painful conjunction between political ideology and human feelings:

Erlach

Had Rossberg sided with his injured country,
Our children's loves had not been crossed thus rudely (I, iii).

The transition from the noble democratic ideals to the stifling impact of politics upon the individual is underscored by Altorf's major psychological conflict and his subsequent yielding to the political cause:

Erlach

'Twas a hard struggle, count,
For my poor boy: but to a father's prayers
At length he yielded. I knew his love
How great, how nourished from his boyhood
up, For your bewitching daughter—And I
feared, His love should prove a tamperer
with his honour,
Should stand betwixt him and his struggling
country,
And in this fear—(I,iii).

Although the play itself is replete with republican principles, attesting to Wright's fervent espousal of the freedom of all people, it, nevertheless, exceeds the one-sidedness of the majority of romantic tragedies written in America during the time the play was produced.[12] More specifically, *Altorf* operates on a multiplicity of ideological levels, breaking through the surface of politics in an attempt to explore human conscience and psyche. The incident of dissension between Altorf and De Rheinthal, Giovanna's brother, stems primarily from their desire for rank and honor, and actually points to the illusory construction of any sense of unity, wholeness, and security, inherent in any political system (I, iv). Their dispute stages the disturbing, yet

unavoidable, instance in human life when personal feelings clash with
such normative values as fidelity and loyalty.

Words, in *Altorf*, as well as ideas have double-edged meanings and
purposes. In a highly philosophical soliloquy, Altorf probes into the
incomprehensible nature of life, into the various contradictions that
reach beyond control, and questions the essential validity of human
causes:

—What is this life?
Some call it a dream, and some—a gossip's
story,
And some—the tricksome acting of a player;
Forgotten soon as ended. Psha! an' 'twere
such,
Should we find in't so many bleeding rubs?
Should we built up so many fairy hopes?
Grasp at such heights of happiness and
greatness
And plan, and feel, and act so many things;
And sigh such sighs, and fret as in the core,
For losses, crosses, wants, and
disappointments?
This life, to angels, looking out from heaven,
May be an idle dream, or passing breath;
But to us men, who have to struggle thro' it,
It's a time most anxious, and most earnest
(II,i).

Almost like an early dramatic heroine, Altorf's melancholy stresses his
own psychological conflict caused by the claustrophobic political
pressures placed upon him. In contrast to Julia Ward Howe's *Leonora*,
here, the power of the social and political forces at work will finally
lead a *man* to madness and death. Reminiscent of Byron's characters,
Altorf's gloominess, his grave disposition, and, at times, his
impenetrable facade, which hides his tormented, torn self, emphasize
the male protagonist's inability to cope with the inexorable pressures of
politics:

I know my face is grave, my temper gloomy:

'Tis my misfortune (II, ii).

For Altorf, any form of bondage to the political ideology, be it the requirement that he marries Giovanna, or that he is unvaried in his allegiance to the rebel cause, is as unacceptable as any form of physical imprisonment because it is incompatible with his own feelings and desires. Altorf's reaction displays his hidden despair as well as his failure to resolve his own conflict:

> Would God I had not yielded. Wherefore did
> I?
> To be a patriot needs it be a husband?
> Tush! We'll not think on't. Oh!—I'm sick at
> heart
> Shield us, my father! (II, iv).

His cry for his father to rescue him from his implacable dilemma, his desperate need for somebody to help him, is only met halfway in the ensuing confrontation with his father. Here, dignity, honor and duty become, on the one hand, laudable qualities, while, on the other, their recurrence underlines the unbearable burden they impose upon the individual. Erlach, who, in fact, represents the clearly-defined distinctions and laws of the male order, exposes with crude pragmatism the absolute necessity of sacrificing one's personal feelings for the good of one's country. Accusing Altorf of pride and "thirst for honour," he reprimands him for failing to come to an agreement with De Rheinthal, and adds to his son's inner turmoil when he asks him to:

> . . . . . search well into thy heart.
> Search—search it clean: whisper this question
> to't:
> When I gave up the trappings of my state,
> Gave up my wealth and my heart's dearest ties,
> My first and trothed;—when all I gave
> Freely and frankly at my country's call,
> Did I then feel I had but done my duty
> Right—and no more than right; or did I think
> That I had done a thing much to admire,
> Felt my heart proud, and said within myself,

My country is my debtor (II,iv).

Altorf attempts to undermine the patriarchal ideals of honor, dignity and courage, by which men are judged in society, as it demystifies the much-celebrated stereotype of the larger-than-life romantic hero by presenting a "proud, weak, foolish" protagonist, who feels that the political cause he has struggled for has now become a suffocating noose around his neck, and who finally succumbs to his own passions:

Erlach

. . . . . .learn again what 'tis you owe to virtue,
What to yourself, what to your fellow men,
What onto God, and, more than all, your
country.

Altorf

Enough! Enough! Behold me on my knee.

Erlach

Your heart, your stubborn heart! bow that my
son.

Altorf

It is; it is; command me, I obey.
I'm proud, weak, foolish; I confess it all
(II,iv).

At the end of Act II, Altorf's regretful speech summarizes his guilt towards his wife for concealing from her the fact that he loved someone else when he married her:

Altorf

Yea, but I have. Oh, it hath weigh'd upon
me,
Weigh'd on my heart like lead! 'Tis now too
late:
To tell thee now, what, had I told before
Had saved us both a cup of agony,
Might now seem insult when the cup is

drank (II,vi).

Giovanna, on the other hand, is portrayed as a self-conscious, independent woman who would never have displayed the same weakness as Altorf:

> Oh, had I known it sooner—Had I known
> You lov'd so deeply, so eternally,
> Never should'st thou have sworn away thy
> freedom.
> Our fathers might have pray'd—pray'd on
> their knees,
> I never would have yielded (II,vi).

In her interesting book about women and film, Mary Ann Doane argues that, in the conventional systems of representation, "masculinity is consistently theorized as a pure, unified, and self-sufficient position," one which the male spectator can easily and comfortably identify with (8). Bearing in mind the Freudian and Lacanian insights concerning sexual development, it is easy to understand how the male has come to occupy a central subject position in our culture, while, the female is placed in a subordinate and derivative position. Sue-Ellen Case, among other theorists, points out that "the male is the subject of the dramatic action"(119). In *Altorf,* however, Wright creates a male protagonist with whom it is difficult to "easily and comfortably" identify. The story deviates from the typical narrative structure according to which the male character is the doer, the promoter of action, the one who makes things happen. Altorf appears to be a victimized and powerless figure, whose frustrated personality and unfulfilled desires isolate him from his social community.

Wright sets up from the start an ambiguous image of Altorf as a source of vexation as well as a figure in search of regaining totality and wholeness, resisting, while, at the same time, being subdued by the conventions and accepted codes of the masculine order he, himself, is part of. Referring to women's experience, Josette Feral argues that, "being in constant movement, women are incapable of reconstituting themselves as unified single subjects and are relegated to the schizoid state that constitutes them"(558). In Wright's *Altorf,* however, it is the "schizoid state," the fragmented identity of the *male* subject, rather than the female one, which attests to the powerful reversal of the dramatic gender conventions. Altorf's mental shifts, hesitations, silences, his own timidity and indecisiveness when faced with his father, his wife, and Rosina, his floating among his various images, as the dutiful son, the brave soldier, the husband, the lover, all testify to his uncentered nature. Altorf's disjointed speech when he unexpectedly meets Rosina injects a frantic, neurotic dimension to his behavior and foregrounds his deterioration into madness:

Altorf (falling on his knees)

Oh! do not curse me! do not curse me, Rosa!
I swear it thee—I swear it thee by Heaven!
I swear it by thyself—thy precious self!
I love but thee—I ne'er have lov'd but thee,
I never will love woman but Rosina.

Rosina

What means thy frenzy? (III,ii)

As dramatic intensity rises in Act III, where the powerful confrontation between Rosina and Altorf takes place, Frances Wright creates a forceful dramatic language that highlights the difference underlying Altorf's and Rosina's being; namely, that between a male order, where self-identity and self-definition depend upon the acceptance of a set of codes, laws, and social roles, and a feminine power that scorns the restraints of social laws and gives privilege to feelings of love and the need for self-articulation and autonomy. In *Altorf*, Rosina breaks out of the snare of silence and verbally attacks Altorf for his weakness and lack of faith:

Rosina

Married! married! to whom? when? where?
Married?
Altorf
Oh, ring not o'er that word! would'st break
my heart?

Rosina

Dost talk to me of breaking hearts? Oh,
Altorf! Thou'st cleav'd mine asunder.
Married! ye Heavens! Where is the faith of
man? where are the oaths
Thou swor'st me, traitor? Where the sighs,
the tears, The burning kisses we've mixed
together (III,ii).

Extremely articulate and self-conscious, Rosina appears to be in control
of language while Altorf, being on the defensive, merely seeks for
excuses to justify his action and attempts to appeal to Rosina's feelings:

Think it, believe it still. I' thine—all thine!
A rigid father, and a bleeding country—

Rosina's power lies in her ability to overthrow parental authority—
"did'st owe thy father all, and Rosa nothing? I have a father too, yet see
me here"(III,ii)—as well as the larger social system which reproduces
the dominant ideology of gender. She clearly rejects the patriarchal
biases that deny her the possibility of personal liberation and self-
definition.

I have loved thee even to forsaking,
And, throwing men's opinions at my back,
Have followed thee o'er mountains such as
these (IV,v).

Aware that she moves within a social and political order, which
controls her and victimizes her love, Rosina refuses to enter the male-
defined linguistic system that shuts out her experiences, feelings, and
thoughts as a woman. Her ensuing words point to the widely-accepted
statement that "women's oppression. . does not merely exist in the
concrete organization of economic, political, or social structure. It is
embedded in the very foundations of the Logos, in the subtle linguistic
and logical processes through which meaning itself is produced"
(Stanton 74):

Altorf

Thou shalt not go. I've thousand things to tell
thee.

Rosina

What use of words? we cannot understand
them (III,ii).

Rosina's language will eventually abide by an economy of death,
culminating in her extreme act of suicide towards the end of the play.

Despite the fact that *Altorf* is confined to a masculine dramatic
mode and, to a certain extent, reproduces some of the classic
representations of women as sensitive, caring, intuitive, loyal, it,
nevertheless, offers a number of possibilities for the exploration of a
new feminist discourse. Taking into consideration Helene Cixous'
statement that "a feminine text brings about an upheaval of the old
property crust, carrier of masculine investments," it appears that *Altorf*
manages to disrupt certain aspects of the ideological codes embedded in
the traditional masculine structures of dramatic representation (258).
Although both Giovanna and Rosina are betrayed by Altorf, they refuse
to submit to the masculine logic that victimizes and silences them
within the respective images of the suffering, submissive wife and the
desperate, abandoned betrothed. In a world of male politics, in a world
of men divided by war, passions, and false definitions of honor and
duty, Wright creates a separate context for her women characters to
move in. It is the context of female solidarity, formed by the
recognition of the existence and uniqueness of female consciousness.
The imprint of a feminine identity is evident in the emotional richness
of the way Rosina and Giovanna think of one another. Despite the fact
that they both love the same man, they are united by bonds of sympathy
and congeniality:

Rosina

Why then I'll pity her,
To have thy company and not thy love;
To call thee husband—and yet find no
fondness (IV,v).

In the larger world of male concerns, power, competition, and hostility, women respect and value one another recognizing the tie of common experiences, anxieties, sorrows and joys that binds them closely together. It is within such a context of a specifically female world of support and understanding that Giovanna utters the closing lines of the play:

> Art gone? Both gone? Poor maid, I envy
> thee.
> In life thou wert belov'd, in death—united;
> And ye shall have one grave, poor, hapless
> lovers!
> And one sad, only mourner there to weep
> you (V,xi).

Throughout the whole play, Wright powerfully subverts the concept of women as objects of exchange in the male market, by having a man—Altorf—'sold out' into marriage.[13] Following the reversal of the most frequently employed theme of the daughter's submission to the father's will to marry the man of his choice, Wright undermines the credibility of the culturally-constructed image of the self-effacing, self-sacrificing wife, by having Giovanna, much to Altorf's surprise, bluntly state that she no longer loves him as a woman:

> I follow you
> Not with a weak and sickly woman's
> dotage. . . .
> No! I have followed you
> For that I saw your stricken soul requir'd
> The tendance of a friend, and for I thought
> You had no friend on earth so true as I.
> I do not say that I now love you, Eberard,
> As when you led me blushing to God's altar,
> And took my maiden troth. No! that is gone.
> The burning flame of love, if left
> uncherished,
> Must wane its fervor (II,vi).

A declared advocate of the idea that people should be together out of mutual attraction and love, Frances Wright sharply hints at the idea of marriage contracted on the grounds of financial, political or any other need, by presenting a most critical picture of the detrimental impact of a loveless union on both parties.[14] The metaphor of marriage as a loveless, conventional union that serves the interest of society, but does not assure the parties' personal happiness, is further reinforced in the play as Wright extends the idea of marriage beyond laws and religion to the higher plane of emotions. In her speech to Altorf, Rosina subtly voices Wright's radical views about sex relations, love, and marriage:[15]

Rosina

Are we not wedded? What, tho' earthly priest
Ne'er joined our hands, have not our hearts been join'd?
What, tho' no altar sanctified our vows,
hath then our love no seal? Ay, that it hath!
Our vows are register'd by angels, Altorf!......
Yes! I am thine, and thou art mine—all mine
(III,ii).

The masculine idea of marriage as the destiny traditionally offered to women is undermined in the play with the introduction of the possibility of divorce in order to dissolve the union between Altorf and Giovanna. "Divorce is easy," Rossberg says (III,i). Altorf will be free to marry his true love, Rosina, and Giovanna will pursue happiness, fulfillment, and love in the arms of another man (IV, viii). It is important to note that *Altorf* is the only tragedy produced in America in the early nineteenth century which presents divorce as a viable solution for an unhappy marriage. Wright's play rejects the fixed, immutable masculine discourse concerning the institution of marriage as a social and economic arrangement defined by patriarchal laws, religion, and culture.

Throughout *Altorf,* the theme of politics, of noble rebellion against the old aristocratic system, does not develop in a linear fashion, but is constantly disrupted by the intersecting theme of personal emotions and conflicts as well as by the recurrence of the patriarchal connotations of the concept of honor. The paradoxical nature of the play can best be described as a major contradiction between the ideal of freedom, represented by the heroic Revolution of the Swiss against tyranny, and the oppressive impact of the political system upon the individual, resulting in the death of Rosina and Altorf at the end of the play. Frances Wright cuts deep into the issue of politics and begins to deconstruct the valorisation of the male dramatic subject, while, at the same time, works towards an exposition and re-definition of the patriarchal ideal of honor The much-celebrated theme in male poetic drama, which focused upon the determining power and significance of the concept of honor in men's lives, comes into question in *Altorf*. Honor, as a notion inherent in the ideology or beliefs of patriarchal culture at large, is undermined in the play. As in Act II, Wright continues to undermine patriarchal values while she manipulates the masculine language of politics. More specifically, Act IV focuses upon the issue of Altorf's honor and the absolute need to:

> Look to thy honour!—As thou art a man,
> As thou art a soldier, as thou art a patriot,
> As thou art a husband—guard thy honour!(IV,
> ii)

The demands made upon Altorf to 'guard' his honor are becoming more and more pressing, thus precipitating his mental derangement and foregrounding his inability to resist the "tempting demons" (IV,ii), in this case Rosina and her father Rossberg. As Altorf himself reveals to Rossberg, "I do so love your daughter that passion might impel me on to madness; to worse—dishonour" (IV,viii).

The general social outcry against Altorf concerning his dishonorable action to abandon his soldiers and leave with Rosina and Rossberg is grounded upon misunderstanding and deception (IV,viii). Falling victim to society's definitions of what is appropriate or acceptable, Altorf finds himself within a reality which is inevitable, while, at the same time, it does not offer any possibilities for escape other than madness and death:

> I am a shipwreck'd man. Where'er I turn,
> Disgrace, dishonour stare me in the face.
> I'm lost beyond redemption. Cursed fool!

> I've err'd—I've sinn'd; nor yet well know I
> how (V,iii).

In Act V, the gothic setting of the gloomy, ancient castle of Rossberg
adds to Altorf's sense of entrapment. His ensuing melancholic desire
for death is a response to the instability of his own fractured sense of
self. Social death precedes his actual suicide. His feelings of guilt
concerning his desertion share the same psychological label with
women's experience in the larger social and political system. Altorf's
grief regarding his loss of honor closely resembles a woman's
lamentation for her loss of virginity and implies the same dreadful
consequences:

> My honour, love; the jewel I have lost;
> My spotless name, my bright integrity,
> My good report on earth (V,iii).

In a very powerful speech, Altorf's father, the figure of righteousness in
the play and the representative of society, curses his son, while his
words seal Altorf's tragic fate:

> *My* son? Thou liest. Thy mother play'd me
> false.
> A son of mine, a traitor and a villain?
> A son of mine, so base a wretch as thou art?
> A son of mine, sell honour and his country,
> Its cause—its righteous cause, for one weak
> woman?
> Look here, thou poor, despised, fallen
> coward!
> . . . .in the revels of thy wanton chambers,
> Cry out aloud in thy appalled ear
> My solemn—dying—curse! (V,iv)

Like a "fallen heroine," Altorf is irretrievably denied his former status
in society, as his reintegration in the social and political order becomes
absolutely impossible. Wright's play provides only one possible
resolution for the hero's tremendous psychological and moral dilemma.
Following a number of references to Altorf's deteriorating mental state,

the play closes with his death, which comes as a release from his emotional torment. However, this climactic scene in the play is sharply undercut by the ironic revelation that Altorf's honor was never really at stake since Rossberg manufactured all these lies against him:

> Live, Altorf, live! Rossberg hath clear'd thy
> fame.
> Wounded, expiring, he reveals the arts
> By which he woo'd thee here (V,xi).

While for Altorf death is the liberation from potential suffering, procured by an imposed sense of social defectiveness, Rosina's suicide occupies a higher level of self-consciousness. Witnessing Altorf's deterioration into madness, his hysterical expressions of anger and fear, his transformation into a figure of ambivalence, Rosina regrets her part in his tragedy and provides him with the ultimate resolution for his conflict:

> Now thou art free: the blasting upas dies.
> Look not so frenzied! Hear me! All is well.
> Return unto thy country—to thy virtue (V,x).

Rosina's suicide, which actually precedes Altorf's death and in a way minimizes its importance, is constructed as a means to reaggregate him into his community. Her power lies in the ability to assume authorship and responsibility for her own destiny as well as Altorf's. Realizing that her love for Altorf "hath been the helping hand to the sire's avarice, the ladder to his aims and worst ambition" (V,vii), Rosina consciously moves to the most radical form of self-expression. Her suicide emerges, on the one hand, as a denial of the constraints and incisions imposed upon her, and, on the other, as a powerful response to the most profane desecration of the one thing she kept beyond male cultural norms and political order—her love for Altorf. Commenting on the rhetoric of suicide as a particularly feminine strategy, Elisabeth Bronfen explains:

> because culture so inextricably connects femininity with the body, and with objectification,. . . . . a woman can gain a subject position only by denying her body. . . . the bind a woman is placed into in the cultural representations is that her position in the symbolic or cultural

order is that of feminine *body*, so that undoing her body, because it is the site of paralysis, because desires connected with it cannot be realized, also means subverting the position cultural laws have ascribed to her (143).

Suicide helps Rosina articulate the limitlessness of her love for Altorf, and, at last, achieve the public recognition of her deep feelings denied to her during her lifetime. Resembling Howe's *Leonora*, Rosina's voluntary death can be read as a revitalising process during which she can reaffirm her control after her disappointment at Altorf's and her father's betrayal. The paradoxical nature of suicide is grounded on the fact that it can simultaneously attest to the disintegration of the self and radically confirm a woman's autonomy. However, unlike Willis' *Bianca Visconti* (1837) and George H. Boker's *Francesca da Rimini* (1855), in which the death of the heroines is staged as the predictable outcome of their horrendous transgressions, the image of death in *Altorf* emerges as the supreme medium for conveying a message. Rosina's suicide largely resembles Louisa's death in Mercy O. Warren's *The Ladies of Castile* in that they both use the rhetoric of suicide as a self-conscious protest against the perpetuation of their claustrophobic presence in the world of male politics and paternal authority.

Both Altorf's death and Rosina's suicide attest to the vagueness and mutability of patriarchal values, like honor and dignity. Suddenly, everything appears to be meaningless: the father's curses, Rosina's sacrifice, Altorf's suicide, even the fact that he is innocent of treason. Frances Wright manages to undermine aspects of the dominant social order and, to some extent, subvert the existing systems of representation. The play explores the myths and ideological codes constructed by patriarchy in order to preserve the illusion of control and order in society and culture at large.[16] The masculine notions inherent in the definitions of love, marriage, sex relations, parental authority, duty, honor, receive serious setbacks in the play. Reversing the common narrative of a woman's 'fall from grace', Wright attempts to deconstruct the wholeness of the 'masculine self', as this is defined by western cultural discourses. The play transcends the culturally-determined gender polarity and examines the impact of the various social and political strategies of repression upon the male as well as the female subject.

Leonora

Like Wright's *Altorf,* Julia W. Howe's *Leonora* manages to undermine aspects of the culturally-determined gender roles through the exploration of the prevalent system of sexual relations. Following a powerful reversal of the traditional roles of 'seducer' and 'seduced', Howe's play has particular disruptive potential. It offers a new image of femininity that bears no resemblance to the typical seduced woman who dies of shame and actually provides an alternative discourse which shuns the traditional male-female power relations. *Leonora* imparts the story of a young woman's revenge upon the married Italian nobleman who seduced and abandoned her. Written within the context of the first organized protests against the social injustices that handicapped American women, the play stands as a mid-nineteenth century piece of subversive drama. As a matter of fact, Howe's social protest conveys the fundamental notion shared by the first generation of American feminists that the double standard of morality epitomized male usurpation of power and actually condemned women to social ostracism and perpetual subordination.

Born in New York in 1819, Julia Ward Howe belongs to a group of early American women, like Lucy Stone, Susan B. Anthony, Elizabeth Cady Stanton, and others, who intended to transform women's position in society and demanded political parity with men. Howe reveals, in her *Reminiscences,* that she was influenced by the ideology of the early women's rights movement and strove for new rights and broader opportunities for women:

> the new domain now made clear to me was that of true womanhood,
> A woman no longer in her ancillary relation to her opposite, man, but
> in her direct relation to the divine plan and purpose, as free agent,
> fully sharing with man every human right and every human
> responsibility"(372).

Poet, playwright, and social reformer, Howe was provided with an excellent education in literature, Roman languages and German philosophy. In 1841, she married Samuel Gridley Howe, the director of the Perkins Institute for the Blind, and for quite some time she helped him publish the *Commonwealth,* an abolitionist newspaper. Immediately after the Civil War, Howe actively involved herself in the woman-suffrage movement and became a founding member of the American Women Suffrage Association, of the Association for the Advancement of Women, and of the New England Woman's Club. Being a frequent speaker at conventions and legislative hearings, Howe sought to achieve higher education for women, "reform of divorce and child custody laws, protection of women's property, and suffrage"(Grant 221).

A close examination of Howe's literary career reveals a broad spectrum of intellectual interests and literary forms ranging from social criticism to poetry to drama. More specifically, Howe put her pen at the service of the burgeoning postwar woman's movement and published a great number of articles, lectures, and speeches concerning women's place in society. In 1870, she founded the weekly *Woman's Journal* and remained an editor and contributor for twenty years. Furthermore, in 1874, she edited *Sex and Education, a de*fense of coeducation and higher education for women.

Always of a literary bent, Howe wrote poetry throughout her whole life and published several volumes of poems—*Passion-Flowers* (1854), *Words for the Hour*(1857), *Later Lyrics*(1866) and *At Sunset*(1910). Unfortunately, her poems had little success and were treated with severity by the great masters of the day, people like Emerson and Hawthorne, mainly because of their conventional and sentimental tone (Adams 193).[17] Far from reflecting radical views concerning woman's social position, Howe's poems mainly constitute an articulate blend of powerful emotions. As a matter of fact, the themes of love and death, inner conflict and disappointment recur in almost all her verses.

Along with this outpouring of poems, Julia Ward Howe also tried her hand at playwriting. Although she was strongly attracted to the stage, she wrote only two poetic tragedies, *Leonora* (1857) and *Hippolytus*(1864).[18] Both her dramatic efforts, however, proved to be a source of disappointment to her. For one thing, *Leonora* was condemned by reviewers as immoral, indecent, and profane, as well as a dramatic failure:

> the critics quite unanimously concede that Mrs. Howe's new play "The World's Own," is a poetic success and a dramatic failure . . . and they all have a great deal to say of the immorality, if not indecency, of the play.

Although most of the adverse criticism of *Leonora* was directed against
the moral precepts it reflected, one critic had something to say about the
play's overall structure:

> In working up the material there are great faults of taste,
> misconceptions of the laws of dramatic art, and an unnecessary
> prolixity.

However, it is my contention that the failure of *Leonora* was not the
result of Howe's ineffectiveness as a playwright, but rather the outcome
of a powerful reaction against the play's radical subject matter as well
as the heroine's audacity and autonomy. As her later active
participation in the women's rights movement indicates, Howe was a
free thinker, ahead of her time. It is safe to infer that *Leonora* stands out
as a self-conscious attempt at the creation of feminist theater.[19] The
truth is that the play voices Julia Ward Howe's feminism with a
particular vehemency, and radicalism which is softened only by her
technique of distant place and time as well as the death of the heroine in
the final scene of the play. After all the above mentioned critic's
generalizations concerning "taste," "dramatic laws," and "prolixity"
become more lucid towards the end of his criticism when he adds:

> Undoubtedly there are offensive expressions which should be cut out,
> as there are whole scenes and characters by whose entire removal the
> play would gain in unity, force and interest.[20]

Although *Leonora* did not meet with public approbation, Howe was not
entirely discouraged and in 1864 she wrote *Hippolytus*. The play retells
the familiar Greek myth in which the hero, son of Theseus and the
Amazon Queen Antiope, refuses to honor Aphrodite and shuns women.
Enraged by his pride, Aphrodite decides to destroy him by causing his
stepmother, Phaedra, to fall in love with him. Though Hippolytus does
not give in to Phaedra's advances and actually repulses her, she lies to
Theseus who curses his son and causes Poseidon to destroy him.

It must be pointed out that Howe wrote this play particularly for
Edwin Booth, the young American actor. She explains, in her
Reminiscences, that she wrote "[her] five-act drama, dreaming of the
fine emphasis which Mr. Booth would give to its best passages and of
the beautiful appearance he would make in classic costume" (239-40).

As a matter of fact, Howe centered thoughtful attention on Hippolytus and drew his character with artistic elegance. More specifically, the play's noble passages of poetry expose the hero's dignity and loftiness. Although *Hippolytus* had a good hope of success—since Charlotte Cushman was chosen to play Phaedra to Booth's Hippolytus—the rehearsals suddenly stopped and the play was not performed.[22] According to Howe, the reasons given were not at all convincing:

> But lo! on a sudden, the manager bethought him that the time was rather late in the season; that the play would require new scenery; and, more than all, that his wife, who was also an actress, was not pleased with a secondary part assigned to her. This was, I think, the greatest "let down" that I ever experienced. It affected me seriously for some days, after which I determined to attempt nothing more for the stage (240).

It is important to note, however, that both *Leonora* and *Hippolytus* are fine examples of high quality blank verse. As a matter of fact, Howe's plays rank among the best that America can offer for the nineteenth century. The characters' speeches with their intensity of passion and suffering best illustrate Howe's dramatic talent. She successfully resorts to poetic language in an attempt to raise her themes to artistic eminence and provide powerful insight into her characters' state of mind, values, longing and desperation. Arthur Hobson Quinn rightly observes that "with any real encouragement [Howe] could have contributed plays to our stage that would have enriched our literature as well as our theater" (367).

Combining numerous instances of impassioned speech, a well—developed female character whose psychological transformation sets the action of the play in swift motion, a powerful story, and a climactic array of events, Howe creates in *Leonora* the picture of a young woman who struggles for autonomy against a male-oriented system of sexual relations. Seduced and abandoned by Lothair, the heroine, Leonora, resolves to resist the sexual inequities of her situation by hunting down her seducer, by disrupting his domestic bliss and family life, and finally by plotting his execution.

In the first scene of the play, the topic of the characters' conversation centers upon the female protagonist, Leonora, once the "hamlet's maiden queen," but now an "ill-counseled girl" who has chosen to "tread those dangerous ways, snatching the flowers that hide the fatal pit" (I,i). From the very beginning, the stage image of Leonora as a figure of applauded purity, a paragon of virtue is established only to be tragically reversed after her sexual transgression. While Jacques, one of the villagers, narrates the story of her loss of honor to Edward, the young man who used to be in love with her, Leonora herself begins to wander about in a labyrinth of signs, images, and metaphors. At first, she assumes the poses of idealized femininity and becomes fixed in the position of the pure object of the villagers' gaze:

> Jacques. At such an evening festival as this
> Just over, ere the dancing was at end,
> The stranger passed, and saw what we have
> seen;
> The band, dividing, passed to either side,
> And from the ranks moved Leonore alone
> To the majestic measure that she loves.
> White were her garments, white her twisted
> scarf,
> And white the flowers that garland her
> brow,
> Proclaiming her the hamlet's maiden queen
> (I,I).

However, Leonora's decision to love Lothair unconditionally, a nobleman who was just passing through her village, cuts deep into her public function as allegorical figure for virtue and glorious merit. In a narcissistic self-assured speech, Leonora shuns society and threatens to overthrow its stabilising powers:

> . . . . . . I could walk abroad,
> Were you so minded, through the market—
> place,
> With dauntless presence—saying to the
> world,
> "Behold Lothair—behold my love for him,
> That seeks its sanction in the face of
> Heaven!" (I, i).

Exchanging her white garments, now for ever tainted, for the "crimson flower of shame," Leonora is no longer the object of the world's admiration and applause, but rather constitutes a most sinister threat against the established order of the small village community (II,i). So, when Lothair abandons her one evening, the villagers function as a cohesive social force set out to punish her:

> Bertha. All has befallen as I told you, Boys:
> Leonora is deserted by her Count.
> She slighted you and all of us for him;
> So, let us raise a friendly voice or two,
> To speed her homeward; Ä rather, let's unite
> To hunt her from our village (II,i)

Throughout Acts I and II, Leonora stands alone "against the world," "against the brutal judgment of the crowd" as a symbol of uncontrolled sexuality. Her sexual transgression is a severe violation of the wider social and ideological codes by which the various sexual practices and relations are established. Viewed as a dangerous woman, one who has momentarily suspended social order, Leonora is forced to enter the marginal position of outsider, a realm beyond the confines of society:

> Leon. . . . .—what mean these words of yours?
> Those mocking looks? Why do you call me
> Countess
> Bertha. Such is your wealthy title, we infer,
> After those sacred nuptials of the heart
> At which the priest, indeed, did not attend,
> Having good cause for absence, as I judge!
> Pardon, your virtuous, blushing excellence.
> We'll call you Countess, Duchess, Paragon,
> Whate'er your la'ship pleases; but
> henceforth
> We please to keep no company with you!
> Leon. I stand amazed at these injurious words
> . . . . These my village mates,
> Have they come to cast their gibes upon
> An unoffending comrade? Loulou! Blanche!

> Suzanne! Are you become my enemies?
> I thought you loved me!
> Suz. Bertha speaks for us (II, i).

Like Altorf, Leonora's social death occurs before her physical demise. As an image of disorder, she is expelled so that the system can maintain its existing patterns. Her banishment from the social community emerges as the requirement for the preservation of existing cultural norms and values:

> Bertha. Well gone.
> Drink friends, in honor of the happy day,
> That rids our village of such wantonness (II,
> ii).

Howe's emphasis upon the social pressures that condemn Leonora's behavior indicates the existence of an essential link between sexuality and social control. As a matter of fact, in the nineteenth-century American society, the appropriate forms of sexual behavior, which were reproduced mainly in medical and etiquette texts, readily linked sexual control with national progress. More specifically, in the decades following the 1830s, virtue and self-denial carried political and economic connotations. Middle-class men differentiated themselves from the lower classes by adopting a specific set of sexual values which celebrated male continence and female passionlessness. As Charles E. Rosenberg explains, "sexual repression served the needs of an increasingly bureaucratized society by helping to create a social discipline appropriate to a middle class of managers, professionals and small entrepreneurs" (132).[22]

However, Leonora's refusal to listen to the voice of the crowd, her refusal to believe that she is "deserted and betrayed" (II,i), as well as her desperate need to "know the truth" (II,i), embody her anguish and fear and reveal her psychological inability to cope with these inexorable pressures placed upon her. Her rebellion against the powerful forces of society can be read in her bewildered, neurotic, even mad-like reaction, which results in her act of revenge near the end of the play:

> Leon. They want to make me mad,
> For cruel laughter—so, I will not rave,—

> I do not doubt my being, person, place,
> Nor that my usual senses help my thought,
> These are my old surroundings—here myself
> (II,i).

Leonora's repressed anger and despair will find an outlet only in her decision to destroy Lothair. Her fascination as a character emanates from her radical refusal to assume the position of the victim. Following a powerful reversal of the traditional roles of 'seducer' and 'seduced', Howe's play has particular disruptive potential. More specifically, it offers a new image of femininity that bears no resemblance to the typical seduced woman who dies of shame and actually provides an alternative discourse which shuns the traditional male-female power relations. As a matter of fact, Leonora derives her distinctive power from her refusal to conform to the submissive silences of the male-prescribed roles. Her decision to confront Lothair undermines the popular myth which proclaimed the literal death of the fallen woman and actually marks her move towards autonomy and power.[23]

In her determination to find Lothair, wherever he is, Leonora acquires a previously inaccessible power: from that moment on, she is transformed into the agent of action. Her power, however, lies beyond the external boundaries of society. As a social outcast, Leonora is forced to remove herself from all cultural symbols, like laws and social roles. Not only does she warn her beloved nanny that she will bring her misfortune and death, but she consciously accepts the fate that has designed her as the instrument of revenge and death:

> Now, Katchen, I must hold you to a bond,
> Or you shall try no further step with me;
> The way I seek is swift and terrible;
> Faith, with its fervent passion, hurries me,
> Even as it blindly guides yon flock in air,
> Whose whitherward is known to Heaven
> alone.
> You must be winged, too, or you will drop,
> A tortoise, to the cruel earth, and die
> For having soared with me. Think on your
> promise;
> Can you be strong and steadfast? (II,i).

Act II closes with Julia Ward Howe's indictment against the archaic masculine ethos which celebrated aggressive sexual behavior as a central component of manliness. Staging a crude conversation between Lothair and his friends regarding women, Howe offers a radical insight into the powerful ideology of sexuality that affects men and women differently. The polarization of the socially prescribed gender roles is particularly illustrated in Lothair's boastfulness, in the fact that he shamelessly brags about having seduced a "virgin heart"(II,iii), Leonora. The primary role model with which the men in this scene strive to identify is the sexually-active man, the "woman-hunter," who

> tires down his prey
> With the true game-dog instinct; 'tis the
> love
> Of conquest, not the feeble thing he hunts,
> incites him (II,iii).

However, the vulgar comments made by Lothair and his friends concerning women are sharply undercut by Lorenzo, a stranger to them. Lorenzo, who is in fact the close friend of Edward, is a powerful character with a high sense of duty and honor. He is appalled by Lothair's vileness and profanity and interprets his behavior towards Leonora as a most hideous crime. Lorenzo's passionate speech actually lays the foundations for Leonora's revenge and Lothair's punishment, and powerfully reveals Julia Ward Howe's protofeminist sentiments, her critical attitude towards male licentiousness and her unmitigated belief in woman's nobility and morality:

> Ev'n the frail creature with a moment's bloom,
> That pays your pleasure with her sacrifice,
> And, having first a marketable price,
> Grows thenceforth valueless,—ev'n such an one,
> Lifted a little from the mire, and purged
> By hands severely kind, will give to view
> The germ of all we honor, in the form
> Of all that we abhor (II, iii).

The seduction of Leonora implies her loss of exchange value. The value of the female body is estimated by its marketability as a medium of exchange among men.[24] The words "marketable," "price," and "valueless," echo Julia Ward Howe's criticism of women's economic and sexual exploitation resulting from the concept of women as both sexual objects and objects of transaction. For Leonora, seduction means the complete destruction of her virtue, the primary value that marked her position in the symbolic order of society. The powerful encounter between Leonora and Lothair in Act III, which takes place in the presence of his wife, Helen, enhances this irrevocable sense of her loss of honor. Explicitly condemned by the social order as a "fallen woman," Leonora now represents for him a "thing [he] would not stoop to pick from off the pavement" (III,iii). In his attempt to explain the true nature of women like Leonora to his wife, Lothair juxtaposes Leonora and Helen as respective/polarized representations of negative and positive femininity, and expresses the idea that women relate to each other "in terms of what they represent in man's desire" (Irigaray, 1985: 188):

> My Child,
> You do not know the world; those wretched
> women
> Can simulate all virtues for their ends;
> Even the blushing gift of modesty
> They trade with, when occasion calls for it.
> But that I could not keep my angel wife
> In such vile presence (III,iii).

The 'pure,' 'angelic' Helen and the 'fallen' Leonora tacitly invoke the paradoxical status of woman in western representational discourse. They represent the archetypal dual image of woman as madonna and whore. Helen embodies the passive qualities of female sexuality. She is a "saint;" she is the "pure," "peerless" (III,iii) woman whose sexual drives are carefully circumscribed within a maternal and reproductive framework. On the other hand, Leonora is portrayed as the primary symbol of willful sexuality. It is precisely this construction of the female body as a culturally-encoded sign when placed in representation that has deprived women of accurate reflections of their personal experiences and emotions.[25] Both Leonora and Helen are presented as they are perceived by Lothair and they are both symbolically constructed in relation to him, as objects of desire within his discourse:

> Loth. This lady is my wife.
> Leon. What strength shall hold me to suffer
> this?
> Let me hear all. Is this your wedded wife?
> ˙Loth. She is.
> . . . .
> Leon. And what was I?
> Loth. A love-lorn village girl,
> The ready partner of a vain amour (III,iii).

However, throughout this scene, Leonora's presence is felt as a sinister threat, as a figurative 'castration' of Lothair's sense of power. She functions as the signifier of disruption because she inspires in him the fear of an ultimate loss of control:

> Loth. [In an undertone to Leonora, showing
> dagger.]
> If e'er you venture in my path again,
> This shall decide between us!
> Leon. . . . God has justice, Count Lothair,
> When it draws nigh your door, remember
> me.

Leonora's gesture of throwing down Lothair's ring before she leaves the stage as well as her refusal to follow Edward, who has come to take her away, mark the beginning of her psychic changes and the process of her transformation into the emblematic figure of an enraged but tormented madwoman:

> Edw. Leonore!
> Come with us, where your faithful Katchen
> waits,
> Grieved at your long delay.
> Leon. I will not come;
> My path is chosen—it is wide of yours.
> Edw. Your brain is crazed, you know not what
> you say. (III, iv)

In her very interesting book about women and madness, Phyllis Chesler maintains that "women who reject or are ambivalent about the female role frighten themselves and society so much that their ostracism and self-destructiveness probably begin very early"(56). A woman like Leonora who exhibits signs of an independent, self-assertive nature, who acts contrary to the rules of culture and society, is considered mentally unhealthy, "crazed," as Edward calls her. If we bear in mind Michel Foucault's statement that "mental illness has its reality and its value qua illness only within a culture that recognizes it as such," then Leonora's descent into "madness" can be read as a marginal state of deviancy in relation to the cultural reality of a particular social group. Rejected or locked out by a society that denounces such passionate behavior, Leonora embarks on a rigorous and lonesome journey that marks, not her reintegration into society, but her alliance with death.

In the last two Acts, where the mood of the play changes with the introduction of gothic presentations of mysterious scenes of manipulation, betrayal, false appearances, and concealed identities, Howe manages to create an atmospheric setting of ambiguity, menace, and death in which Leonora, as a dark figure of disorder, reigns. The plan that she has devised for punishing Lothair indicates how far she has moved beyond passivity to action. In the first place, she has mysteriously become the favorite of the Prince of the small Ducal Court where Lothair lives. As a matter of fact, the Prince has so much fallen under her spell that:

> . . . she draws him with a hair,
> She binds him with a chain of perfumed breath,
> Padlocked with kisses. What she wills, he does,
> Our lives are in her hand (IV,ii).

Leonora has become the embodiment of the powerful and the unknown that threatens male authority. Described by the male characters as a dreadful figure, a "monstrous woman," she, in fact, represents all the archaic fears about woman marked as "Other" because she embodies a fascinating passion and sensuality which is disruptive of masculine order, reason and control. Her seductive nature, her strength, autonomy and decisive action inspire fear in all the characters. Nobody really knows anything about her and very few people have seen her:

> Orzetto. Have any seen her?
> Berto. Would she walk abroad,
> Think you, for common men to look upon?
> She's veiled, and does not pass her
> chamber door;
> Yet her malignant eyes are everywhere
> (IV,i).

This almost monster-like dimension in Leonora's behavior is indicative of a dual personality, of a "mad-double" that lurks inside her foreshadowing her merciless revenge.[26] Like the other powerful images of assertive femininity—Delilah, Salome, Medea, the Sirens, the Witch—Leonora overtly rejects the strictures of patriarchal society and seeks the power of self-articulation. She has become an all-powerful militant rebel figure manipulating the characters to serve her needs. She sends Amalfi , her servant, to Lothair in order to fool him into signing his own death sentence. Her scheme is to make Lothair appear as a traitor to the Prince, thus achieving his immediate execution. At first, Lothair has no idea who this "dark lady" really is. Witnessing the inevitability of his own ruin, however, Lothair feels particularly threatened by her power and autonomy; he becomes weak and helpless, and bears no resemblance, whatsoever, to the mighty "woman-hunter" at the beginning of the play:

> Loth. Can I not fly?
> Amalf. Your every step is watched
> Spies are about you in your very bed.
> Loth. Great Heaven! What help remains ?
> Amalf. One sole resource,—
> The deed of Brutus, swift and terrible ! (IV,
> ii).

The final confrontation between Leonora and Lothair in Act V, attests to the reversal of power relations. The scene of their second encounter introduces in essence the difference between a masculine order, whose codes and laws are clearly-defined and preserved, and a feminine disruption and transgression of such an order. Leonora's triumph over Lothair is evident; her revenge almost complete:

> Leon. Death to the traitor first!
> Loth. What do I see!
> Vengeance of Heaven!
> Leon. Do you remember me?
> Loth. Oh, fool! I am betrayed (V,i).

Not only is Lothair betrayed and condemned to die, but his wife is also arrested as an accomplice, and his child, kidnapped by a gypsy woman, is now in the hands of Leonora. He has lost everything a man strives for in society, his social status, the respect of the people, his wife, and his child. The likelihood of Lothair's punishment actually undermines the double standard of sexual morality according to which men escaped the consequences of illicit sexual relations. Trapped within a system of reversed gender roles, Lothair is unable to react. He can only verbally attack Leonora, in a speech that conveys his own repressed rage:

> Fiend! Are you satisfied? Is this enough?
> Could not my ruin glut your greed of blood,
> But my pure wife, my guiltless child must perish
> To heap the measure of your fell revenge?
> 'Twas little that a nobleman should die,
> Vilest of spiders, strangled in your web! (V,i).

However, throughout Act V, Leonora, as the agent of revenge and rebellion, is possessed by her "mad-double," which directs her and controls all her actions. When left alone in her chamber, Leonora's triumphant revelry resembles the delirium of real madness:

> 'Twas great! 'twas godlike! I have drunk to the
> full
> The costly wine of vengeance, and I feel
> Its mighty madness coursing through my veins.
> What pang was left forgotten? what disgrace?
> Oh, man! so gallant and so reckless once,
> Crushing the poor girl's heart in your white
> hands,
> Shaking your wanton lockets to the wind,
> Where are you now? your glozing tongue is
> dumb,

> The flashing falsehoods of your eyes are spent;
> And death and you, of all disguises stript,
> Glare grimly on each other (V,iii).

Her lack of penitence, however, which reaches the point of exaltation, must be punished by death. Given her subversive possibilities, and the fact that Leonora incorporates the qualities of powerful and destructive femininity, which may turn her into another "Lucretia Borgia," or another "Messalina," (V,iii) it is imperative that she dies at the end of the play.

Although Leonora's victory over Lothair is complete, a masked man, who is really Edward, sneaks into her room and forces her to face her split personality, her "mad-double." The process by which Leonora comes to realize her dual personality can be read in terms of Case's interpretation of Lacan's "mirror stage." When Leonora looks into the mirror, she sees her split self; her younger, innocent, undefiled self sharply contrasts with her present, alienated, rebellious self. Her stepping into the subject position as creator of the drama, making the other characters the objects of her hatred, revenge, and triumph, is marked by the realization of her own split identity.[27] Leonora's psychological conflict, which stems from her dual personality, can only be resolved through her death:

> Leon. This man seems risen from the depths of
> hell,
> With all its torments burning in his speech!
> Speak! what remains?
> Mask. The fate of ruined souls,
> To prosper and grow fat in wickedness.
> I need not draw the portrait of the future,
> I've seen its prototype a thousand times:
> Lucretia—not the heaven-avenging one;
> The poisoning Borgia, fiend-like, false, and
> cruel;
> Or Messalina, with the cold, shy look;
> Or other dames, whose picture give us fright,
> Lest they should claim our human
> fellowship.
> Rather than you should grow a thing so vile.

[*Shows a dagger*]
Methinks 'twere merciful to slay you here.
Leon. [Snatches the dagger]. Give here the
steel;
Wrest not from me my right of sacrifice;
(V,iii).

Leonora's sacrifice, however, should not be read as an act of contrition and submission. Her death can be seen as an act of purification, as an attempt to return to her innocence of youth, to escape her male-identified subjectivity as a 'vengeful,' 'monstrous' woman.

Why should you grieve?
See how this life-blood lets the madness out
That pressed, so closely packed, upon my
heart.
And I grow calm at last, and, as in dreams,
Behold the peaceful visions of my youth
(V,iii).

Leonora turns to death, the "most radical form of disruption of the integrity and unity of human existence," in order to reassert her control (Bronfen 149). Her death scene emerges as a perfect form of self-authorship as she manages to escape the social and cultural constraints and representations that reduce the feminine body to the position of dependency and submission. By staging her death as a violent weaning from the world, Leonora is bent upon eradicating the image of her body as the vulnerable object of sexual incursions. Her suicide gives authority to the privilege of death as the most meaningful and powerful instance of rebellion. Her suicide, self-defeating as it seems, is exemplary, in the sense that it is different from the conventionally expected outcome of seduction, since it is not imposed by any explicit social constraints—after all, Leonora has now extreme power near the Prince. Rather, her death emerges as a conscious strategy for setting an effective final mark on her story, for destroying her violated feminine body in order to construct an autonomous self-image. Leonora's death, as a form of liberation, signifies an absolute refusal of those social and sexual values that victimised and alienated her. It is only through the death of her body that Leonora can exchange the destruction of her sexual integrity with the restoration of her former virtuous image. In the final scene of the play, as she enfolds the image with which she wants to leave the world, Leonora forgives Lothair.

However, the social resonance of Leonora's suicide implies the reconfirmation of cultural norms and the reestablishment of social order. As an outsider, a social outcast, and a dangerous `Other,' Leonora has come to stand for a complete negation of the ruling norm, for a force disruptive of the security of masculine order. What is circumscribed with Leonora's death is Otherness as uncontrollable sexuality, femininity as a sign of the subversive.

It can be argued that the end of the play partly conveys Howe's awareness of the nineteenth-century middle-class audiences' sensibilities and the fact that she wanted to see her play produced in a society that justified the double standard of morality. In my view, however, Julia Ward Howe succeeds in developing strategies of resistance in order to counter the cultural construction of woman as object and commodity, and actually utilizes the portrait of the `fallen,' the `other' woman in an attempt to resist the ideology of passive, self-controlled womanhood, of sexual repression and the masculinization of desire. Leonora's death serves as the site where cultural norms and social conventions can be debated.

It is my contention that the story of Leonora can be read as a dramatization of women's struggle for autonomy against a patriarchal system of sexual relations. Her transformation from the passive victim of seduction to a powerful female figure coincides with women's social move towards political and economic independence and social authority. The image of Leonora reflects the image of a woman in transition from the social and cultural inheritance of repression and denial to independence and self-definition.

Both Wright's and Howe's vision and perspective are essentially society-conscious and feminine. Employing the techniques of romantic tragedy, they manage to reveal their own awareness of the complex implications of political and sexual ideology in women's struggle for autonomy and self-definition. In their dramatic world, as their characters wander about in a labyrinth of values and ideological codes, they question the validity and immutability of the various social and political forms which have become the normative structure for defining female reality.

NOTES

1. A similar trend began to flourish in England at the end of the eighteenth century. More specifically, the English `poet' dramatists, like Shelley, Coleridge, Byron, and Tennyson, were greatly influenced by the dramas of the German romantics, like Schiller and Goethe. In their vast majority, romantic dramatists injected rich tragic emotion into their scenes and adapted historical material for dramatic purposes. The influence of Schiller and Byron is evident in Wright's *Altorf*. For one thing, the play's plot is founded on the Swiss War of Independence which had already been celebrated in Schiller's drama of William Tell (1804). Also, the influence of Byron can be located in the character of Altorf himself, a gloomy, sensitive young man.

2. Being relegated to secondary roles next to exaggeratedly heroic and powerful male figures—like John H. Payne's Brutus, Stone's Metamora, Bird's Pelopidas, Oralloosa and Spartacus, Richard Penn Smith's Caius Marius, and, finally, Conrad's Jack Cade,—the female characters were left little room for action and self-expression. Morally superior and sexually passive, the women in poetic plays revolved around the need to love and be loved, while, in certain cases, like Juana in Robert M. Bird's *The Broker of Bogota* (1834), wavered between love and their deep moral sense of duty and honor.

3. The major difference of Boker's Francesca, however, when compared to Wright's Rosina and Howe's Leonora, is mainly grounded on the fact that Francesca's assertive and sexually active nature, her frank physical desire for Paolo, her transformation from an obedient daughter to a willful, passionate woman, are regrettably subordinated to the prevalent `passion' of the play: the love between the two brothers, Paolo and Lanciotto. For an analysis of George Henry Boker's *Francesca da Rimini* (1855), one of the greatest poetic dramas in the nineteenth century, see Voelker, 1972: 383-95; Zangler, 1973: 410-19.

4. *Leonora* was the first play to tackle the issue of the double standard with such vehemency. Towards the end of the nineteenth century and with the rise of American realism, James A. Herne wrote *Margaret Fleming* (1890), a play dealing with women's increasing demand for a single standard of morality for both men and women. For more information regarding the way *Margaret Fleming* challenges the status quo by portraying a strong female character, see Stephens, 1989: 45-55.

5. In her very interesting study about women in Victorian America, Carroll Smith-Rosenberg explains that "some nineteenth-century women channeled their frustration with women's restricted roles combined with a sense

of superior righteousness legitimized by the Cult of True Womanhood into the reform movements of the first half of the nineteenth
century" (109).

6. It must be noted that, at first, reform was an instant outgrowth of evangelical fervor. During the second Great Awakening in the early nineteenth century, the first large-scale female organizations to promote religion were formed. Catherine Clinton argues that "missionary zeal, the need to disseminate Christian knowledge, and other spiritual causes, stimulated females to band together against what they perceived as the weakening of religious fervor" (55). However, later on, women began to participate in social organizations in order to eliminate social evils, like drink, debt, violence, and prostitution that threatened many American families. A number of books have been written regarding the nineteenth-century female organizations in America. For example, see Berg, 1978; Dubois, 1978; Flexner, 1975; Kraditor, 1968; Lerner, 1967; Martin, 1972; Matthews, 1992.

7. The theme of Howe's *Leonora* precisely tackles the issue of the double standard of morality and elaborates on the early American feminists' opposition to the dominant sexual ideology which entrenched the physical, mental, and functional separateness of men and women.

8. Emma Willard and Mary Lyon defended women's right to advanced education. Elizabeth Blackwell was the first woman doctor in either the United States or Great Britain. Also, reformers like Frances Wright and Ernestine Rose fought for married women's property rights as well as their right to divorce. After all, Wright's *Altorf* presents divorce as a viable possibility for an unhappy marriage.

9. For biographical information, see James, 1971: 675-80; Malone, 1929/1957: 549-50; Martin, 1974: 273-78; Van Doren, 1974: 1163; Woodward, 1953: 24-52; Wright, 1963.

10. Catharine Esther Beecher, one of the first domestic reformers, called for the elevation of women's status in the home and the recognition of their contribution to family and community life in general. More specifically, Beecher did not seek to subvert the prevailing gender system of her time, but she attempted to expand women's role and power within it. In a series of letters, she attacked as 'unfeminine' those women who deviated from her own ideal vision of domesticity.

11. Also, the critic for the *New York Evening Post* (Feb. 22, 1819) contended that:

The plot is neither dark nor intricate, nor is their

> any difficulty in following its details; the
> language is clear and elegant, the characters
> natural and interesting, the morality pure, the
> probabilities and rules of drama all observed.

12. As I have already pointed out in the first part of this chapter, the majority of American dramatists strove to provide noble themes of freedom and patriotism, but, at the expense of the characters who were denied human dimensions. Altorf bears no resemblance to Spartacus or Brutus. He is a weak and helpless individual who suffers from a major internal conflict.

13. The tradition of heroines promised in marriage to men they have no feelings for, is prevalent in a vast number of plays written in America in the late-eighteenth and nineteenth centuries, ranging from melodramas to comedies to romantic tragedies. Starting with Royall Tyler's Maria Van Rough in *The Contrast* (1787) and George W. P. Custis' *Pocahontas* (1830), there are quite a few early American plays which tackle the theme of the heroine's wavering between her duty to her father and her love for the hero. For example, Izidora, in Epes Sargent's *Velasco* (1837), is unhappily betrothed by her father to Hernado. Also, in Nathaniel Parker Willis' *Tortesa the Usurer* (1839), Isabella is the price Count Falcone pays to Tortesa in order to save his property. Later in the nineteenth century, Francesca's tragic fate is sealed, in Boker's *Francesca da Rimini* (1855), when she is forced to marry Lancioto in order to help cement relations between Ravenna and Rimini. Finally, in Steele Mackaye's sentimental melodrama, *Hazel Kirke* (1880), the heroine is driven out of her house because she loves another and refuses to marry the man of her father's choice.

14. For information concerning the marital status of women in early American society, see Calhoun, 1945; Ditzion, 1953; Earle, 1895; Foster, 1913; Hymowitz, 1978; Norton, 1980.

15. Wright's radical views about marriage as well as a wholesale attack upon racial taboos in sex relations, racially segregated schools, and organized religion appeared in a widely circulated article published in the *Memphis Advocate* (1827). For information about her published papers, see Perkins, 1939.

16. For an understanding of the function of myths and ideological codes in legitimising cultural norms, see Barthes, 1972. For biographical information, see Adams, 1913: 178-214; Faust, 1983: 322-25; Hall,1913; James, 1971: 225-29; Kunitz, 1966: 391—92; Van Doren, 1974: 513-14.

17. However, Mrs. Howe won national fame when she published her poem "The Battle-Hymn of the Republic" in the Atlantic Monthly in 1862, which actually became the semi—official Civil War song of the Union Army and secured her a place in the American Academy of Arts and Letters.

18. Julia Ward Howe's play, *Leonora*, was produced in New York's Lyceum Theater in 1857, and in Boston Theater in 1858 with Matilda Heron in the leading role.

19. By "feminist," I refer to the political value of the play as an explicit attempt towards the exploration of gender-specific concerns regarding the problem of female identity and experience. Furthermore, the play explicitly reveals a critical awareness of the fact that women's positioning within existing social, cultural, and ideological structures differs fundamentally from that of men. It must be noted that a number of early American female playwrights like Mercy O. Warren, Susanna H. Rowson, Anna C. Mowatt, Sidney F. Bateman, and Frances Wright, treated social and political issues in their plays and actually showed an acute awareness of women's position in American society. However, Howe's *Leonora* capsulizes certain feminist issues of the time which receive powerful, searing dramatization in the play.

20. All the quotations regarding the adverse critical reception of Hippolytus was successfully *Leonora* are taken from the *New York Daily Times*. March 30, 1857.

21. *Hippolytus* was successfully performed after Howe's death, in 1911, when Miss Margaret Anglin produced it in Boston.

22. For details about the prevalent nineteenth-century sexual ideology in America, see Degler, 1974: 1467-90; D' Emilio, 1988; Freedman, 1982: 196-215; R. M. Ireland, 1989-90: 27-44; Kusher, 1978: 34-49; Napheys, 1870; C. E. Rosenberg, 1973: 131-53; Smith—Rosenberg, 1985, 1974: 23-37, 1973: 332-56.

23. From Richardson's *Clarissa* to Hardy's *Tess*, western literature abounds in images of seduced women who eventually die. In the American drama of the nineteenth century, the treatment of the theme of seduction in a number of plays reiterated the message that women were subject to a stricter moral code than men. For example, Ardelia's and Lucretia's suicide in Warren's *The Sack of Rome* and John H. Payne's *Brutus* respectively attest to the general belief that the loss of a woman's honor prevented her from being reintegrated into society. Later in the century, Lena, the seduced woman in James A. Herne's *Margaret Fleming* (1890), dies giving birth to her illegitimate child.

24. In nineteenth-century America, the social and economic values of the rising middle-class reinforced the dependence of women on marriage for economic survival. In this bourgeois economic system, "virtue [was] a commodity to be sold to the highest bidder, and virginity relinquished before marriage inevitably [meant] that a woman [was] less marketable and [was] therefore less likely to survive economically" (Martin 259).

25. Luce Irigaray offers a very interesting insight into the symbolic representation of women as sexual objects existing only to reflect male image and male desire, and observes that "just as a commodity has no mirror it can use to reflect itself, so woman serves as reflection, as image of and for man, but lacks specific qualities of her own. Her value-invested form amounts to what man inscribes in and on its matter: that is, her body"(187).

26. In *The Madwoman in the Attic*, Gilbert and Gubar argue that "it is, after all, through the violence of the double that the female author enacts her own raging desire to escape male houses and male texts, while at the same time it is through the double's violence that this anxious author articulates for herself the costly destructiveness of anger repressed until it can no longer be contained"(85).

27. In a very interesting study concerning female subjectivity in dramatic representation, Sue-Ellen Case appropriates the term 'split subject' from Lacanian discourse in order to account for the "split between a feminine consciousness and its male—identified symbolic role"(132). Since the subject of discourse or representation has been gendered as male, women can inhabit that position only as male-identified subjects. However, Sue-Ellen Case attempts to include the possibility of a female subject by arguing that:

'she' also sees in that mirror that she is a woman. At that moment she further fractures, split once as the male-identified subject and his subjectivity and split once more as the woman who observes her own subject position as both male-identified and female. She acts in the system in the male position, but she also marks that position with her own feminine action"(130-31).

CHAPTER 5

Conclusion

Examining the available published material, one easily discovers that early American women dramatists began to use their writing as a means of participation in the formation of a uniquely American literary tradition as well as a point of entry to the debate about women's status and rights within the social, political, and economic systems of the newly-born democratic nation. It is possible to say that the plays I have focused on in this study call attention to women's position in early American society, tend to deal, directly or indirectly, with social and political issues from a woman's point of view, and certainly bear evidence to the existence of feminist dramatic writing that dates back to the beginnings of American drama. In the preceding chapters, I have tried to show that women playwrights, and more specifically, Warren, Rowson, Mowatt, Bateman, Howe and Wright turned the potent art of theater into a unique source of strength, into an instrument to raise their collective female consciousness. Their plays stand as the most obvious and direct reflection of the striking changes that were taking place in American society in the late-eighteenth and early-nineteenth centuries, and the tremendous impact these changes had on women's lives. Despite the absence of any cultural assistance and encouragement, the women in this book found ways to channel their creative urge into communicating their experiences, feelings, perspectives and apprehensions.

Their strength as dramatists rests in the combination of their theatrical imagination and their political and social awareness. All of them were self-consciously concerned about the status of American women and dared to give dramatic shape to the struggles and limitations of women in early American society. They all placed their characters in historically meaningful contexts in an attempt to explore new areas of women's lives as well as alternative social roles and definitions. By appropriating certain dramatic conventions and methods, the six female playwrights discussed extensively in this work developed strategies which foreground women's reality on the stage as well as strategies of resistance to counter the ideology of the increasing polarization of public and private spheres, of commodified womanhood and sexual repression. What is particularly interesting is that the plays of my study focus upon urgent social issues, highlight the playwrights' political and social consciousness, without sliding into any form of personal outrage and bitterness. The dichotomy prevalent in all the plays is between a fixed masculine order and ideology—be it republican, industrial, sexual—and female exploration at the outskirts of such an order for any possibilities for change

The pioneering spirit in which the plays foreground female characters does not center around women's seeking emancipation from conventional gender roles, but rather, it is inextricably linked with a regenerating attitude towards the reconstruction of women's understanding of the relationship between female identity and social values, images, and roles. All these women dramatists explore the insidious power of cultural images that are not only forced upon women, but are also at times embraced by them, and provoke questions that are addressed simultaneously to the female self and to society in general. By writing plays, women exploited the political, social, and cultural opening of the American theater in the late-eighteenth and early-nineteenth centuries, and saw in the art of theater a potential venue for their common reality and the general ideological framework of social myths and cultural images.

When I decided to engage myself in recovering and reassessing texts by early American women playwrights, I aimed at elaborating on the powerful interplay between the social and political role of the theater and the female dramatists' ongoing effort to document women's realities through their own looking glass. Redressing the neglect of many years, I have tried to bring to light the hidden or otherwise unknown legacy of women dramatists in early American society. By shifting my focus to an exploration of largely ignored figures in both the business and the art of theater, I managed to gain new insights into the untold story of women's important and, sometimes, original role in the development of early American theater. Hopefully, this study will fill in some of the still sparsely occupied space in feminist theater criticism.

Appendix

The following appendix is an accurate, though not exhaustive, record of extant plays written by women writers in America between 1769 and 1860. It is designed to make accessible the dramatic works by a number of neglected writers in order to establish the range and variety of printed plays by women published during that time. Entries are made by title, and for each one of them, there is about half a page of commentary on the play's subject matter and plot, while, at the same time, information is provided about the production of the play—if it was ever produced,—together with parenthetical information referring to the publication of the play. I would like to point out that I have not included any plays that were produced only but not printed; all the entries on this appendix are known to be available in print. This was done primarily because of my intention to aid researchers and readers in their attempt to locate extant plays by early American women playwrights.

It should also be mentioned that the more central issue, what constitutes a dramatic work, was at first difficult to resolve. To restrict myself to original plays published in acting editions or the author's collected works would present only a portion of women's dramatic writing. Consequently, translations and adaptations of classic plays or popular novels for the stage are included as they constitute an entirely new work. Furthermore, this appendix covers a number of moral dialogues, pastorals, dramatic sketches and dramatic poems. The authors listed here were almost all native born. Those who were not, like Frances Wright, Fanny Kemble, and others, did the significant majority of their work in the United States and are therefore included. The issue of the writers' nationality is rather complicated by the number of trans-Atlantic careers. Finally, I would like to add that some of playwrights listed here also published in other genres, like poetry, juvenile literature, and especially fiction, while others contributed essays for periodicals or wrote political and feminist tracts.

SELECTED SOURCES

Adams, Oscar. *A Dictionary of American Authors*. Detroit: Gale, 1969.

Alston, R. C. *A Checklist of Women Writers*, 1801-1900. Boston: G. K. Hall, 1990.

Bergquist, William G. *Three Centuries of English and American Plays: A Checklist*. New York: Hafner, 1963.

Bibliography of American Literature. Comp. Jacob Blank. New Haven: Yale UP, 1955.

Boos, Florence and Lynn Miller. *Bibliography of Women and Literature*. New York: Holmes & Meier, 1989.

Brown, T. Allston. *A History of the New York Stage from the First Performance in 1732 to 1901*. New York: 1903. Repr. New York: Blom, 1964.

Checklist of American Drama. Comp. Albert von Chorba, Jr. Philadelphia: The U of Pennsylvania Library, 1951.

Clark, Barret H. *America's Lost Plays*. 20 vols. Princeton: Princeton UP, 1940-49.

Davis, Gwenn and Beverly A. Joyce, eds. *Drama by Women to 1900: A Bibliography of American and British Writers*. London: Mansell, 1992.

Dunlap, William. *History of the American Theater*. New York: Burt Franklin, 1963.

Elliott, Emory, ed. *Dictionary of Literary Biography*. Detroit, Michigan: Gale Research Company, 1984.

Hartman, John Geoffrey. *The Development of American Social Comedy from 1787 to 1936*. Philadelphia: U of Pennsylvania P, 1939.

Hill, Frank. *American Plays Printed 1714-1830*. Stanford: Stanford UP, 1934.

Hixon, Donald L. and Don A. Hennessee. *Nineteenth Century American Drama: A Finding Guide*. Metuchen, NJ: Scarecrow, 1977.

Hutton, Laurence. *Plays and Players*. New York: Hurd and Houghton, 1875.

Ireland, Joseph Norton. *Records of the New York Stage, from 1750 to 1860*. New York: T. H. Morrell, 1866-7.

Kunitz, Stanley J. and Howard Haycraft, eds. *American Authors, 1600-1900*. New York: H. W. Wilson, 1938.

Mainiero, Linda, ed. *American Women Writers: A Critical Reference Guide from Colonial Times to the Present.* New York: Ungar, 1977.

Meserve, Walter J. *American Drama to 1900: A Guide to Information Sources.* Detroit: Gale, 1980.

Moses, Montrose J. and John Mason Brown, eds. *The American Theater as Seen by Its Critics, 1752-1934.* New York: W. W. Norton, 1934.

Odell, George Clinton Densmore. *Annals of the New York Stage.* New York: Columbia UP, 1927-49.

Read, Thomas Buchanan. *The Female Poets of America.* Philadelphia: E. H. Butler, 1849.

Rees, James. *The Dramatic Authors of America.* Philadelphia: G. B. Zieber, 1845.

Ware, Ralph H. *American Adaptations of French Plays on the New York and Philadelphia Stages from 1834 to Civil War.* Philadelphia: s. n. , 1930.

Wegelin, Oscar. *Early American Plays,* 1714-1830. New York: Haskell, 1968.

Wells, Henry Willis. *Three Centuries of Drama: American and English, 1500-1800.* New York: Readex Microprint, 1952.

Anonymous with indications of female authorship:

Americana; or, A New Tale of the Genii: being an Allegorical Mask in five acts. (Baltimore: W. Pechin, 1802).

This anonymous masque was performed at the City Theater in Charleston, Feb. 9, 1798. The play is devoted exclusively to the celebration of the fight for freedom and constitutes one of the most interesting examples of the masque used as a patriotic spectacle. Although there are extremely long and wearisome speeches in the play, its blank verse manages, at times, to rise to a certain degree of beauty and vigor, while the characters are a curious mixture of symbolic personalities and mountain nymphs. The action is prompted by a sincere love of freedom and an atmosphere of intense patriotic feelings and moral values pervades the play's theme. The scene is set in the utmost summit of the Allegany Mountains and the story involves the coming of Elutheria, Genius of Liberty, from Britain to America to seek Americana's help against Typhon, Genius of Tyranny, and Fastidio, Genius of Pride, who reign in Britain. In their battles against these evil forces, Americana and Elutheria are aided by Galiana, Genius of France, and Fulmenifer, who symbolically represents Benjamin Franklin. Of particular interest in the play are the elaborate stage directions and the spectacular setting. The scene in which Americana literally clips Typhon's and Fastidio's wings, and the one where Fulmenifer appears with an electrical rod in his hand to destroy evil must have been really intriguing to eighteenth century audiences. Equally exciting must have been the concluding scene of the play in which Elutheria is restored to life by placing her two feet upon the necks of her two enemies.

Catherine Brown, the Converted Cherokee, a missionary drama founded on fact by a Lady. (New Haven, 1819).

An essentially moral and religious piece, Catherine Brown is a long one-act play in six scenes. It is evidently an amateur effort by an unidentified lady that was not intended as a commercial play, but to be performed by church missionary groups. There is no action in the play, just long discussions between the characters. It could be said that it is a simple propaganda piece meant to attract attention to the Presbyterian missionary stations in the old Southwest and their attempts to christianize the Indians. The story focuses upon Catherine, an Indian girl (her Cherokee name is never given in the play) whose parents brought her to the Brainerd missionary school to be educated in white ways. The missionary teachers manage to turn Catherine nearly 'white.' She has learned English perfectly and has become a good and intensely religious young girl. Catherine feels particularly happy at Brainerd where she teaches and acts as a surrogate mother to the other Cherokee children at the school. However, one day her parents return and arbitrarily insist that she go back to her old Indian life with them. Having being indoctrinated into a more 'civilized' and 'better' form of life at Brainerd, Catherine is really disappointed, but as a truly sentimental heroine she must obey the will of her parents and follow them. The play simply reiterates the most popular idea that native Americans were always improved by white contact, particularly by religious influence. Almost all the professional plays that were produced in America between 1808 and the 1870s and focused on the Indian as a stage-type shared this attitude. More specifically, the native American woman, since the appearance of Pocahontas, has been portrayed as particularly eloquent in English; she spurned the supposedly crude, savage manners and mores of her upbringing, and learned to mouth Christian tenets. American playwrights showed the Indian woman to be very much alike her white sister in her attempt to emulate the white lady's Christian understanding and humility as well as in her determination to aid white men in the conquest of the continent.

The Little Trifler, a Drama in Three Parts. (Boston: W. Spotswood, 1798).

The play is simply a moralizing lecture, intended for the instruction of young ladies. The story focuses on Laura, the youngest of Mrs. Mildmay's daughters, who is always late and does not seem willing to conform to the rules of good housekeeping. Mrs. Cecil, the girls' governess, reprimands her for being idle, curious, impertinent, untidy, and not as submissive as her sisters. This dramatic piece greatly resembles a conduct book, or advice manual for women, as it emphasizes the proper behavior of young ladies, the observance of etiquette, religious values and domestic principles.

The Little Country Visitor, a Drama in two parts. (Boston: W. Spotswood, 1798).

Like the majority of instructive dramatic pieces, *The Little Country Visitor* also employs an all-female cast of characters aiming primarily at instilling solid principles and moral values in young girls. The play is about Mrs. Montfort and her daughters, Matilda and Harriot, who are visiting the countryside. In the first part of the play, the contrast between living close to nature and living in the city becomes evident. Matilda is really surprised and excited about all the beauties of nature. She looks at the colorful flowers, the herbs and the fruit, she watches the bees and the cattle, while Rosetta, a farmer's daughter, explains to her what it means to live on a farm. Rosetta, with her modesty and her admirable accomplishments, helps Matilda to see her own faults, her impertinence and arrogance, and decide to become a better person.

The Lover, a Dramatic Fragment. In *The Witch of New England.* (Philadelphia: H. C. Carey, 1824).

Set in the gothic atmosphere of a chapel at midnight, the play is written in blank verse and centers around the story of Antonio who has gone mad with grief after Ines, his wife, died. Alice, his sister, and a Friar start looking for Antonio who is wandering half mad in the shadows of the night. When they find him, it becomes clear to them that it is impossible to reclaim him "from madness wild," as "his paleness now more death-like grows and o'er his fixed eye the film of death is passing."

Mary of Scotland; or, The Heir of Avenel, A Drama in Three Acts founded on the popular novel of The Abbot, and originally performed at the Theater, New York, with universal applause. (New York: Henry I. Megarey, 1821).

According to the play's preface, *Mary of Scotland* was favorably received by the American audience as an "indigenous effort" and was really successful, with Mrs. Barnes showing "prodigious talent" in the role of Mary. It is a poetic drama written in blank verse, blending elements of romance and melodrama with the gothic surroundings of Scottish castles, Queen Mary's prison and strange apparitions. As in most romantic tragedies, the characters in *Mary of Scotland* reveal little psychological insight on the part of the playwright while their thoughts and motivations evaporate in the midst of lifeless rhetorical speeches. The action of the play centers upon the efforts of Roland Graeme, David Douglas, and Catherine Seyton, to free the Queen from the castle of Lady Lochleven where she is kept a prisoner. The scene of the Queen's escape and the ensuing battle scene are the most dramatic and powerful ones. At the end of the play, Queen Mary is forced to leave her native land in order to save herself while Roland Graeme, the Queen's page, proves to be the rightful heir of Avenel.

The Misfortunes of Anger, a Drama in two parts. (Boston: W. Spotswood, 1798).

As the title itself suggests, this dramatic piece focuses on the consequences of fury and passionate behavior. In the preface to the play, the author explains that she did not "intend her dramatic dialogues to be performed; well aware that the length of the scenes in some places, and the simplicity of the plot in all, would render them flat and heavy in representation." As was the case with most didactic pieces, here, too, the emphasis is less on structure and plot development than on instruction and moral guidance. The story centers around the passionate behavior of Juliet, a young girl, whose mother died when she was still a baby, thus having no-one to advise and instruct her. Juliet's quick temper makes her disagreeable to other people who fear her and avoid her company. So uncontrollable is Juliet's temper that she does not even hesitate to throw a knife at her younger brother because he dared to make her angry. It is Pauline, her sensible and virtuous cousin, who helps her come to terms with her inappropriate behavior and violent attitude.

Morning Visitors; or, A Trip To Quebec, a farce. (1830)

The play has been attributed to A. B. Lindsley, but her authorship of the piece is really doubtful. According to the play's preface, "the following farce was got up at Quebec, in the course of last winter, for a charitable purpose. It has no pretensions to literary merit." The action in *Morning Visitors* takes place in Quebec and the characters form a curious amalgam of various nationalities and social classes: there is the vulgar but straightforward and honest American Yankee, the arrogant British merchant, the cunning Glasgow speculator, and the well-meaning Irish gentleman. However, the attempt to satirize the representative national and cultural traits of the characters as well as the use of dialect and slang do not really make up for the weak structure of the plot and the total lack of character delineation. The story of the play focuses upon Miss Cleopatra Patience Bunker, a very wealthy girl, daughter to old Bunker, the American Yankee. Having an eye on her large fortune, Mr. Ludgate, a London commission merchant seeks to marry Cleopatra purely for her money. But, Cleopatra, being a sensible American girl, falls in love with the good-natured and honest Captain McGraw.

Shepherdess of the Alps, a play in four acts by a citizen of New York (New York: T. Low, 1815). The play has been attributed to Almira Selden but there is no evidence of her authorship.

Following the romantic tradition that was prevalent on the American theatrical scene in the 1820s, the play is set in the spectacular summits of the Alps where Adelaide, the shepherdess, lives in a hut with Baucis and Philemon, an aged couple who treat her like a daughter. From the very beginning, we become aware of the fact that Adelaide does not really belong in her wild surroundings. Her air and refined manners betray a more aristocratic background. The Marquis and Marchioness are the first to notice that when they meet her after their carriage has broken down. They become curious about this young lady's past but nobody knows who she really is and where she comes from. It is obvious that some great secret is hanging over Adelaide's past, that some terrible misfortune has befallen on her. But what? In the course of the play, Adelaide reveals her secret to Fonrose, son of the Marquis and Marchioness, whom she takes for a humble shepherd. Adelaide feels responsible for her beloved husband's death because she detained him while his regiment was fighting a battle thus preventing him from performing his duty. Dishonored and ashamed, her husband killed himself in front of her own eyes. It should be noted that the playwright's attempts towards adding greater sensational effect by presenting a mysterious woman, victim of fatal circumstances, by adding a number of melodramatic devices—disguises, concealed identities, suspense—do not really make up for the play's loose structure, dull dialogues, and lack of action.

Armand; or, The Child of the People (1847), a play in five acts by Anna Cora Mowatt (New York: S. French, 1849). Also, in *Plays* (Boston: Ticknor, 1855).

The play was first performed at Park Theater, Sept. 27, 1847, and it was later acted in England with the subtitle *The Peer and the Peasant*. *Armand* is a romantic drama written in blank verse and set in eighteenth-century France, at the court of Louis XV. The plot centers around Blanche, the daughter of the Duke of Richelieu by a clandestine marriage, who lives with an old peasant woman unaware of her noble parentage. Blanche attracts the attention of the King, and a major conflict develops between the king and Armand, her lover. In a very powerful scene, Armand expresses his democratic ideas before the king, and so he is shipped off to wars where he eventually gains wealth, fame, and high rank, and also manages to save the king's life. In the meantime, and in order to save Blanche from the clutches of the lustful king, her father, the Duke, gives her a sleeping potion to suggest death and places her in a convent, away from the king. At the end of the play, Blanche and Armand are reunited by the king who appears remorseful and grateful to Armand for saving his life. Mowatt's play was really successful, and as the *Spirit of the Times* argued, it contained "living and suggestive outlines of character, scenes of pathos whose power is testified by the emotions of the audience, and a pervading simplicity, truth and loveliness, both of though and language which act as a charm and are full of fascination (Feb. 24, 1849).

The Benevolent Lawyers; or, Villainy Detected, a comedy in five acts by Mary Carr Clarke. (Philadelphia, 1823).

In the preface to her play, Clarke dedicates her dramatic creation to the "gentlemen of the bar," while in her prologue she cleverly satirizes corrupt lawyers who "laugh at their client, if the cause he has lost, And fill their own pockets at other men's cost." The play is intensely melodramatic with a beautiful heroine in distress, unscrupulous villains, scenes of recognition between parents and children, conspiracies and suspense. The story focuses upon Mrs. Campbell, a beautiful young mother whose husband, a ship captain, is away at sea. Mrs. Campbell, who lives alone with her two children and her husband's sister, is in great need of money. The person who offers to lend her money to pay her rent, ironically called Mr. Fairface, is a lecherous man who attempts to force himself on her. In a very interesting scene, which was later imitated by other playwrights, the heroine allows her disguised black maid to take her place in meeting with the villain. The subplot deals with the sad story of Mr. Trueman who was forced to abandon his pregnant beloved one by his cruel father. As it turns out at the end of the play, Mrs. Campbell is Mr. Trueman's long-lost daughter and her mother the landlady who was trying to evict her. Father and daughter are reunited but the mother, Mrs. Loverule, has grown so harsh after her many misfortunes that she practically turns her back on her. Throughout the play, it is made quite clear that lawyers are divided into two categories: there are those who help people and put morals before money, but there are others who charge 100 percent interest on money loaned, intrigue with their clients, foreclose without warning, and force their attention on helpless and innocent women. What is also worth mentioning about the play, is Clarke's interest in the variety of people who make up the American social landscape. Among her characters are an Irish gentleman and a German moneylender, both of whom speak in dialect, two black servants, as well as a Yankee hero, Trueman.

The Blockheads; or, The Affrighted Officers, a farce (1776), attributed to Mercy Otis Warren. In Norman Philbrick, *Trumpets Sounding: Propaganda Plays of the American Revolution* (New York: Benjamin Blom, 1972).

The play, which was published anonymously in pamphlet form, satirizes the English retreat from Boston when the American forces besieged Dorchester Heights, thus restricting the British to the confines of the city, leaving them no escape except by sea. The historical characters of the play are the grumbling, starving, defeated British officers and the panic-stricken Loyalists who found themselves caught between the retreating British and the advancing Americans. Following the pattern of most propaganda plays written at the time, the central trajectory in *The Blockheads* is determined by the dominant thematic polarization between right and wrong, between American virtue and British vice. As in Warren's *The Group*, the play focuses on the British and their Tory sympathizers and exposes their cowardly and corrupt nature. What is particularly worth mentioning about the plot is that it operates on two levels: the public and the private, the impersonal and the personal, as it shifts from the British reaction to the siege, the frustration and friction among the British troops, to the Simples, a Tory family, who have sided with the British and do not share their countrymen's values. The farcical aspect of the play is best demonstrated in Simple's regrets at his decision to become a Tory, in his inability to control his wife's insatiable desire to become a gentlewoman, and in his daughter's scheme to use marriage to Lord Dapper as a means to enter London's fashionable society.

Camille; or, The Fate of a Coquette, adapted from Dumas', fils, *La Dame aux Camélias* by Matilda Heron. (Cincinnati: T. Wrightson, 1856).

The play retells the familiar story of Camille and Armand Duval and was first produced in Philadelphia at the Walnut Street Theater, October 3, 1855. However, it was not until two years later, in 1857, when Matilda Heron staged her production at Wallack's Theater in New York, that the play became a real hit and ran for one hundred nights. It should be noted that Matilda Heron's *Camille* is the only American adaptation of Dumas' play that has survived. Compared to the original piece, it appears that Heron's version was written in a more realistic style than the standard drama of the period; in fact, so realistic that the reviewer in the New York *Herald* responded with a brutally short summary of the plot: "the heroine is a bad woman, who secures a spooney young man, then makes extraordinary sacrifices for him, and finally dies of consumption" (Jan. 23, 1857). However, as the most influential actress of the school of emotionalism, Heron tended to sentimentalize the character of Camille, presumably a technique that afforded her wider scope for the display of both emotionalism and naturalism, of the overt manifestations of passion. Finally, reading her play and Dumas' original, one cannot help noticing that Heron also added length to some of the speeches and frequently a moralizing turn, perhaps in an attempt to conform to the conventionalities sanctioned by the American stage.

The Defeat, by Mercy Otis Warren (1773). In her *Poems, Dramatic and Miscellaneous* (Boston: Thomas and Andrews, 1790).

The Defeat, which exists only in fragmentary form, appeared in the *Boston Gazette* in two installments (May 24 and July 19, 1773). The play was written as a reaction to the publication of incriminating letters of Hutchinson to his friends in England, letters that actually proved that Hutchinson was in fact a duplicitous manipulator. As in *The Adulateur,* Warren depicts the corruption of Tory officials, projects the evil nature of Rapatio and predicts his political downfall. Unlike *The Adulateur,* however, in which the patriot Brutus was sharply contrasted to Rapatio, *The Defeat* focuses almost entirely on Rapatio and his devilish machinations.

Dramatic Poems, by Harriette Fanning Read. (Boston: Crosby & Nichols, 1848).

This is a collection of three plays, *Medea, Erminia,* and *The New World,* all romantic tragedies written in black verse and modeled after Shakespearean drama. *Medea* retells the familiar Greek story of Medea's passionate love for Jason, his betrayal, and her extreme action of killing her children. Read's play is far from being a modest dramatic attempt since it successfully elaborates on themes of arbitrary power, passive submission and individual freedom, and actually creates a portrait of Medea as a talented, strong, and independent woman trapped within a male-dominated social system. The play also raises questions about woman's role and status in nineteenth-century American society and suggests an awareness of women's frustrations over their lack of options and personal rights.

Erminia: A Tale of Florence is a typical romantic tragedy in stilted blank verse full of declamatory and sentimental speeches that dramatizes the tragic love story between Erminia and Guido. Faithful to the tradition of poetic tragedy, the action of the play is centered around incidents of intrigue, betrayal, revenge, and a final denouement of death. When, on the eve of their wedding, Guido jilts Erminia, the latter decides to avenge her honor by having her family and friends seek out and punish Guido. However, when it is too late to save him from execution, she dies of remorse and love for him.

The New World is set in the romantic atmosphere of the Province of Haragua, in the island of Haiti. The characters are Spaniards and Indians and the theme of the play focuses upon the Spanish colonial exploitation. The universal issues of freedom and tyranny are raised in the play against a background of resentment of any from of oppression. The two young lovers, Hernando de Guevara, the Spanish noble, and Alana, the daughter of the local chief, commit suicide in order to foil the plans of the island's corrupt Spanish governor to marry Alana.

Effusions of the Heart, Contained in a Number of Original Poetical Pieces, on Various Subjects by Almira Selden. (Bennington, VT: D. Clark, 1820).

This collection of poems contains three short dramatic pieces: *Naomi*, *Lady Jane Gray*, and *The Irish Exiles in America*. The first one, *Naomi, a sacred drama in five scenes*, is in fact a religious sermon in dialogue transmitting a message of faith and fortitude in times of misfortune and despair. Naomi, bereaved of her husband aand children, returns to Bethleem, her native land, where she once lived happily. She is followed by Ruth, a young girl who is now her only companion in life and who loves her like a mother. In Bethleem, she finds Boaz, her late husband's kinsman, who falls in love with Ruth, and the two finally give meaning and a sense of fulfillment to Naomi's life.

Lady Jane and Lord Guilford Dudley is a dramatic poem that focuses upon the tragic story of Lady Jane, "the eldest daughter of Henry Gray, Marquis of Dorset and Duke of Suffolk, and great grand daughter to Henry VIII of England." This short dramatic piece describes the last moments of Lady Jane and her husband, Lord Guilford, both imprisoned in the Tower of London awaiting their execution. The Earl of Northumberland and the Duke of Suffolk convinced king Edward VI to "declare his sisters Mary and Elizabeth illegitimate, to reject the claims of the Queen of Scotts, and appoint Lady Jane his successor." However, on the death of the young king, lady Jane and her husband were imprisoned and sentenced to death.

The Irish Exiles in America, a drama in five scenes. As the author herself explains in the preface to her play, "this little dramatic piece was written for the purpose of having it represented by her youthful pupils." The play centers around the nostalgic memories of Mrs. Balfour and Evelina, her daughter, Irish immigrants who fled to America, the land of democracy and freedom.

Ernest Maltravers, a drama in three acts adapted from Bulwer-Lytton's novel by Louisa Medina. (New York: French's Standard Drama, no. CLXIII, 1857).

An exceptionally prolific dramatist, Medina wrote a substantial number of plays (about 34) between 1833 and 1838 and achieved a popular success that no woman and very few men would surpass or equal in the early years of the nineteenth century. Only eleven of her plays have been documented from stage histories and only three of these appear to have survived. She began to write plays working almost exclusively with Hamblin during his management of the Bowery Theater and made an astonishing career by dramatizing popular novels of the time. *Ernest Maltravers* was first performed at Wallack's National Theater, March 28, 1838. Shortly after the opening of the play, *The New York Mirror* observed that Medina's "power of composition is said to be astonishingly rapid. She is partial to startling and terrible catastrophes. Her knowledge of stage effects is very great, and there is an impassioned ardour in her poetry, which enhances the thrilling interest of her pieces" (April 28, 1838).

The first scene of *Ernest Maltravers* is set in the gothic atmosphere of a darkened wood where Ernest, "heir to the oldest and wealthiest family in Cumberland, and just returning to [his] paternal home" (I, i), meets Richard Darvil, "the most notorious thief, vagabond—poacher" (I, ii). Darvil persuades Ernest to spend the night at his house while intending to murder him in his sleep and rob him of all his money. However, Alice, Darvil's daughter, foils her father's plans and rescues Ernest who, in turn, falls in love with her. They run off together and they secretly get married. But, before they reach Ernest's paternal home, an evil advisor, a false friend, Lumley Ferres, who wants Alice for himself, deceives Ernest into believing that he actually got married to a "lascivious wanton" (II, i). He also persuades him to present Alice to his father as his mistress and not his wife since Sir W. Maltravers intends his son to marry the wealthy and aristocratic Lady Florence. Alice refuses to act as his mistress and leaves for Maltravers Hall to make herself known. Luckily, she arrives just in time to interrupt the robbery planned by her father in the course of which Ernest's father is killed. Employing all the popular techniques of melodrama, Medina adds suspense as well as ample opportunity for complication and adventure and she closes the second act of the play with Darvil's revelation that he is really the brother of Ernest's father and that Alice is Ernest's sister. The third act takes us to the spectacular scenery of the Lake Como in northern Italy where Alice, presumably driven mad by her discovery, is roaming the hills with her father. Ernest arrives with friends and all is happily resolved by a letter from Darvil's wife which explains that Ernest and Alice are merely first cousins. The play ends happily while soft music is playing in the background.

Essays Religious, Moral, Dramatic, and Poetical, Addressed to Youth; and Published for a Benevolent Purpose by Maria Henrietta Pinckney. (Charleston: A. E. Miller, 1818).

This collection, which has been erroneously attributed to Sarah Pogson Smith by some biographers, consists of a number of religious essays on Christian virtue and moral failings, as well as three five-act plays mainly intended for reading rather than for production. The first one, *The Young Carolinians; or, Americans in Algiers*, deals with a most important political issue, the continual struggle between Americans and the pirates of the Barbary States. The romantic adventures of the American sailors, captured and put into slavery in the mysterious, faraway land of Algeria, was particularly popular material with the American dramatists. *The Young Carolinians* uses spectacular scenes of the Barbary Coast war—the sea fight and eventual capture of the American ship, a grand procession to the accompaniment of Turkish music—to add a certain degree of romance and splendor. The story is about Ellinor and her friend Margaret who are captured by Algerian pirates on their way to England. While much is made of the suffering of these Christian slaves at the hands of their cruel and cunning Moslem captors, Ellinor's fiance, already a prisoner of the Turks manages to escape and save the girls and they all finally return to England. Throughout the play, Pinckney touches upon the issue of slavery and the slave-based economic system of American society.

The second play, *A Tyrant's Victim*, is a tragedy laid near Carthage. The plot of the play revolves round Agathocles, the king of Syracuse, whose "soaring ambition" and overcoming selfishness make him one detestable tyrant. It is quite clear in the play that Pinckney wrote this piece for a particular purpose: she was trying to express her concern for social morality and her interest in democratic nationalism.

In the last play, *The Orphans*, a five-act melodrama set in England, Pinckney dramatized social manners and morality through the actions of the shrewish Lady Flinty who did not hesitate to cast three orphaned young girls unprotected into the world. Fortunately, they are rescued just in time by their sea-going brother. Probably using the drama as a social weapon, Pinckney presents a bad-tempered and ignorant character such as Lady Flinty—more easily found in England than in America of course—in order to warn young girls against the snares of maliciousness.

Francis the First, an historical drama in five acts by Frances Ann Kemble. (London: John Murray, 1832).

The play was performed at Park Theater on February 19, 1833, and enjoyed a moderate success in production. Conforming to the prevalent dramatic trend of the time, the play is a romantic tragedy written in blank verse and focusing on the universal issues of love, hate, passion, corruption, freedom and tyranny. The first four acts are set in France while the fifth act takes place in Pavia, Italy. The dramatic element of *Francis the First* is built around a web of incidents of revenge, conspiracy, treason, and intrigue from which we get no relief. When the play opens, the Duke of Bourbon is due to return to the Court after a long absence. He has been recalled from Italy by the Queen, Francis' mother, who is in love with him and determined to "lift him to the dizziest height of power this hand can grant, or kingdom can confer" (I, ii). However, Bourbon spurns the Queen when she offers herself to him together with her crown because he scorns her devious ways and really loves Lady Margaret, the Queen's daughter. Hurt by this outright effrontery, the Queen vows to take revenge and has Bourbon arrested on the charge of treason. In all her schemes, the Queen is aided by a most dark figure, Gonzales, who pretends to be a Spanish monk. Gonzales visits Bourbon in jail and lures him to join the Spanish forces and fight against France that has so readily cast him off. The subplot of the play deals with the king's sexual desire for Francoise, the sister of Lautrec, and the promised wife of Laval. In order to avoid Francis' sexual advances, Francoise leaves the Court and goes to her parent's castle when her brother together with Laval is sent to Italy as governor of Milan. However, when Lautrec is accused of treachery and taken prisoner, Francoise goes back to the Court and pleads with the King for his release. Francis seizes this opportunity and seduces her in return for her brother's freedom. Not being able to reconcile herself with her shameful act, Francoise descends into madness and finally commits suicide. In the last act of the play, the perverse King and the corrupted Queen are punished when Lautrec joins Bourbon and the two manage to overthrow the tyrants.

The Golden Calf; or, Marriage a la Mode, a comedy in three acts by Sidney Frances Cowell Bateman. (St. Louis: Mo. Republican office, 1857).

The play was first produced in St. Louis at Woods Theater, Aug. 31, 1857. Falling into the category of social comedy, *The Golden Calf* maintains a satiric tone and, like most mid-nineteenth-century American comedies, portrays socially ambitious people and centers around the parvenu. The characters are mainly social caricatures and the mood of the play is explicitly didactic and melodramatic. The play presents an essentially international amalgam of fashions, values and morals since it shifts its action from London to Paris, involving American, British and French characters. The opening scene of the play is laid in London where we are first introduced to the main character, Edward L'Estrange, an American, who lives with his wealthy aunt, Miss Rosalie Ricketts, and is her sole heir. Although Edward is in love with Alethea Arkwright, the play's heroine, he feels that he cannot marry her because his aunt would then disinherit him and, left penniless, he wouldn't be able to support Alethea. However, Edward plans to elope with an English lady, Hebe Haugh, the estranged wife of Sir Stephen Haugh, because she turned to him for emotional support in a moment of weakness and aroused his sympathy. Sir Stephen discovers his wife's plans and challenges Edward to a duel where the latter is wounded. Alethea runs to his side and Edward is ready to renounce his aunt's fortune to be with his beloved one when by some magic trick she is divested of all her money which falls into Edward's possession at the end of the play. An amusing character is Colonel Parasite who, as the name itself suggests, is the representative of vain affectation and moral decadence in the play. He has befriended Edward for his money and trails after his aunt hoping that he may eventually marry her. The idea of marriage as loveless union contracted only for money is prevalent throughout the play. Another issue that Bateman tackles in *The Golden Calf* is the desire of the otherwise crude and vulgar nouveaux riche to rise socially. The play presents Crassus Styearine, a very wealthy American, who goes to Europe and tries to buy his daughter a position in society. He actually exemplifies the type of American who has just emerged from the business boom of the 1850s and feels that anything can be gotten if you have the money to pay for it. Of course, the play ends with a moral which warns Americans not to fall down in worship of the mighty dollar.

Isadore, a Dramatic Sketch by Caroline Howard Gilman. In her *Tales and Ballads* (Boston: W. Crosby, 1839).

This is a short dramatic dialogue between Isadore and her father in two scenes. The piece clearly exhibits Gilman's skill at poetic composition with its metaphors and similes as well as with its overwhelming nature imagery. The theme of this dramatic sketch centers around Isadore's rather hasty choice of Julian as her husband-to-be. Her father warns her against this man who, "caught by sensual low desires," has descended to alcoholism. Of course, at the end of the piece, Isadore realizes her mistake and frees herself from Julian. Her father, really proud of his daughter exclaims: "Heroic child! thine was a high resolve, And followed up in nobleness of soul! I knew thou wouldst not compromise with sin, Nor give soft names to foul intemperance." While reading this sketch, it becomes obvious that Gilman was probably aiming at expressing implicitly one aspect of female victimization as she warns women about the danger of choosing alcoholic men for their husbands.

The Last Days of Pompeii, a Dramatic Spectacle in three acts adapted from Bulwer-Lytton's novel by Louisa Medina. (New York: French's Standard Drama, no. CXLVI, 1844).

The play opened at Bowery Theater on February 9, 1835, and except for one night in March ran continuously for twenty-nine performances. It is a historical drama, set in ancient Pompeii and concentrates solely on the love story of Glaucus and Ione. *The Last Days of Pompeii* incorporates all those melodramatic elements that so much entranced nineteenth-century American audiences: scenes of seduction, jealousy and betrayal, banquets, gladiatorial games, erotic religious ceremonies, boat trips, and of course the earthquake itself. The action of the story is spurred by the machinations of the villain, Arbaces the "Egyptian, the terrible magician" (I, i), who is the guardian of Ione and secretly in love with her. Throughout the play, Arbaces devises a number of plans to get rid of Glaucus. He deceives Lydon into believing that Glaucus is the 'paramour' of his sister, Nydia, "the blind girl of Thessaly," thus persuading him to kill Glaucus in order to defend his sister's honor. He also accuses Glaucus of a murder he himself committed, thus sending him to prison. Amazingly enough, Nydia is the one who saves Glaucus and brings him and Ione together. Taking into account the stage directions, it appears that the final scene of the play must have been particularly spectacular as it takes place in the amphitheater at the time the earthquake begins: "at this moment, the fire breaks forth from the mountain, and the walls of arena fall— everybody cries, The earthquake—the earthquake!—Arbaces is killed by the falling of a statue—all in confusion and screams till curtain falls on a grand tableau" (III, v). As a final note, I would like to add that Medina introduces a rather extraordinary character, Stratonice, a female gladiator, an outspoken, strong woman who playfully "strikes [her husband] on the head" (I, i).

Le Demi-Monde, A Satire on Society, adaptation of Dumas' *fils Demi-Monde* by Miriam Florence Folline Squier Leslie. (Philadephia: Lippincott, 1858).

The play, which is, in fact, a comedy of manners, is a study of Parisian social life in the 1850s. It combines elements of melodrama, scenes of intrigue, episodes of duels and love affairs, and the social chitchat of the *Demi-Monde*. It is obvious that Leslie was primarily concerned with pointing a moral as well as presenting as accurately as possible the social system in which the characters live and interact. The plot focuses on the efforts of Olivier, who used to be the lover of La Baronne Suzanne d'Ange, a woman of false title and questionable morals, to prevent his friend De Nanjac from marrying her. In order to achieve his purpose, Olivier uses a number of tricks: he denies Suzanne's title and social position, insults her by hinting that she accessible without marriage, and gives De Nanjac the letters she has written him. On her part, however, Suzanne, with rare diplomacy, uses her own weapons to counter Olivier's attack. She forges certificates of birth and marriage, she manages to obtain a settlement from a former lover, and she even proves that the love letters are not in her own handwriting. Nevertheless, at the end of the play, her plottings are unmasked and she succumbs to Olivier's scheme. Besides Suzanne, the other female characters, who also constitute the *Demi-Monde*, that is neither aristocracy nor plebianism, have an unsavory past, some spot on their name. For example, Valentine de Santis is a heartless woman who pretends to be a widow, while at the same time, she ruthlessly blackmails her husband. Countess de Vernieres in turn is a real widow, a dissolute woman with loose morals. It should be noted that thirty-five years later, Leslie returned to this play and adapted it for the New York stage, changing its title to *The Froth of Society*. So, on April 24, 1893, *The Froth of Society* opened at the Union Square Theater, but was not at all favorably received by either critics or public.

Miriam, a dramatic poem, by Louisa J. Hall. (Boston: Crosby & Nichols, 1850).

Hall began to compose verse at an early age, publishing it anonymously in newspapers in the 1820s and 1830s. Her verse drama, *Miriam*, which was written in 1837, was intended primarily for private reading and not for the stage. The play is a highly didactic dramatic piece built around a religious theme and conveying a message of morality and Christianity. It is written in rather tedious and stilted blank verse with long monologues and extensive nature imagery. *Miriam* is set in Rome at the time of the persecutions of the early Christians and depicts the doomed love between, Paulus, the son of a proud and cruel Roman governor and Miriam, a devout young Christian girl, ready to fight and die for her faith. When Miriam's father is arrested by the Romans, Paulus agrees to be taken hostage by Euphas, Miriam's brother, and the other Christians so that Piso, his father, will be forced to release the prisoner. However, when Piso finds out that his son is in love with a Christian girl, he reacts in a highly unpredictable way. He becomes furious and refuses to set the prisoner free at the cost of his son's life. When Miriam goes to see him, it turns out that she is the daughter of the Christian woman he used to be in love with as a young soldier but who finally married someone else. Blinded by jealousy and revenge, Piso kills Miriam's father while he lets her and her brother go. In the final scene of the play, Paulus converts to Christianity but Miriam dies in a sudden and completely unjustifiable way.

The Motley Assembly, a farce (1779), attributed to Mercy Otis Warren. In Norman Philbrick, *Trumpets Sounding: Propaganda Plays of the American Revolution* (New York: Benjamin Blom, 1972).

The play was published anonymously in 1779, it takes place in Boston several years after the British were driven from the city, and centers around the frivolity of those in the upper colonial classes who were still aspiring to English values. The satire of the piece is directed against the social rather than the political world, against those American citizens who pretended to be in favor of the Patriot cause while they were secretly drawn to the British culture. Although the structure of the play is really weak and there are no scenes of conflict or confrontation, the playwright manages to expose the social pretense and affectation evident in the 'assemblies' or dances sponsored by the Bostonian elite. The characters in the play are all Loyalists with the exception of Captain Aid of the army and Captain Careless of the navy. The women in *The Motley Assembly,* Mrs. Flourish and Mrs. Taxall, with their fashionable daughters, complain about the lack of elegant and refined entertainment and actually lament the 'motley' nature of the social assemblies, more democratic but much ruder for their taste. It is made clear throughout the play that the playwright urges Americans to reject the cultural residue of the British social decorum and try to cultivate American values and mores.

Nick of the Woods; or, Telie, The Renegade's Daughter, adapted from Robert Montgomery Bird's novel by Louisa Medina. (New York: French's Standard Drama, no. CCLXIX, 1843).

The play was first produced at Bowery Theater on February 20, 1843, and immediately became one of the most popular and highly colorful melodramas of the time. Like her other plays, *Nick of the Woods* is also replete with action, adventure, mystery, disguises, romantic love and most spectacular scenery of raging cataracts, bridges dangling over rocky passes. The setting of the play is the romantic landscape of the American frontier where Roland Forrester and his cousin and bride-to-be, Edith Forrester, are traveling "through the pathless wilderness" (I,i) with a group of emigrants. Among the travelers, there is Richard Braxley, the villain of the play, who has cheated Roland and Edith of their legacy by destroying their uncle's will. In the course of the action, Braxley tries to kill Roland and kidnaps Edith with the intention of forcing her to marry him in order to be able to lay his hands on the girl's Virginia estate. In this scheme, he is aided by Abel Doe a renegade man and Telie's presumed 'father.' The play's subplot deals with a Quaker woodsman, Nathan, who is, in fact, Jibbenainosay, the dread Indian killer, who seeks to avenge himself upon the Indians, particularly Wenonga, who murdered his bride and his family. Fortunately, Nathan appears at the right moment and rescues Edith from Braxley. This is accomplished in an extremely spectacular scene in which "the Jibbenainosay is precipitated down the cataract in a canoe of fire; the Indians all utter a yell of horror, and fall on their faces" (II, v). In the final act of *Nick of the Woods*, things are becoming even more complicated, in a truly melodramatic fashion: Telie is revealed to be the dead uncle's lost child, born of a secret marriage, Nathan accomplishes his revenge and is recognized as Reginald Ashburn, Telie throws herself in front of Roland and intercepts a bullet which Braxley fires at him, thus leaving Roland and Edith free to return to an undisputed inheritance in Virginia. Finally, Braxley is killed by Ralph Stackpole, a horse thief, while the audience watches the brave Jibbenainosay die in peace.

Poems, on Various Subjects by Isabella Oliver Sharp. (Carslile: A. Loudon, 1805).

This collection of poems includes two dramatic dialogues, one between Philander and Lucinda and the other between Frances and Mila. In both dialogues, Sharp's skill at composing beautiful lines and employing pleasantly musical phrases and ingenious images becomes evident. Her purpose in writing these dramatic dialogues must have been highly didactic. In *Philander and Lucinda*, Sharp stresses the importance of the cultivation of female intellect, while at the same time, emphasizes women's inner worth and value as opposed to the superficiality of physical beauty. Philander confesses to his sister, Lucinda, that what particularly attracted him to Frances was her virtuous nature, her "refined thoughts" and the "holy elevation" of her mind. On the other hand, a woman like Mila, whose "capricious beauty" has been a "gilded snare" for many men, is to be avoided. In the second dialogue, Frances, the embodiment of virtue, modesty, and common sense is sharply juxtaposed to Mila, the personification of pride, selfishness, jealousy, and folly.

The Star of Seville, a drama in five acts by Frances Ann Kemble Butler. (London: Saunders & Otley, 1837).

The play was performed at Walnut Street Theater on August 7, 1837. Similar in technique and theme with her earlier tragedy, *Francis the First, The Star of Seville* elaborates on the theme of tyranny and corruption as it builds its story on a series of incidents of intrigue, betrayal, and sexual passion. Conforming to the codes of romantic tragedy, the play shows little concern for character development and is written in dull and stilted blank verse. The main action of the play involves the King's sexual desire for Estrella, Don Pedro's sister and Don Carlos' finacee, and his attempt to seduce her when he secretly breaks into her house in disguise. Fortunately, however, she is rescued by her brother, who, not recognizing the king, inflicts a number of blows on the intruder. The king runs away but seeks revenge. He asks Don Carlos to punish the man "who hath incurred all these against his King—'Gainst me, the Lord and Sovereign of Castille, he rais'd his arm" (III, ii). Of course, he does not reveal the identity of this man to Carlos but writes his name on a piece of paper and gives it to him. When Carlos finds out who this man really is, he is torn between his love for his friend and the duty to his king. Not knowing what to do, he goes into an inn and tries to drown his misery. Drunk as he is, he encounters Pedro in the street and, without realizing what he is doing, kills him. He is arrested for Pedro's murder and condemned to death by the Council. In the meantime, Estrella is getting ready for her wedding day when she hears the news about her brother's death and Carlos' sentence. Feeling desperate and confused, she starts raving with sorrow as she deteriorates into madness. The ending of the play, with its final denouement of death, establishes the belief in the perversity and corruption of tyrannical rule. In a very dramatic scene, Carlos and Estrella die together.

The Traveller Returned, by Judith Sargent Murray. (*The Gleaner* III, 1798).

It was performed at the Federal Street Theater in Boston, March 9, 1796. In this play, Murray attempts to experiment with accents and dialects as she introduces a curious amalgam of such characters like a Yankee named Obadiah, Irish servants and a German couple. Nevertheless, Murray fails to break free from her tendency to create stock characters with no real depth, loosely-constructed stories and unbalanced scenes. In a typical and rather sentimental plot, Mr. Rambleton arrives in his native country, America, after an absence of nineteen years and stays at Major Camden's lodgings. The scene in the second act changes to Mrs. Montague's house where Harriot Montague, fiancée of Camden, and Emily Lovegrove, her cousin, are discussing Camden. Emily really loves him but Harriot agreed to become engaged to him to please her mother. Mrs. Montague, however, realizing her daughter's lack of interest in her fiancé, talks to her about the importance of reason, and not passion, in the sensible choice of marital partner. Many years ago, Mrs. Montague's husband abandoned her and Harriot and left with their four-year-old son because he thought that she was in love with another man. Of course, after an number of complications, and in a most spectacular ballroom scene, Mrs. Montague mysteriously receives a picture of herself and becomes aware that Major Camden, whom she wishes her daughter to marry, is her son, and Mr. Rambleton is really Mr. Montague. It is a happy reunion for all the characters and they all join in a dance at Mrs. Montague's house.

Xerxes the Great; or, The Battle of Thermopyle, a patriotic drama in five acts. (Philadelphia: G. Palmer, 1815).

The play, which has been attributed to Frances Wright, dramatizes in romantic fashion the activities of Xerxes the Great. Elaborating on a particular historical incident, the war between the Greeks and the Persians, the play conforms to the pattern of poetic drama that was most prevalent in America in the early decades of the nineteenth century. Like the majority of verse plays, it employs an ancient setting, the characters' speeches are written in stilted and lifeless blank verse which in fact resembles rhetorical sermons rather than real speech, while, at the same time, it treats the universal passions of love, jealousy, hatred and revenge alongside the theme of tyranny, patriotism and freedom. The romantic atmosphere of the play is further enhanced with Xerxes' vision of the Genius of dreams which descends in a bright cloud on the stage as well as the most spectacular appearance of the Ghost of Darius in "armor, bearing sword and laurel wreath," thus prophesying Xerxes' victory (IV, v). The main focus of the play is on the Persians' preparations to invade Greece and the Spartans' plans to defend themselves and their country. Leonidas, the king of Sparta, and his three hundred soldiers become the embodiment of courage, patriotism and heroism; they alone stand up against Xerxes' army. Although at the end of the play the Greeks are defeated, their democratic spirit and their love for freedom continue to live for ever.

Zamba; or, The Insurrection, a Dramatic Poem in five acts by Elizabeth Ricord. (Cambridge: Metcalf, Keith, and Nichols, 1842).

Interspersed with songs and nature imagery, the play attempts to offer a truthful picture of the slaves' life on the plantation conveying, at the same time, religious and anti-slavery sentiments. The action of *Zamba* takes place on an island of the West Indies and involves the insurrection of the slaves against their cruel and oppressive proprietors. The play offers details about the slaves' brutal capture, the way they are taken away from their families and sold to cruel masters. Zamba, a former African Prince, but now a slave of the despotic Count de Nouville, is presented as a passionate and elevated character who mourns for his wife's death and seeks revenge. However, in a truly Christian fashion, he warns his master about the slaves' uprising on the eve of the intended massacre and saves him and his family. In return, the Count shows his gratitude by making him a free man. Although the rest of the play is filled with long speeches in the form of sermons, the chronicle of the insurrection is presented in a highly dramatic way with all the horrid details of the slaves' attack and the ensuing disaster.

Works Cited

PRIMARY SOURCES

Anonymous with indications of female authorship:

Catharine Brown; or, The Converted Cherokee. A Missionary Drama Founded on Fact. By a Lady. New Haven, 1819.

Mary V. V.

A Dialogue between a Southern Delegate and his Spouse on his Return from the Grand Continental Congress: A Fragment Inscribed to the Married Ladies of America, by their Most Sincere and Affectionate Friend and Servant. In Norman Philbrick, *Trumpets Sounding: Propaganda Plays of the American Revolution* (New York: Benjamin Blom, 1972).

May Day; or, The Celebration of the Return of Spring. Being a Play for the Amusement of Young Girls on the First Day of May. Carlyle, Pa., 1819.

The Misfortunes of Anger. A Drama in Two Parts. Boston: W. Spotswood, 1798.

The Search After Happiness. A Pastoral Drama; From the Poetry of Miss More. By a Lady in Connecticut. Catskill: M. Croswell, 1794.

Bacon, Delia Salter (1811-1859).

The Bride of Fort Edward, founded on a Incident of the Revolution. New York: S. Colman, 1839.

Barnes, Charlotte Mary Sanford (1818-1863).

Octavia Bragaldi; or, The Confession. Performed in New York: National
Theater, Nov. 8, 1837. In *Plays, Prose, and Poetry* (Philadelphia: E. H.
Butler, 1848).

The Forest Princess; or, Two Centuries Ago (1844). In *Plays, Prose and
Plenty.*

Bateman, Sidney Frances Cowell (1823-1881).

Self. An Original Comedy. Performed in St. Louis: People's Theater, 1856;
Woods Theater, Aug. 31, 1857. In Montrose J. Moses, *Representative
Plays by American Dramatists, From 1765 to the Present Day* (New York:
Arno, 1978).

Clarke, Mary Carr (no dates).

The Fair Americans. An Original Comedy in Five Acts. Philadelphia, 1815.

Ellet, Elizabeth Fries Lummis (1818-1877).

Teresa Contarini. A Tragedy in Five Acts. New York: Park Theater, March
1835. In her *Poems, Translated and Original* (Philadelphia: Key and
Biddle, 1835).

Faugeres, Margaretta V. (1771-1801).

Belisarius. A Tragedy. New York: T. and J. Swords, 1795.

Hentz, Caroline Lee Whiting (1800-1856).

De Lara; or, The Moorish Bride. Tuscaloosa, Ala.: Woodruff and Olcott, 1843.

Howe, Julia Ward (1819-1910).

Leonore; or, The World's Own. New York: Wallack's Theater, March 16,
1857. Pub. Ticknor and Fields, 1857.

Kemble, Frances Ann (1809-1893).

Francis the First. An Historical Drama. (Adapt. From Spanish). Park
Theater, Feb. 19, 1833. London: John Murray, 1832.

The Star of Seville. A Drama in Five Acts. (Adapt. of La Estrella de
   Sevilla). Walnut, Aug. 7, 1837. London: Saunders and Othey, 1837.

Lindsley, A.B.

Love and Friendship; or, Yankee Notions. New York: D. Longworth, 1809.

Marriott, Mrs.

The Chimera; or, Effusions of Fancy. New York: I. and J. Swords, 1795.

Mowatt, Anna Cora Ogden (1819—1870).

Fashion; or, Life in New York. A Comedy. Park Theater, March 24, 1845. New
   York: S. French, 1849. Republished Boston: Ticknor and Fields, 1855.

Murray, Judith Sargent Stevens (1751-1821).

Virtue Triumphant (Original title: *The Medium; or, The Happy Tea Party*.)
   Boston: Federal Theater, March 2, 1795. Published in The Gleaner III
   (1798): 15-87.

Rowson, Susanna Haswell (1762-1824).

Slaves in Algiers; or, A Struggle for Freedom. A Play Interspersed with Songs,
   in Three Acts. Philadelphia: Chestnut St. Theater, Dec. 22, 1794.
   Philadelphia: Wrigley and Berriman, 1794.

Smith, Sarah Pogson (no dates).

The Female Enthusiast. A Tragedy in Five Acts. Charleston: J. Hoff, 1807.

Warren, Mercy Otis (1728-1814).

The Group, 1775.
Poems, Dramatic and Miscellaneous. Boston: Thomas and Andrews, 1790.
   Includes: *The Ladies of Castile* and *The Sack of Rome*.

Wright, Frances (1795-1852).

Altorf. A Tragedy. New York: Park Theater, Feb. 19, 1819. Philadelphia: M.
   Carey, 1819.

SECONDARY SOURCES

Adams, Elmer C. and Warren D. Foster. *Heroines of Modern Progress.* New York: Sturgis, 1913.

Alcott, W. A. *The Young Husband; or, Duties of Man in the Marriage Relation.* New York: Derby, 1855.

———. *The Young Wife.* Boston: Light, 1838.

Anthony, Katharine. *First Lady of the Revolution: The Life of Mercy Otis Warren.* Garden City, New York: Double Day, 1958.

Argetsinger, Gerald. "Dunlap's Andre: Beginning of American Tragedy." *Players* 49 (1975): 62-64.

Armstrong, Isobel, ed. *New Feminist Discourses.* New York: Routledge, 1992.

Arthur, T.S. *Advice to Young Ladies on their Duties and Conduct in Life.* Boston: Phillips, 1848.

Aster, Jane. *The Ladies' and Gentlemen's Etiquette Book of the Best Society.* New York: Carleton, 1878.

Austin, Gayle. *Feminist Theories for Dramatic Criticism.* Ann Arbor: The U of Michigan P, 1990.

Bacon, Theodore. *Delia Bacon, A Biographical Sketch.* Boston: Houghton, 1888.

Bailey, Thomas A. and David M. Kennedy. *The American Pageant.* Lexington, Mass.: Heath, 1987.

Bailyn, Bernard. *The Ideological Origins of the American Revolution.* Cambridge: Harvard UP, 1967.

Barnes, Eric W. *The Lady of Fashion, The Life and Theatre of Anna Cora Mowatt.* New York: Scribner, 1954.

Barrett, Michele. *Women's Oppression Today.* London: Verso, 1988.

Barthes, Roland. *Mythologies.* New York: Hill, 1972

Basch, Norma. *In the Eyes of the Law: Women, Marriage, and Property in Nineteenth-Century New York.* Ithaca: Cornell UP, 1982.

Baym, Nina. "Mercy Otis Warren's Gendered Melodrama of the Revolution." *The South Atlantic Quarterly* 90 (1991): 531-54.

———. *American Women Writers and the Work of History, 1790-1860.* New Brunswick, : Rutgers UP, 1995.

Benson, Mary S. *Women in Eighteenth-Century America, A Study of Opinion and Social Usage.* New York: Columbia UP, 1935.

Bercovitch, Sacvan. *The American Puritan Imagination.* Cambridge: Cambridge UP, 1974.

Berg, Barbara. *The Remembered Gate: Origins of American Feminism*. New York: Oxford UP, 1978.

Berquist, William G. *Three Centuries of English and American Plays: A Checklist*. New York: Hafner, 1963.

Billington, Ray. *American History Before 1877*. Totowa, New Jersey: Rowman, 1988.

Bloch, Ruth H. "The Gendered Meanings of Virtue in Revolutionary America." *Signs* 13 (1987) : 37-58.

Boydston, Jeanne, Mary Kelley and Ann Margolis. *The Limits of Sisterhood*. Chapel Hill: The U. of North Carolina Press, 1988.

Brandt, Ellen B. *Susanna Haswell Rowson, America's First Best-Selling Novelist*. Chicago, Illinois: Sebra, 1975.

Bronfen, Elizabeth. *Over Her Dead Body*. Manchester: Manchester UP, 1992.

Brooks, Peter. *The Melodramatic Imagination*. New Haven: Yale UP, 1976.

Brown, Alice. *Mercy Warren*. New York: Scribner, 1896.

Brown, Thomas Allston. *A History of the New York Stage from the First Performance in 1732 to 1901*. 3 vols. New York: Dodd, 1903.

Butler, Judith. "Performative Acts and Gender Constitution: An Essay in Phenomenology and Feminist Theory." *Theatre Journal* 40 (1988): 519-31.

Calhoun, Arthur W. *A Social History of the American Family from Colonial Times to the Present*. New York: Barnes, 1945.

Carroll, Peter N. and W. Noble. *The Free and the Unfree: A History of the United States*. New York: Penguin, 1977.

Case, Sue-Ellen. *Feminism and Theatre*. London: Macmillan, 1988.

———. "From Split Subject to Split Britches." *Feminine Focus: The New Women Playwrights*. Ed. Enoch Brater. New York:Oxford UP, 1989. 126-46.

———, ed. *Performing Feminisms: Feminist Critical Theory and Theatre*. Baltimore: The Johns Hopkins UP, 1990.

Checklist of American Drama. Comp. Albert von Chorba, Jr. Philadelphia: The U of Pennsylvania Library, 1951.

Chesler, Phyllis. *Women and Madness*. New York: Harcourt, 1989.

Chinoy, Helen Krich and Linda Walsh Jenkins. *Women in American Theatre*. New York: Theatre Communications Group, 1987. 57-92.

Citizen Snub. *A Rub from Snub; or, A Cursory Analytical Epistle: Addressed to Peter Porcupine*. Philadelphia, 1795.

Cixous, Helene. "The Laugh of the Medusa." *New French Feminisms.* Ed. Elaine Marks and Isabelle de Coutrivron. Brighton, Sussex: Harvester, 1981. 245-67.

Clark, Barret H. *America's Lost Plays.* 20 vols. Princeton: Princeton UP, 1940-49.

Clinton, Catherine. *The Other Civil War.* New York: Hill, 1984.

Coad, Oral S. "The American Theatre in the Eighteenth Century." *South Atlantic Quarterly* xvii (1918): 190-7.

Cobbett, William (Peter Porcupine). *A Kick for a Bite; or, Review upon Review with a Critical Essay on the Works of Mrs. S. Rowson.* 2nd ed. Philadelphia: Bradford, 1796.

Cogan, Frances B. *All-American Girl: The Ideal of Real Womanhood in Mid-Nineteenth-Century America.* Athens: The U of Georgia P, 1989.

Cohen, Lester H. "Explaining the Revolution: Ideology and Ethics in Mercy Otis Warren's Historical Theory." *William and Mary Quarterly* xxxvii (1980): 200-18.

———. "Mercy Otis Warren: The Politics of Language and the Aesthetics of Self." *American Quarterly* 35.5 (1983): 481-98.

———. Ed. *History of the Rise, Progress and Termination of the American Revolution.* Mercy Otis Warren. Indianapolis, Indiana: Liberty, 1988.

Cott, Nancy F. *The Bonds of Womanhood: "Woman's Sphere" in New England, 1780-1835.* New Haven: Yale UP, 1977.

———. *Root of Bitterness: Documents of the Social History of American Women.* Boston: Northeastern UP, 1986.

———. "Divorce and the Changing Status of Women in Eighteenth-Century Massachusetts." *William and Mary Quarterly* 33 (1976) 586-614.

Coxe, Margaret. *The Young Lady's Companion.* Columbus: Whiting, 1839.

Davis, Tracy C. "Questions for a Feminist Methodology in Theatre History." *Interpreting the Theatrical Past.* Ed. Thomas Postlewait and Bruce A. McConachie. Iowa: U of Iowa P, 1989. 59-81.

D'Emilio, John and Estelle B. *Freedman. Intimate Matters: A History of Sexuality in America.* New York: Harper, 1989.

De Beauvoir, Simone. *The Second Sex.* New York: Vintage, 1989.

Degler, Carl N. "What Ought To Be and What Was: Women's Sexuality in the Nineteenth Century." *American Historical Review* 79 (1974): 1467-90.

De Lauretis, Teresa. *Alice Doesn't, Feminism, Semiotics, Cinema.* Bloomington: Indiana UP, 1984.

Diamond, Elin. "Mimesis, Mimicry, and the 'True Real'," *Modern Drama* XXXII (1989): 58-72

Dingwall, Eric John. *The American Woman*. New York: Rinehart, 1957.

Ditzion, Sidney. *Marriage, Morals and Sex in America, A History of Ideas*. New York: Bookman, 1953.

Doane, Mary Ann. *The Desire to Desire*. Bloomington: Indiana UP, 1987.

Dolan, Jill. *The Feminist Spectator As Critic*. Ann Arbor: U of Michigan P, 1988.

———. *Presence and Desire: Essays on Gender, Sexuality, Performance*. Ann Arbor: The U of Michigan P, 1993.

Donovan, Josephine, ed. *Feminist Literary Criticism*. Kentucky: Kentucky UP, 1989.

———. "Toward A Women's Poetics," *Feminist Issues in Literary Scholarship*. Ed. Shari Benstock. Bloomington: Indiana UP, 1987. 98-109.

Dubois, Ellen Carol. *Feminism and Suffrage, The Emergence of an Independent Women's Movement in America, 1848-1869*. Ithaca: Cornell UP, 1978.

Dudden Faye E. *Women in the American Theatre*. New Haven: Yale UP, 1994.

Dunlap, William. *History of the American Theatre*. New York: Burt Franklin, 1963.

Earle, Alice Morse. *Colonial Dames and Good Wives*. Boston: Houghton, 1895.

Ellet, Elizabeth. "The Women of the American Revolution." *America Through Women's Eyes*. Ed. Mary Beard. New York: Macmillan, 1933.

Elliott, Emory, ed. *Dictionary of Literary Biography*. Detriot: Gale, 1985.

Ellis, Joseph J. *After the Revolution: Profile of Early American Culture*. New York: Norton, 1979.

Farello, Elene Wilson. *A History of the Education of Women in the United States*. New York: Vantage, 1970.

Farrar, Mrs. John. *The Young Lady's Friend*. New York: Larkin, 1853.

Faust, Langdon L. Ed. *American Women Writers*. New York: Ungar, 1983.

Feral, Josette. "Writing and Displacement: Women in Theatre." *Modern Drama* 27 (1984): 549-63.

Field, Vena Bernadette. *Constantia: A Study of the Life and Works of Judith Sargent Murray, 1751-1820*. Orono: U of Maine, 1931.

Flexner, Eleanor. *Century of Struggle, The Woman's Rights Movement in the United States*. Cambridge: Harvard UP, 1975.

Forte, Jeanie. "Women's Performance Art: Feminism and Postmodernism" *Theatre Journal* 40 (1988): 217-35.

———. "Focus on the Body: Pain, Praxis, and Pleasure in Feminist Performance." *Critical Theory and Performance*. Ed. Janelle Reinelt and Joseph R. Roach. Ann Arbor: The U of Michigan P, 1992. 248-62.

Foster, Lemuel H. *The Legal Rights of Women*. Detroit, Michigan: Woman's, 1913.

Foucault, Michel. *Mental Illness and Psychology*. Trans. Alan Sheridan. Berkeley: U of California P, 1987.

Franklin, Benjamin V. "Introduction." *The Plays and Poems of Mercy Otis Warren*. New York: Scholar's Fascimiles, 1980.

Freedman, Estelle B. "Sexuality in Nineteenth-Century America: Behavior, Ideology, and Politics." *Reviews in American History* 10 (1982): 196-215.

Freibert, Lucy M. and Barbara A. White. *Hidden Hands, An Anthology of Women Writers, 1790-1870*. New Brunswick, New Jersey: Rutgers UP, 1985. 14.

Fritz, Jean. *A Cast for a Revolution: Some American Friends and Enemies, 1728-1814*. Boston: Houghton, 1972.

Gilbert, Sandra M. and Sandra Gubar. *The Madwoman in the Attic, The Woman Writer and the Nineteenth-Century Imagination*. New Haven: Yale UP, 1979.

Gordon, Linda. "What's New in Women's History," *Feminist Studies/Critical Studies*. Ed. Teresa de Lauretis. Bloomington: Indiana UP, 1986. 20-30.

Grant, Mary H. "Domestic Experience and Feminist Theory: The Case of Julia Ward Howe." *Woman's Being, Woman's Place: Female Identity and Vocation in American History*. Ed. Mary Kelley. Boston: Hall, 1979. 220-32.

Greene, Gayle and Coppelia Kahn, eds. *Making A Difference*. London: Routledge, 1985.

Grossberg, Michael. *Governing the Hearth: Law and the Family in Nineteenth-Century America*. Chapel Hill: U of North Carolina P, 1985.

Gundersen, Joan R. and Gwen Victor Gampel, "Married Women's Legal Status in Eighteenth-Century New York and Virginia." *William and Mary Quarterly* XXXIX (1982): 114-34.

Hall, Florence Howe. *Julia Ward Howe and the Woman Suffrage Movement*. Boston: Estes, 1913.

Halttunen, Karen. *Confidence Men and Painted Women, A Study of Middle-Class Culture in America, 1830-1870*. New Haven UP, 1982.

Hart, Lynda, ed. *Making a Spectacle, Feminist Essays on Contemporary Women's Theatre*. Ann Arbor: The U of Michigan P, 1989.

Hartman, Mary and Lois W. Banner. *Clio's Consciousness Raised, New Perspectives on the History of Women*. New York: Harper, 1974.

Hartman, John Geoffrey. *The Development of American Social Comedy from 1787 to 1936*. Diss. U of Pennsylvania, 1939.

Havens, Daniel F. *The Columbian Muse of Comedy*. Carbondale: Southern Illinois UP, 1973.

Hill, Frank P. *American Plays Printed, 1714-1830*. New York: Blom, 1968.

Hixon, Donald L. and Don A. Hennessee. *Nineteenth Century American Drama: A Finding Guide*. Metuchen, New Jersey: Scarecrow, 1977.

Hoole, W. Stanley. *The Ante-Bellum Charleston Theatre*. Tuscaloosa: U of Alabama P, 1946.

Howe, Julia Ward. *Reminiscences 1819-1899*. Boston: Houghton, 1900.

Hutton, Laurence. *Curiosities of the American Stage*. New York: Harper, 1891.

Hymowitz, Carol and Michaele Meissman. *A History of Women in America*. New York: Bantam, 1978.

Ireland, Joseph N. *Records of the New York Stage from 1750 to 1860*. New York: Franklin, 1860-7.

Ireland, Robert M. "The Libertine Must Die: Sexual Dishonor and the Unwritten Law in the Nineteenth-Century United States" *Journal of Social History* 23 (1989-90): 27-44.

Irigaray, Luce. *This Sex Which Is Not One*. Ithaca: Cornell UP, 1985.

———. *Speculum of the Other Woman*. Ithaca: Cornell UP, 1985.

Jacobus, Mary, ed. *Women Writing and Writing about Women*. New York: Barnes, 1979.

Jacobus, Evelyn Fox Keller and Sally Shuttleworth, eds. *Body/Politics, Women and The Discourses of Science*. New York: Routledge, 1990.

James, Edward T., Janet Wilson James and Paul S. Boyer. *Notable American Women 1607-1950, A Biographical Dictionary*. Cambridge: Belknap, 1971.

Jardine, Alice A. "Gynesis." *Critical Theory Since 1965*. Ed. Hazard Adams & Leroy Searle. Tallahassee: Florida State UP, 1986.

Johnson, Claudia. *American Actress: Perspective on the Nineteenth Century*. Chicago: Nelson-Hall, 1984.

Jones, Ann Rosalind. "Writing the Body: Toward An Understanding of L'Ecriture Feminine." *Feminist Studies* 7 (1981): 247-263.

Kaplan, E. Ann. *Women and Film*. New York: Methuen, 1981.

Kelley, Mary. *Private Woman, Public Stage*. New York: Oxford UP, 1984.

Kerber, Linda K. *Women of the Republic, Intellect and Ideology i n Revolutionary America*. Chapel Hill: U of North Carolina P, 1980.

———, Alice Kessler-Harris, Kathryn Kish Sklar, eds. *U.S. History as Women's History*. Chapel Hill: U of North Carolina P, 1995.

Kofman, Sarah. *The Enigma of Woman, Woman in Freud's Writings*. Ithaca: Cornell UP, 1985.

Kolodny, Annette. "Dancing Through the Minefield: Some Observations on the Theory, Practice, and Politics of a Feminist Literary Criticism." *Critical Theory Since 1965.* Ed. Hazard Adams & Leroy Searle. Tallahassee: Florida State UP, 1986. 499-512.

———. "A Map for Rereading: Gender and the Interpretation of Literary Texts." *The New Feminist Criticism.* Ed. Elaine Showalter. London: Virago, 1986. 46-62.

Kornfeld, Eve. "Women in Post-Revolutionary American Culture: Susanna Haswell Rowson's American Career 1793-1824." *Journal of American Culture* 6 (1983): 56-62.

Kraditor, Aileen S. *Up from the Pedestal.* Chicago: Quadrangle, 1968.

Kristeva, Julia. "Women's Time." *Critical Theory Since 1965* (1986). 471-84.

Kunitz, Stanley J. and Howard Haycraft. *American Authors, 1600-1900.* New York: Wilson, 1966.

Kushner, Howard I. "Nineteenth-Century Sexuality and the 'Sexual Revolution' of the Progressive Era." *The Canadian Review of American Studies* IX (1978): 34-49.

Lerner, Gerda. *The Woman in American History.* Menlo-Park, California: Addison, 1971.

———. "Placing Women in History: Definitions and Challenges." *Feminist Studies* 3 (1975): 5-14.

———. *The Grimke Sisters from South Carolina: Pioneers for Women's Rights and Abolition.* Boston: Houghton, 1967.

———. *The Creation of Patriarchy.* New York: Oxford UP, 1986.

Leslie, Eliza. *The Behavior Book: A Manual for Ladies.* Philadelphia: Hazard, 1854.

Lewis, Jan. "The Republican Wife: Virtue and Seduction in the Early Republic." *William and Mary Quarterly* XLIV (1987): 689-721.

McConachie, Bruce. *Melodramatic Formations: American Theatre and Society, 1820-1870.* Iowa: U of Iowa P, 1992.

Mainiero, Linda, ed. *American Women Writers: A Critical Reference Guide from Colonial Times to the Present.* New York: Ungar, 1979.

Malone, Dumas. *Dictionary of American Biography.* New York: Scribner, 1929/1957.

Marble, Annie Russell. "Mistress Mercy Warren: Real Daughter of the American Revolution." *New England Magazine, An Illustrated Monthly* 28 (1903): 163-80.

Martin, Wendy. "Profile: Frances Wright, 1725-1852." *Women's Studies* 2 (1974): 273-78.

———. "Seduced and Abandoned, The Fallen Woman in American Fiction." *The American Sisterhood*. Ed. Wendy Martin. New York: Harper, 1972. 257-72.

Mates, Julian. *The American Musical Stage Before 1800*. New Brunswick, New Jersey: Rutgers UP, 1962.

Matthaei, Julie A. *An Economic History of Women in America*. New York: Schocken, 1982.

Matthews, Brander. *A Book About the Theatre*. New York: Scribner, 1916.

Matthews, Glenna. *The Rise of Public Woman*. New York: Oxford UP, 1992.

Meserve, Walter J. *An Emerging Entertainment, The Drama of the American People to 1828*. Bloomington: Indiana UP, 1977.

———. *An Outline History of American Drama*. Totowa, New Jersey: Littlefield, 1965.

———. *Heralds of Promise*. New York: Greenwood, 1986.

———. *American Drama to 1900: A Guide to Information Sources*. Detriot: Gale, 1980.

Miller, Nancy K. *Subject to Change, Reading Feminist Writing*. New York: Columbia UP, 1988.

———. "Emphasis Added: Plots and Plausibilities in Women's Fiction." *PMLA* 96 (1981): 36-48.

Miller, Perry. *The American Puritans*. New York: Anchor, 1956.

———. *The Puritans* 2 vols New York: Harper, 1963.

Millett, Kate. *Sexual Politics*. New York: Ballantine, 1988.

Moers, Ellen. *Literary Women*. New York: Anchor, 1977.

Moody, Richard. *America Takes the Stage*. Millwood, New York: Kraus, 1977.

Morgan, Edmund S. *Visible Saints, The History of a Puritan Idea*. Ithaca, New York: Cornell UP, 1963.

Moses, Montrose J. *The American Dramatist*. New York: Blom, 1964.

——— and John Mason Brown, eds., *The American Theatre as Seen by Its Critics, 1752-1934*. New York: Norton , 1934. 59-66.

Mowatt, Anna Cora. *Autobiography of an Actress*. New York: Arno, 1980.

———. *Plays*. Boston: Ticknor, 1855.

Napheys, George H. *The Physical Life of Woman, Advice to the Maiden, Wife and Mother*. Philadelphia: McKay, 1870.

Nason, Elias. *A Memoir of Mrs. Susanna Rowson*. Albany, New York: Joel, 1870.

Nichols, Kathleen L. "Earlier American Women Dramatists: From National to Sexual Politics." *Theatre History Studies* XI (1991): 129-49.

Nicolay, Theresa Freda. *Gender Roles, Literary Authority, and Three American Women Writers*. New York: Peter Lang, 1995.

Norton, Mary Beth. *Liberty's Daughters: The Revolutionary Experience of American Women*. Boston: Little, 1980.

Nye, Russel B. *This Almost Chosen People: Essays in the History of American Ideas*. East Lansing: Michigan State UP, 1966.

Odell, George C.D. *Annals of the New York Stage*. 15 vols. New York: Columbia UP, 1927-1949.

Parrington, Vernon Louis. *Main Currents in American Thought*. New York: Harcourt, 1958.

Perkins, A.J.G. and Theresa Wolfson. *Frances Wright, Free Enquirer*. New York: Harper, 1939.

Philbrick, Norman. *Trumpets Sounding: Propaganda Plays of The American Revolution*. New York: Blom, 1972.

Pollock, Thomas Clark. *The Philadelphia Theater in the Eighteenth Century*. Philadelphia: U of Pennsylvania P, 1933.

Quinn, Arthur Hobson. *A History of the American Drama from the Beginning to the Civil War*. New York: Crofts , 1944.

Reinelt, Janelle G. and Joseph R. Roach, eds. *Critical Theory and Performance*. Ann Arbor: The U of Michigan P, 1992.

Richards, Jeffrey H. *Theatre Enough, American Culture and the Metaphor of the World Stage, 1607-1789*. Durham Duke UP, 1991.

———. *Mercy Otis Warren*. New York: Twayne, 1995.

Richardson, Gary A. *American Drama from the Colonial Period Through World War I: A Critical History*. New York: Twayne, 1993.

Robinson, Alice M. "Mercy Warren, Satirist of the Revolution." *Women in American Theatre*. Ed. Helen Krich Chinoy and Linda Walsh Jenkins. New York: Crown, 1981.

———. *Notable Women in the American Theatre*. Westport, Connecticut: Greenwood, 1989. 757-61

Robinson, Lillian S. "Treason Our Text: Feminist Challenges to the Literary Canon." *Critical Theory Since 1965* (1986). 572-582.

Roden, Robert F. *Later American Plays, 1831-1900*. New York: Franklin, 1900.

Rosenberg, Charles. "Sexuality, Class and Role in Nineteenth-Century America." *American Quarterly* 25 (1973): 131-53.

Rush, Benjamin. "Thoughts upon Female Education." *Early American Women*. Ed. Nancy Woloch. Belmont, California: Wadsworth, 1992.

Russ, Joanna. *How to Suppress Women's Writing*. Austin: U of Texas P, 1983.

Ryan, Mary P. "The Power of Women's Networks: A Case Study of Female Moral Reform in Antebellum America." *Feminist Studies* 5 (1979): 66-85.

Sargent, Epes. *The Modern Standard Drama: A Collection of the Most Popular Acting Plays.* New York: Taylor, 1846.

Seilhamer, George O. *History of the American Theatre.* Philadelphia: Globe, 1889.

Scullion, Adrienne. *Female Playwright of the Nineteenth Century.* Rutland, Vt.: C. E. Tuttle, 1996.

Showalter, Elaine, ed. *The New Feminist Criticism.* London: Virago, 1986. 125-43, 243-70.

———. *A Literature of their Own.* London: Virago, 1988.

———. "Feminist Criticism in the Wilderness." *Writing and Sexual Difference.* Ed. Elizabeth Abel. Sussex: Harvester, 1982. 9-35.

———. *Sister's Choice: Tradition and Change in American Women's Writing.* Oxford: Clanderon, 1991.

Silverman, Kenneth. *A Cultural History of the American Revolution.* New York: Crowell, 1976.

Simpson, Alan. *Puritanism in Old and New England.* Chicago, Illinois: The U of Chicago P, 1955.

Slotkin, Richard. *Regeneration Through Violence.* Middletown, Connecticut: Wesleyan UP, 1973.

Smith, Page. *Daughters of the Promised Land.* Boston: Little, 1970.

Smith, William Raymond. "Mercy Otis Warren's Radical View of the American Revolution." *The Colonial Legacy.* Ed. Lawrence H. Leder. New York: Harper, 1971. 203-25.

———. *History as Argument, Three Patriot Historians of the American Revolution.* The Hague, Paris: Mouton , 1966. 73-119.

Smith-Rosenberg, Carroll. *Disorderly Conduct, Visions of Gender in Victorian America.* New York: Knopf, 1985.

———. "The New Woman and the New History." *Feminist Studies* 3 (1975): 185-198.

———. "Puberty to Menopause, The Cycle of Femininity in Nineteenth-Century America." *Clio's Consciousness Raised.* Ed. Mary Hartman and Lois Banner. New York: Harper, 1974. 23-37.

——— and Charles Rosenberg, "The Female Animal: Medical and Biological Views of Women in Nineteenth Century America." *Journal of American History* 60 (1973): 332-56.

Spacks, Patricia Meyer. *The Female Imagination.* London: Allen, 1976.

Spritz, Kenneth. *Theatrical Evolution: 1776-1976.* New York: The Hudson River Museum, 1976.

Stansell, Christine. *City of Women: Sex and Class In New York, 1789-1860.* Urbana: U of Illinois P. 1987.

Stanton, Domna. "Language and Revolution: The Franco-American Dis-Connection." *The Future of Difference.* Ed. Hester Eisenstein and Alice Jardine. New Brunswick, New Jersey: Rutgers UP, 1985.

Stephens, Judith L. "Gender Ideology and Dramatic Convention in Progressive Era Plays, 1890-1920." *Theatre Journal* 41 (1989): 45-55.

Styan, J.L. *Drama, Stage, and Audience.* New York: Cambridge UP, 1975.

Taubman, Howard. *The Making of the American Theatre.* New York: McCann, 1965.

Tocqueville, Alexis de. *Democracy in America.* Ed. J.P. Mayer. New York: Harper Perennial, 1988.

Tompkins, Eugene. *The History of the Boston Theatre, 1854-1901.* Boston: Houghton, 1908.

Trollope, Frances. *Domestic Manners if the Americans.* Ed. Donald Smalley. Gloucester, Mass.: Smith, 1974.

Turner, Mary M. *Forgotten Leading Ladies of the American Theatre.* North Carolina: McFarland, c1990.

Tuthill, Louisa C. *The Young Lady's Home.* New Haven: Babcock, 1839.

Van Doren, Charles, ed. *Webster's American Biographies.* Springfield, Mass.: Merriam, 1974.

Vaughn, Jack A. *Early American Dramatists from the Beginnings to 1900.* New York: Ungar, 1981.

Voelker, Paul D. "George Henry Boker's Francesca da Rimini: An Interpretation and Evaluation." *Educational Theatre Journal* 24 (1972): 383-95.

Wandor, Michelene. *Carry On, Understudies. Theatre and Sexual Politics.* London: Routledge, 1986.

Weales, Gerald. "The Quality of Mercy, or Mrs. Warren's Profession." *Georgia Review* 33 (1979): 881-94.

Weedon, Chris. *Feminist Practice and Poststructuralist Theory.* Oxford: Blackwell, 1987.

Wegelin, Oscar. *Early American Plays, 1714-1830.* New York: Literary Collection, 1905.

Weil, Dorothy. *In Defense of Women: Susanna Rowson (1762-1824).* University Park: Pennsylvania State UP, 1976.

Welter, Barbara. *Dimity Convictions, The American Woman in the Nineteenth Century.* Athens, Ohio: Ohio UP, 1976.

Wilson, Arthur Herman. *A History of the Philadelphia Theatre, 1835 to 1855.* Philadelphia: U of Pennsylvania P, 1935.

Wilson, Garff B. *Three Hundred Years of American drama and Theatre.* Englewood Cliffs, New Jersey: Prentice, 1973.

———. *A History of American Acting.* Bloomington: Indiana UP, 1966.

Wollstonecraft, Mary. *A Vindication of the Rights of Woman.* London: Norton, 1975.

Woodward, Helene Beal. *The Bold Women.* New York: Farrar, 1953.

Wright, Frances. *Views of Society and Manners in America.* Ed. Paul R . Baker. Cambridge, Mass.: Belknap, 1963.

Wright, Louis B. *The Cultural Life of the American Colonies.* New York: Harper, 1957.

Zagarri, Rosemarie. *Mercy Otis Warren and the American Revolution: A Woman's Dilemma.* Wheeling, Ill.: Davidson, 1995.

Zanger, Jules. "Boker's *Francesca da Rimini*: The Brother's Tragedy." *Educational Theatre Journal* 25 (1973): 410-19.

Index

For Product Safety Concerns and Information please contact our EU
representative GPSR@taylorandfrancis.com
Taylor & Francis Verlag GmbH, Kaufingerstraße 24, 80331 München, Germany

www.ingramcontent.com/pod-product-compliance
Lightning Source LLC
Chambersburg PA
CBHW060019100426
42740CB00010B/1536